SOLARO

STUDY GUIDE

English 11 University Preparation (ENG3U)

SOLARO Study Guide is designed to help students achieve success in school. The content in each study guide is 100% curriculum aligned and serves as an excellent source of material for review and practice. To create this book, teachers, curriculum specialists, and assessment experts have worked closely to develop the instructional pieces that explain each of the key concepts for the course. The practice questions and sample tests have detailed solutions that show problem-solving methods, highlight concepts that are likely to be tested, and point out potential sources of errors. ***SOLARO Study Guide*** is a complete guide to be used by students throughout the school year for reviewing and understanding course content, and to prepare for assessments.

Rao, Gautam, 1961 –
SOLARO Study Guide:
English 11 – University Preparation (ENG3U) Ontario
ISBN: 978-1-77044-476-8

1. English Language Arts – Juvenile Literature. I. Title

Published by
Castle Rock Research Corp.
2000 First & Jasper
10065 Jasper Avenue
Edmonton, AB T5J 3B1

10 9 8 7 6 5 4 3

Publisher
Gautam Rao

Contributors
Brigitta Goerres
Wayne Defer
Lois Westerlund

CASTLE ROCK
RESEARCH CORP

Dedicated to the memory of Dr. V.S. Rao

SOLARO STUDY GUIDE—English 11 University Preparation (ENG3U)

SOLARO Study Guide consists of the following sections:

Key Tips for Being Successful at School gives examples of study and review strategies. It includes information about learning styles, study schedules, and note taking for test preparation.

Class Focus includes a unit on each area of the curriculum. Units are divided into sections, each focusing on one of the specific expectations, or main ideas, that students must learn about in that unit. Examples, definitions, and visuals help to explain each main idea. Practice questions on the main ideas are also included. At the end of each unit is a test on the important ideas covered. The practice questions and unit tests help students identify areas they know and those they need to study more. They can also be used as preparation for tests and quizzes. Most questions are of average difficulty, though some are easy and some are hard—the harder questions are called *Challenger Questions*. Each unit is prefaced by a ***Table of Correlations***, which correlates questions in the unit (and in the practice tests at the end of the book) to the specific curriculum expectations. Answers and solutions are found at the end of each unit.

Key Strategies for Success on Tests helps students get ready for tests. It shows students different types of questions they might see, word clues to look for when reading them, and hints for answering them.

Practice Tests includes one to three tests based on the entire course. They are very similar to the format and level of difficulty that students may encounter on final tests. In some regions, these tests may be reprinted versions of official tests, or reflect the same difficulty levels and formats as official versions. This gives students the chance to practice using real-world examples. Answers and complete solutions are provided at the end of the section.

For the complete curriculum document (including specific expectations along with examples and sample problems), visit www.edu.gov.on.ca/eng/curriculum/secondary.

SOLARO Study Guide *Study Guides* are available for many courses. Check www.castlerockresearch.com for a complete listing of books available for your area.

For information about any of our resources or services, please call Castle Rock Research at 1.800.840.6224 or visit our website at http://www.castlerockresearch.com.

At Castle Rock Research, we strive to produce an error-free resource. If you should find an error, please contact us so that future editions can be corrected.

TABLE OF CONTENTS

Key Tips for being Successful at School

KEY TIPS FOR BEING SUCCESSFUL AT SCHOOL

KEY FACTORS CONTRIBUTING TO SCHOOL SUCCESS

In addition to learning the content of your courses, there are some other things that you can do to help you do your best at school. You can try some of the following strategies:

- **Keep a positive attitude:** Always reflect on what you can already do and what you already know.

- **Be prepared to learn:** Have the necessary pencils, pens, notebooks, and other required materials for participating in class ready.
- **Complete all of your assignments:** Do your best to finish all of your assignments. Even if you know the material well, practice will reinforce your knowledge. If an assignment or question is difficult for you, work through it as far as you can so that your teacher can see exactly where you are having difficulty.
- **Set small goals for yourself when you are learning new material:** For example, when learning the parts of speech, do not try to learn everything in one night. Work on only one part or section each study session. When you have memorized one particular part of speech and understand it, move on to another one. Continue this process until you have memorized and learned all the parts of speech.
- **Review your classroom work regularly at home:** Review to make sure you understand the material you learned in class.
- **Ask your teacher for help:** Your teacher will help you if you do not understand something or if you are having a difficult time completing your assignments.

- **Get plenty of rest and exercise:** Concentrating in class is hard work. It is important to be well-rested and have time to relax and socialize with your friends. This helps you keep a positive attitude about your schoolwork.
- **Eat healthy meals:** A balanced diet keeps you healthy and gives you the energy you need for studying at school and at home.

How to Find Your Learning Style

Every student learns differently. The manner in which you learn best is called your learning style. By knowing your learning style, you can increase your success at school. Most students use a combination of learning styles. Do you know what type of learner you are? Read the following descriptions. Which of these common learning styles do you use most often?

- **Linguistic Learner:** You may learn best by saying, hearing, and seeing words. You are probably really good at memorizing things such as dates, places, names, and facts. You may need to write down the steps in a process, a formula, or the actions that lead up to a significant event, and then say them out loud.
- **Spatial Learner:** You may learn best by looking at and working with pictures. You are probably really good at puzzles, imagining things, and reading maps and charts. You may need to use strategies like mind mapping and webbing to organize your information and study notes.
- **Kinesthetic Learner:** You may learn best by touching, moving, and figuring things out using manipulatives. You are probably really good at physical activities and learning through movement. You may need to draw your finger over a diagram to remember it, tap out the steps needed to solve a problem, or feel yourself writing or typing a formula.

SCHEDULING STUDY TIME

You should review your class notes regularly to ensure that you have a clear understanding of all the new material you learned. Reviewing your lessons on a regular basis helps you to learn and remember ideas and concepts. It also reduces the quantity of material that you need to study prior to a test. Establishing a study schedule will help you to make the best use of your time.

Regardless of the type of study schedule you use, you may want to consider the following suggestions to maximize your study time and effort:

- Organize your work so that you begin with the most challenging material first.
- Divide the subject's content into small, manageable chunks.
- Alternate regularly between your different subjects and types of study activities in order to maintain your interest and motivation.
- Make a daily list with headings like "Must Do," "Should Do," and "Could Do."
- Begin each study session by quickly reviewing what you studied the day before.
- Maintain your usual routine of eating, sleeping, and exercising to help you concentrate better for extended periods of time.

Creating Study Notes

Mind-Mapping or Webbing

Use the key words, ideas, or concepts from your class notes to create a mind map or web, which is a diagram or visual representation of the given information. A mind map or web is sometimes referred to as a knowledge map. Use the following steps to create a mind map or web:

1. Write the key word, concept, theory, or formula in the centre of your page.
2. Write down related facts, ideas, events, and information, and link them to the central concept with lines.
3. Use coloured markers, underlining, or symbols to emphasize things such as relationships, timelines, and important information.

The following mind map is an example of one that could help you develop an essay:

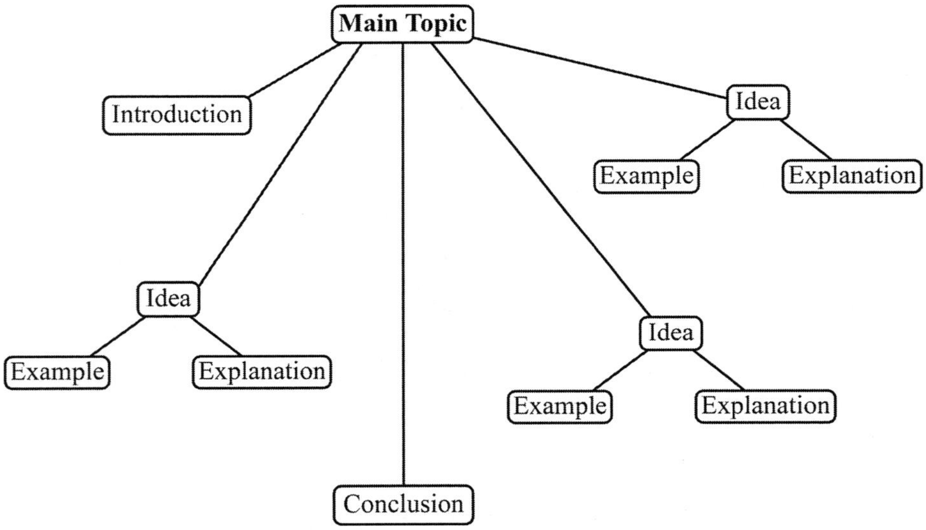

Index Cards

To use index cards while studying, follow these steps:

1. Write a key word or question on one side of an index card.
2. On the reverse side, write the definition of the word, answer to the question, or any other important information that you want to remember.

What are synonyms?

What are synonyms?
Synonyms are words that have the same or almost the same meaning.

For example, "coarse" is a synonym for "rough"

Symbols and Sticky Notes—Identifying Important Information

Use symbols to mark your class notes. The following are some examples:

- An exclamation mark (!) might be used to point out something that must be learned well because it is a very important idea.
- A question mark (?) may highlight something you are not certain about
- A diamond (◊) or asterisk (*) could highlight interesting information that you want to remember.

Sticky notes are useful in the following situations:

- Use sticky notes when you are not allowed to put marks in books.
- Use sticky notes to mark a page in a book that contains an important diagram, formula, explanation, or other information.
- Use sticky notes to mark important facts in research books.

Memorization Techniques

- **Association** relates new learning to something you already know. For example, to remember the spelling difference between dessert and desert, recall that the word *sand* has only one *s*. So, because there is sand in a desert, the word *desert* has only one *s*.
- **Mnemonic** devices are sentences that you create to remember a list or group of items. For example, the first letter of each word in the phrase "Every Good Boy Deserves Fudge" helps you to remember the names of the lines on the treble-clef staff (E, G, B, D, and F) in music.

- **Acronyms** are words that are formed from the first letters or parts of the words in a group. For example, RADAR is actually an acronym for Radio Detecting and Ranging, and MASH is an acronym for Mobile Army Surgical Hospital. HOMES helps you to remember the names of the five Great Lakes (Huron, Ontario, Michigan, Erie, and Superior).
- **Visualizing** requires you to use your mind's eye to "see" a chart, list, map, diagram, or sentence as it is in your textbook or notes, on the chalkboard or computer screen, or in a display.
- **Initialisms** are abbreviations that are formed from the first letters or parts of the words in a group. Unlike acronyms, an initialism cannot be pronounced as a word itself. For example, GCF is an initialism for **G**reatest **C**ommon **F**actor.

Key Strategies for Reviewing

Reviewing textbook material, class notes, and handouts should be an ongoing activity. Spending time reviewing becomes more critical when you are preparing for a test. You may find some of the following review strategies useful when studying during your scheduled study time:

- Before reading a selection, preview it by noting the headings, charts, graphs, and chapter questions.
- Before reviewing a unit, note the headings, charts, graphs, and chapter questions.
- Highlight key concepts, vocabulary, definitions, and formulas.
- Skim the paragraph, and note the key words, phrases, and information.
- Carefully read over each step in a procedure.
- Draw a picture or diagram to help make the concept clearer.

KEY STRATEGIES FOR SUCCESS: A CHECKLIST

Reviewing is a huge part of doing well at school and preparing for tests. Here is a checklist for you to keep track of how many suggested strategies for success you are using. Read each question, and put a check mark (✓) in the correct column. Look at the questions where you have checked the "No" column. Think about how you might try using some of these strategies to help you do your best at school.

Key Strategies for Success	Yes	No
Do you attend school regularly?		
Do you know your personal learning style—how you learn best?		
Do you spend 15 to 30 minutes a day reviewing your notes?		
Do you study in a quiet place at home?		
Do you clearly mark the most important ideas in your study notes?		
Do you use sticky notes to mark texts and research books?		
Do you practise answering multiple-choice and written-response questions?		
Do you ask your teacher for help when you need it?		
Are you maintaining a healthy diet and sleep routine?		
Are you participating in regular physical activity?		

Reading

READING

Table of Correlations

Specific Expectation	Practice Questions	Unit Test Questions
Students are expected to:		
11R1.0 read and demonstrate an understanding of a variety of literary, informational, and graphic texts, using a range of strategies to construct meaning		
11R1.3 identify the most important ideas and supporting details in texts, including increasingly complex ordifficult texts	12, 13, 17, 30, 41, 42, 50	31
11R1.4 make and explain inferences of increasing subtlety about texts, including increasingly complex or difficult texts, supporting their explanations with well-chosen stated and implied ideas from the texts	4, 19, 33, 35, 36, 37, 39, 40, 47	6, 7, 14, 17 26, 28, 34, 40, 44, 45, 47, 57
11R1.5 extend understanding of texts, including increasingly complex or difficult texts, by making appropriate and increasingly rich connections between the ideas in them and personal knowledge, experience, and insights; other texts; and the world around them		19, 53, 54
11R1.6 analyse texts in terms of the information, ideas, issues, or themes they explore, examining how various aspects of the texts contribute to the presentation or development of these elements	25, 43, 46, 48, 51	36, 37, 42, 51
11R1.7 evaluate the effectiveness of texts, including increasingly complex or difficult texts using evidence from the text to support their opinions	24	8, 39, 46
11R1.8 identify and analyse the perspectives and/or biases evident in texts, including increasingly complex or difficult texts, commenting with growing understanding on any questions they may raise about beliefs, values, identity, and power	3, 10, 22, 32, 44, 45, 49	1, 10, 38, 50
11R2.0 recognize a variety of text forms, text features, and stylistic elements and demonstrate understanding of how they help communicate meaning		
11R2.2 identify a variety of text features and explain how they help communicate meaning	8, 18	
11R2.3 identify a variety of elements of style in texts and explain how they help communicate meaning and enhance the effectiveness of the text	1, 2, 6, 7, 14, 16, 20, 23, 26, 29, 38	2, 3, 4, 5, 9, 13, 15, 16, 18, 22, 23, 24, 29, 30, 35, 43, 48, 49, 55, 58, 59
11R3.0 use knowledge of words and cueing systems to read fluently		
11R3.1 automatically understand most words in a variety of reading contexts	5, 11, 21, 28, 31, 34	20, 21, 25, 27, 32, 33, 41, 56, 52
11R3.2 use decoding strategies effectively to read and understand unfamiliar words, including words of increasing difficulty	9, 15, 27	12
11R3.3 use a variety of strategies, with increasing regularity, to explore and expand vocabulary, focusing on the precision with which words are used in the texts they are reading		11

Practice Questions = 46/51 = 90%

Unit Test = 54/59 = 92%

READING

Reading for Meaning

11R1.2 select and use the most appropriate reading comprehension strategies to understand texts, including increasingly complex or difficult texts

Reading Strategies

Reading may seem like a passive activity—you sit down and absorb what someone else has written. This could not be farther from the truth; good readers read actively. Imagine, for example, that someone is writing a biography of your life, and the writer has asked you to review it before it is published. Since you know all of the facts of your life quite well, you would probably be quite critical in analysing the writer's work. You would probably ask a lot of questions about where the writer got his or her information and how the writer reached certain conclusions about who you are. Because you know so much about yourself, it is easy to be critical of a text that is about something in which you have expertise. You can apply this same level of analysis to *all* texts you read. Reading requires an active, critical mind, no matter how much you may know about a text.

Reading should be an ongoing interaction between your thoughts and a text. As you read, questions and ideas should flow, images of descriptions should be conjured in your mind, and analysis of the meaning of a text should be built in to your reading process. The strategies described in this section of your ***KEY*** can be used to help you be as observant, critical, and curious as possible when reading.

Step-by-step Critical Reading

The following steps are useful as a general guide to reading carefully. You may find that you already perform some of these steps without thinking about it.

1. Quickly scan the text without pausing to determine the

- intended audience
- kind of text (for example, is it a play, essay, report, short story, informal letter, formal letter, article, or advertisement?)
- writer's purpose (is it to describe, to inform, to explain, to instruct, to persuade?)
- general contents of the text

2. Take time to look for information about the writer and the work itself in the front or the back of the book or in outside sources (such as other books or online). The writer's country of origin or dates of birth and death, for instance, can be useful information. Knowing when and where a writer lived can help you interpret his or her meaning.

3. As you read, make note of significant words in the text. Highlighting, underlining, circling words, or writing notes in the margin are all effective methods of documenting your observations.

4. Connect the words on the page to what you already know.
For example, if you like sports, reading the sports page is easy because you already have a framework for reading, understanding, and analysing the language that is used in sports articles. When you read any text, think about what you already know about the subject and connect it with what you are reading.

5. Look at the context and structure of unfamiliar words to figure out meaning if the definitions are not given at the bottom of the page. Roots, prefixes, and endings can help you find relationships between familiar and unfamiliar words as a strategy for determining meaning. Taking into account the context of the passage in which the word is used can help you figure out its meaning. Read the following short passage and see if there are any words you do not recognize. Can you guess at the meaning of any unfamiliar words?

Example

- The committee members left the boardroom close to midnight. Although they were exhausted after the sederunt, they agreed that they would meet again in the morning to complete the discussion.

  You may not know the meaning of an unusual word like sederunt, but the context supplies the clues: words and phrases such as "committee," "boardroom," "midnight," "exhausted," and "complete the discussion" contribute to a solid context. You can guess with reasonable confidence that a sederunt is a kind of meeting or discussion, probably a long one.

6. Use the features of the text to help you to determine meaning. Text features include

- titles or thesis statements
- organization of ideas
- punctuation

The first paragraph of a non-fiction passage often contains the controlling idea or a thesis statement. The main idea is also sometimes contained in the title and/or conclusion.

Take particular note of titles and endings. Titles often give clues or reinforce meaning. Your interpretation of a text must take into account the ending. If it does not, you could end up with an incomplete interpretation. Ignoring an ending can result in a contradictory interpretation of the text.

Observe how a text is organized. If there is a lot of dialogue in a text, perhaps the writer is trying to use a lot of indirect characterization. If there are charts or diagrams, the writer could be trying to persuade the reader by using statistics. Question how a text is organized and you can find out more about the writer's intent in designing that text. Use punctuation as important cues to meaning. Stopping at the end of a line of poetry when there is no punctuation, for example, often breaks it up into meaningless chunks. In poetry, as in all writing, punctuation marks can clarify meaning, show relationships, and help to reinforce mood. When reading scripts, use stage directions as important clues to meaning.

7. Know commonly used figurative language. This will help you to better understand the texts and questions, since some of the questions and answers will use these terms. An analysis of different types of figurative language is included in your ***KEY***.

11R1.3 identify the most important ideas and supporting details in texts, including increasingly complex or difficult texts

Main Ideas and Supporting Details

All texts share basic elements. In general, a writer states an idea and then supports it with details that lead to a logical conclusion. To better understand the writing, you must first be able to define the writer's idea. You should be able to clearly interpret the intent of the work from the supporting information that has been included in the text. The final step is to make reasonable inferences from the conclusions that the writer has drawn.

You are often asked to identify the main idea of a text. You should also be able to find details and supporting information. From the conclusion that you draw, you must be able to make a logical extension of the writer's ideas. The following steps form a good method for identifying a main idea in a text and expanding on that idea using support from the text.

Finding the Main Idea Step by Step

1. To begin defining the main idea of a passage, poem, or dramatic piece, first ask yourself the following basic questions:

- What is the title of this work, and why was it chosen? The answer to this question may immediately point to the main idea of the passage.
- Why did the writer write this piece? By understanding the writer's purpose, you may see where the passage is heading.
- What main idea is the writer conveying directly or through characters, dialogue, or imagery? If the writer does not speak directly to the reader, one of the characters may be the writer's mouthpiece.
- What is the topic sentence of the paragraph(s), the subject of the stanza(s), or the interest of the character(s)? Sometimes, the main idea is not explicitly stated but can be found by interpreting dialogue or deciphering verse.

Ask yourself these questions either during reading or after you have read the passage in its entirety. Either way, the answers you form will help expand your knowledge of the main ideas in a text.

2. Next, find clues that support the main idea through additional details or developments. When applicable to a text, ask yourself the following questions:

- Does the writer supply proof or supporting information to back up his or her arguments? Use any supporting information to reinforce your interpretation of the writer's ideas.
- What specifics are given to expand upon the general idea? A general idea needs specific details in order to advance an argument or position.
- Is there a comparison to other related or parallel ideas? An indirect writing style will require you to sift through rhetorical devices or figures of speech to find a coherent position.
- What information conforms to this position and what information presents an opposite view in contrast? A writer may illustrate his or her own central idea by discussing opposing viewpoints.

3. The last step is to connect the information that is directly stated with the information that is implied to reach a conclusion that is a logical extension of these ideas.

- While watching a movie, you may find yourself wondering or guessing what will happen next. When you speculate like this, you are using your interpretative skills to infer possible outcomes. Reading can be approached in the same way. The following questions can help you find the main idea at this stage in the process.
  - From the information that has been presented, what outcomes or results can be expected?
  - What is implied or suggested by the writer, narrator, or characters?
  - What else would fit within the framework of the writer's position?
  - How can someone apply the information contained in this passage?
- All of these questions can lead you to logical conclusions drawn from the information provided directly by the writer or through dialogue and actions.

The three steps outlined in this section can help you improve your reading comprehension of poetry and prose. Some of the questions are useful to think about while you are reading, while others may be best answered after you have had a chance to read the whole selection. Being as curious as possible about a text can help you discover different layers of meaning and will help you to form ideas about the meaning of a text for assignments and tests.

11R.1.4 make and explain inferences of increasing subtlety about texts, including increasingly complex or difficult texts, supporting their explanations with well-chosen stated and implied ideas from the texts

Inferring Ideas from Texts

To make an inference is to draw a reasonable conclusion based on evidence and clues that are left behind in the text. One of the pleasures of reading, and one of the skills that develops with more reading, is to keep track of a variety of clues on several levels and see how they lead to different events and meanings in the text.

Often, many of the main ideas in a piece of writing are not stated directly, so when you read, you make assumptions or *inferences*. To make an inference, you need to use all the given information to decide what the text is about. It is also useful to think about your own experiences with the subject in order to determine correctly what the writer means.

Read the short story "Sanctuary," by Laurie Halse Anderson, and then look at the outline showing conclusions and generalizations supported by evidence inferred from the story. None of the points is explicitly given, but all can be inferred from the text. When you read, remember to consider what is implied as well as what is actually stated. The writer explicitly states how Mr. Freeman looks (ugly, big, and old), but does not tell us about Mr. Freeman's character. To get to know the real Mr. Freeman, you have to observe his words and actions in the story.

SANCTUARY

Art follows lunch, like dream follows nightmare. The classroom is at the far end of the building and has long, south-facing windows. The sun doesn't shine much in Syracuse, so the art room is designed to get every bit of light it can. It is dusty in a clean-dirt kind of way. The floor is layered with dry splotches of paint, the walls plastered with sketches of tormented teenagers and fat puppies, the shelves crowded with clay pots. A radio plays my favorite station.

Mr. Freeman is ugly. Big old grasshopper body, like a stilt-walking circus guy. Nose like a credit card sunk between his eyes. But he smiles at us as we file into class.

He is hunched over a spinning pot, his hands muddy red. "Welcome to the only class that will teach you how to survive," he says. "Welcome to Art."

I sit at a table close to his desk. Ivy is in this class. She sits by the door. I keep staring at her, trying to make her look at me. That happens in movies—people can feel it when other people stare at them and they just have to turn around and say something. Either Ivy has a great force field, or my laser vision isn't very strong. She won't look back at me. I wish I could sit with her. She knows art.

Mr. Freeman turns off the wheel and grabs a piece of chalk without washing his hands. "SOUL," he writes on the board. The clay streaks the word like dried blood. "This is where you can find your soul, if you dare. Where you can touch that part of you that you've never dared look at before. Do not come here and ask me to show you how to draw a face. Ask me to help you find the wind."

I sneak a peek behind me. The eyebrow telegraph is flashing fast. This guy is weird. He must see it; he must know what we are thinking. He keeps on talking. He says we will graduate knowing how to read and write because we'll spend a million hours learning how to read and write. (I could argue that point.)

Mr. Freeman: "Why not spend that time on art; painting, sculpting, charcoal, pastel, oils? Are words or numbers more important than images? Who decided this? Does algebra move you to tears?" (Hands raise, thinking he wants answers.) "Can the plural possessive express the feelings in your heart? If you don't learn art now, you will never learn to breathe!!!"

There is more. For someone who questions the value of words, he sure uses a lot of them. I tune out for a while and come back when he holds up a huge globe that is missing half of the Northern Hemisphere. "Can anyone tell me what this is?" he asks. "A globe?" ventures a voice in the back. Mr. Freeman rolls his eyes. "Was it an expensive sculpture that some kid dropped and he had to pay for it out of his own money or they didn't let him graduate?" asks another.

Mr. Freeman sighs. "No imagination. What are you, thirteen? Fourteen? You've already let them beat your creativity out of you! This is an old globe I used to let my daughters kick around my studio when it was too wet to play outside. One day Jenny put her foot right through Texas, and the United States crumbled into the sea. And *voilà*—an idea! This broken ball could be used to express such powerful visions—you could paint a picture of it with people fleeing from the hole, with a wet-muzzled dog chewing Alaska—the opportunities are endless. It's almost too much, but you are important enough to give it to."

Huh?

"You will each pick a piece of paper out of the globe." He walks around the room so we can pull red scraps from the center of the earth. "On the paper you will find one word, the name of an object. I hope you like it. You will spend the rest of the year learning how to turn that object into a piece of art. You will sculpt it. You will sketch it, papier-mâché it, carve it. If the computer teacher is talking to me this year, you can use the lab for computer-aided designs. But there's a catch—by the end of the year, you must figure out how to make your object say something, express an emotion, speak to every person who looks at it."

Some people groan. My stomach flutters. Can he really let us do this? It sounds like too much fun. He stops at my table. I plunge my hand into the bottom of the globe and fish out my paper. "Tree." Tree? It's too easy. I learned how to draw a tree in second grade. I reach in for another piece of paper. Mr. Freeman shakes his head. "Ah-ah-ah," he says. "You just chose your destiny, you can't change that."

He pulls a bucket of clay from under the pottery wheel, breaks off fist-sized balls and tosses one to each of us. Then he turns up the radio and laughs. "Welcome to the journey."

—*by* Laurie Halse Anderson

Inferences are assumptions. You have probably made many assumptions about this story after reading it just once. What is the narrator's character like, for example? How does he feel about art? What are his feelings toward Ivy? How does he approach school; do you think he is a good student?

The answers you have to these questions are inferences you have made from the text. Think of some more inferences about the teacher in the story, Mr. Freeman. What kind of man is he? What does he seem to value? Do you think he has a sense of humour?

Read the following example of a student's inferences about the narrator of the story and the teacher.

Example

POSSIBLE INFERENCES FROM "SANCTUARY"

The Narrator:

- likes art
- likes Ivy
- is not a particularly academic student—he does not see himself doing a lot of reading before he graduates
- does not realize the extent of the assignment

Mr. Freeman:

- believes art is part of the soul
- believes art infuses great emotions
- believes art is more important than the "core" subjects
- is imaginative
- has a sense of humour
- enjoys teaching and the students

Thinking more about inferences will help your essay writing. Being able to find evidence from the text to support your thesis statement begins with something you already do when you read: making inferences. You already make inferences about texts you read, so being able to pinpoint exactly what part of the text led you to draw those inferences is important. If you can tell what part of a text caused you to make an assumption, you can quote that part of the text in your essay. Backing up your thesis statement using evidence from the text is extremely important. To help your reading and writing skills, start thinking more about the inferences you already make during reading.

11R1.5 extend understanding of texts, including increasingly complex or difficult texts, by making appropriate and increasingly rich connections between the ideas in them and personal knowledge, experience, and insights; other texts; and the world around them

Extending Understanding of Texts

One of the ways you can enjoy texts is through the experience of the emotions they inspire within you. You can deepen your understanding of the technical aspects of a text and appreciate the level of expertise that is required to create a compelling piece of writing. At the same time, your responses to what you read tell you something about yourself. You might find yourself supporting characters you typically would not support or resisting those with whom you would typically identify. This movement in and out of the text, from the craft of the writer to the interpretation of the reader, gives an exciting variety to the range of meanings in any one text.

To better understand what you read, you should connect, compare, and contrast.

Connect: As you read different things about a subject, look for connections between the ideas, themes, and issues that are presented. First of all, are there connections? Is the subject the same? Do the writers feel the same way about it? Even when two pieces of writing seem to be about different subjects, you can often find connections.

Compare: When you compare pieces of writing, you think about how they are similar to each another. Perhaps they are very different in style, but they give the same basic information. When you compare, similarities are your focus.

Contrast: When you contrast pieces of writing, you think about how they are different from each another. Perhaps the writers give the same information, but the way they go about it is very different. When you contrast, differences are your focus.

11R1.6 analyse texts in terms of the information, ideas, issues, or themes they explore, examining how various aspects of the texts contribute to the presentation or development of these elements

Analysing Texts

Sometimes, students say that analysing a text is what ruins it for them; that doing analysis is like dissecting a frog in a biology class. After you are finished dissecting the poor creature, there is nothing left of the original living, breathing frog. But it is possible to analyse a text and not ruin it completely for yourself by keeping in mind what you are really doing. Analysis is not like frog dissecting; instead, it is a way to return to a text you have really enjoyed and ask yourself some technical questions about what makes the text enjoyable. Here, analysis refers primarily to the craft of composition, the art of fine writing. In order to find ways to talk about the finer points of a text you have enjoyed, you will need some special terms. As you become a better reader, you will want to become more skilled at analysing texts while continuing to enjoy them for your own personal reasons. Analytical skills develop as you explore and assess ideas, themes, concepts, and arguments while reading.

Multiple Perspectives and Theme in the Novel

Theme can be defined as the controlling or core idea of a narrative. All elements of a narrative contribute to its theme, as illustrated in the diagram:

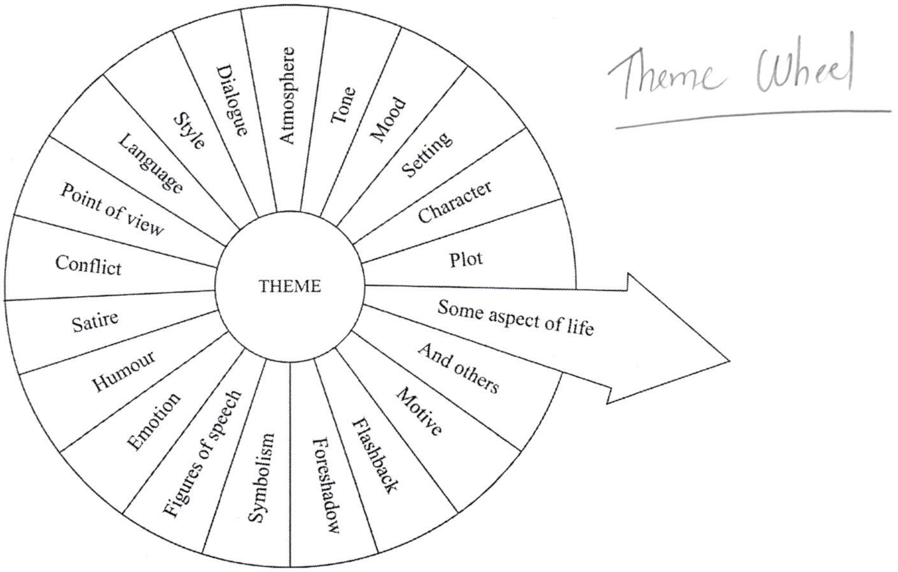

It is also important to recognize universal themes in literature that have existed in various time periods and cultures. Some frequently encountered universal themes include the

- fear of the unknown
- struggle between good and evil
- desire for meaningful relationships
- desire for understanding and search for meaning or truth
- desire to control our environment
- desire to be understood
- struggle to meet challenges or overcome adversity

The fact that universal themes remain constant and recur contributes to the enduring appeal of cross-cultural and classical literature. The novel *Oliver Twist*, for instance, deals extensively with the theme of good struggling against evil. In the novel, written approximately 200 years ago, multiple perspectives contribute to the theme.

Consider some of the following perspectives:

Setting

The dark, dank workhouse environment, the dark, closed casket where Oliver hides at Sowerberry's undertaking establishment, and the dark, seamy underbelly of criminal London contrast sharply with the airy open windows of Mr. Brownlow's home looking out over the sunny square bustling with legitimate human endeavours and business.

Character

The novel is filled with contrasting good/evil characters, but of note are the following two characters who especially contrast: Bill Sikes, the very epitome of evil, contrasted with Oliver's gracious and benevolent grandfather, Mr. Brownlow.

Mood

The mood of suspense and foreboding lurks in the deep shadows of the London Bridge, at night, contrasting with the mood of salvation and anticipation evident in Mr. Brownlow's hurrying steps as he hastens toward his fateful meeting with Nancy.

Conflict

In the climactic struggle under the bridge, evil temporarily seems to triumph over good, as Bill Sikes takes Nancy's life in a fit of rage.

Plot

Many of the episodes comprising the rising action of the novel reflect the universal theme of the struggle between good and evil: the old nurse stealing the locket from Oliver's mother; the struggle for fair treatment in the workhouse which climaxes in Oliver asking for more food; the struggles at the undertaking establishment; Fagin's constant indecision between good intentions and his profitable-but-evil lifestyle, and so on.

Point of View

The omniscient narrator viewpoint allows the revelation of the ongoing struggle between good and evil to be revealed through character viewpoints in the novel, including Nancy's gradual transformation from cynical exploiter (evil) to heroic saviour (good).

Foreshadowing

Bill Sikes' threats against Nancy foreshadow the evil outcome that will result from her courageous choice, while the ironic surrender of a small gold locket to Mr. Brownlow by the greedy Bumbles foreshadows the golden outcome that lies ahead for Oliver.

If you refer back to the theme diagram, you will see that other elements of the narrative also contribute to the universal theme underlying the novel.

11R1.8 identify and analyse the perspectives and/or biases evident in texts, including increasingly complex or difficult texts, commenting with growing understanding on any questions they may raise about beliefs, values, identity, and power

Critical Literacy = Looking beyond the surface of the storyline.

Here the term "critical" does not imply a negative, or even skeptical, attitude toward everything that one reads as one becomes more "literate." Instead, being "critical" involves looking beyond the surface of the storyline to understand the motives of characters or the meanings of events. Together with this attitude of curiosity and understanding, the term "critical" also refers to the development of your own stance in relation to a variety of topics, issues, lifestyles, and values. The ultimate purpose here is not to dismiss those texts that you do not "agree with," but to understand on a deeper level your own reasons for the opinions you form. Reading "critically" also means becoming aware of those messages that try to manipulate the reader into accepting points of view he or she would normally resist.

Literature presents the reader with values, perspectives, and world views in a way that invites engagement, discussion, interpretation, and comparison. Good literature makes you think about the ideas it presents and how these ideas might relate to the real world.

Values = influence your perspective and point of you on life and issues.

Values are invisible, but they are based on the beliefs and principles that influence your *perspective*, or point of view, on the experiences of your life, and on the issues you encounter. Your values ultimately shape your *world view*. This world view influences your judgments, the way you feel toward and treat others, and the motivations that govern your actions.

Literature, like life, is an arena of *values*, *perspectives*, and *world views*. In literature, these world views are revealed through the writer's narration and descriptions of settings. In particular, characters in literature often become voices for values, perspectives, and world views. Poetry is also a vehicle for expressing a single or multifaceted viewpoint. Stories offer perspectives and world views for exploration, interpretation, and comparison. As a reader, you are invited to join the discussion, to analyse descriptions and motivations you see in the text, and to agree or disagree with the writer or characters.

Values, perspectives, and world views can be presented in different ways:

By the Author

Henry David Thoreau (1817–1862) was an American author and philosopher. He was an advocate of independence and simple living who opposed slavery. Can you find clues about his values, perspective, or world view in the opening paragraph of one of his most well-known essays?

Example

***from* WALDEN OR, LIFE IN THE WOODS**

The mass of men lead lives of quiet desperation. What is called resignation is confirmed desperation. From the desperate city you go into the desperate country, and have to console yourself with the bravery of minks and muskrats. A stereotyped but unconscious despair is concealed even under what are called the games and amusements of mankind. There is no play in them, for this comes after work. But it is a characteristic of wisdom not to do desperate things.

From a Character

Lester Burnham is the main protagonist in the movie *American Beauty*, the screenplay for which was written by Alan Ball. As a middle-aged man who values fulfillment in life, Lester finds himself trapped in a rut, wherein he hates the mundane predictability of his job and comes home at night to a wife consumed by materialism. One day, Lester meets his daughter's friend, whose youth and beauty jars Lester alive. His quest to recapture his lost youth motivates him to begin working out, to try drugs, to quit his job, and to buy an expensive car. Lester's twisted and adolescent views of self-fulfillment eventually lead him to attempt the seduction of his daughter's teenage friend, foreshadowing the tragic denouement of the story. As a cautionary tale, the movie ends with the visual of a simple plastic bag dancing in the wind, reflecting simplicity. Simplicity, as evidenced in Thoreau's view, cited earlier in the excerpt of *Walden*, is that which makes life beautiful and meaningful.

From a Setting

The setting contributes to a set of assumptions and value systems that can often reinforce theme.

Example

In William Faulkner's short story, "A Rose for Emily," the description of Miss Emily's house reinforces the decline of Miss Emily's influence in the town, and by inference, her resistance to change, along with the changing economic climate.

"It was a big squarish frame house that had once been white, decorated with cupolas and spires and scrolled balconies in the heavily lightsome style of the seventies, set on what has once been our most select street. But garages and cotton gins had encroached and obliterated even the august names of that neighborhood; only Miss Emily's house was left, lifting its stubborn and coquettish decay above the cotton wagons and the gasoline pumps—an eyesore among eyesores."

From a Poem

In the poem "Swimmer's Moment," the lure of seeking self-fulfillment is compared to a swimmer taking a risk by diving into a whirlpool. The world view or perspective that self-fulfillment requires risk is a theme also present in *American Beauty*. In John Milton's poem, "On His Blindness," the poet expresses a less narcissistic, more spiritual worldview. The poet, upon reflecting on the personal challenge of losing his vision, concludes that, while it is a natural outreach of the human condition to question God or fate, dark times do not have to cause the death of dreams. "They also serve who only stand and wait."

Change in Character Perspective = Dynamic Character.

Developed characters in literature are motivated by their values and perspectives. Because they are not static, their world views, particularly in a novel, tend to evolve through conflict and experience. Consider Nancy, the tragic character in *Oliver Twist*:

Early in the Novel

Bawdy, self-mocking, and irreverent, Nancy survives as a hardened prostitute in London. Street life is all she has known since her earliest association with Fagin, who exhibits the same fancy and superficial airs of the "gentlemen" she so despises. The closest emotion to love that Nancy has encountered is her love/hate relationship with the violent and unpredictable Bill Sikes, a professional thief who verbally and physically abuses her.

Later in the Novel

Nancy meets young Oliver when he is brought into Fagin's gang by the Artful Dodger. Although she sneeringly teases the new recruit, some long-dead softness in her heart is awakened by the vulnerability and innocence of the young orphan. Nancy's world view opens to admit a ray of generosity, hope, and optimism. However, at this point, Nancy's world view is still opportunistic and cynical enough that she relentlessly participates in kidnapping Oliver back from Mr. Brownlow.

Near the End of the Novel

Nancy's world view has changed dramatically. The opportunistic, cynical view that has influenced Nancy to submit to a violent life of criminal activity has been replaced by hope, not for herself, but for the disarming child, Oliver Twist. Although it is too late for her, Nancy realizes that the world represented by Mr. Brownlow is a truly good place, full of opportunities for Oliver if he can escape the criminal slums of London. So completely has Nancy embraced her moral, philanthropic, and optimistic world view that she is willing to sacrifice everything, even her life, to return the child she has stolen to his grandfather. Nancy does indeed sacrifice her life for her new world view.

As you look at literature, it is fascinating to connect the changes in developing characters to evolving world views. These are the memorable connections that link characters in a work of fiction to the ever-evolving complexities of our real lives.

Understanding Form and Style

11R2.1 Identify a variety of characteristics of literary, informational, and graphic text forms and explain how they help communicate meaning

Text Forms

Understanding the meaning of the term form is easier if you first consider the meaning of the term *content*. Content is the message the text is expressing through symbols, settings, events, and characters' responses. Content is often considered to express the meaning of a text. In contrast, the form of a text refers to the way in which meaning is expressed. Formal questions about a text might deal with organization and the sequence of ideas, relating this ordering to the general effectiveness of the text in presenting the content, or meaning.

Poetry

Every part of a poem is carefully chosen to create a particular message, experience, or idea. The words, the sounds of the words, the line breaks, the stanzas, and the spaces are all aspects of a poem that are deliberately chosen by a poet. There are many different styles of poetry, but all poems contain some or all of these elements: form, sound, a speaker, figurative language, and imagery.

Short Stories

The elements of a short story, such as character, plot, theme, and setting, are related to each other in such a way that the reader is left with a definite impression.

Setting

Setting is the time and place in which the story takes place. Many texts begin with a detailed description of the setting so the reader has a foundation for imagining the environment in which the action between characters takes place.

Character and Action

Character and action are two essential elements in all stories. Without characters, there would be no story.

Historical Novels

Historical novels use elements of reality from a given time period and may portray fictitious characters or historical characters. Writers of historical novels depend on imagery to transport their readers into the realms of the past, and they use symbols to represent ideas or emotions. The writer of a realistic novel tries to create characters that could actually have existed in the historical setting in which the novel is placed.

Essays

Essays are compositions of several paragraphs in which a writer discusses a certain subject in detail. Essayists have a purpose for writing, organize their ideas clearly, and come up with creative and original details in order to enhance their essays.

Elements of an Essay

The Introduction

- must grab the reader's attention and be creative and imaginative
- must introduce the main idea and provide a preview of supporting details that will be discussed

The Body

- Definition: defines key terms and elaborates on them
- Comparison: explores similarities and differences between things
- Cause and Effect: considers causes for events and behaviours and discusses their outcomes
- Problem-Solution: states a problem, giving details and offering solutions supported with evidence andfacts that will solve the problem

Conclusion

- Short and to-the-point endings
- Brief summary of main points
- Should not include new information

There are many different types of essays, but by examining a few, you can see how organization can strengthen a writer's argument.

Descriptive Essays

Descriptive essays are essays in which the writer provides concrete details describing people, places, experiences, or ideas. Writers use descriptive essays to enable readers to have the fullest, most sensory experience of the writer's topic. The main focus of a descriptive essay is to make readers feel as though they are really experiencing what the writer is describing.

Narrative Essays

Narrative essays allow the writer to present real or imagined events in the first-person perspective. The writer uses his or her essay to make a comment about life or to present ideas about a particular situation.

Expository Essays

Expository essays give information about events, issues, or ideas. The purpose of an expository essay is to expose, explain, analyse, or clarify a topic. The writer does this using comparison and contrast, cause-and-effect logical reasoning, or definition. Expository essays are informative; a writer will try to remain objective and avoid emotional language.

Persuasive or Argumentative Essay

The main purpose of a persuasive or argumentative essay is to convince the reader to agree with the writer's point of view or ideas on a topic. The writer presents his or her arguments and uses factual examples to support and convince the reader. The basic text is expository because it uses definition, examples, and comparison/contrast to present the arguments. Persuasive, emotional language can also be used in order to sway the reader to agree with the writer's ideas.

Form

Form describes the structure of a text. The following chart contains examples and definitions of common text forms.

Examples of Forms	Characteristics
letter	generally begins with an inside address and date; uses conventional greeting and closings such as *Dear*——— and *Yours sincerely*
memorandum	often brief and addressed to a limited group, such as the employees of a company; limited to essential information
short story	20 000 words or less; usually few characters, one main character; a single plot
novella	20 000 to 50 000 words; a shorter version of a novel
novel	over 50 000 words; usually 90 000 to 100 000 or more; may contain many characters and multiple plots within the main story
screenplay	contains mainly dialogue and directions for the action; special rules for margins and font size give a standard length of approximately one page to one minute of screen time

Genre

Genre refers to content or subject matter. Works that are categorized in a literary genre will share certain characteristic elements. A western, for example, usually includes a gunfight. Science fiction often includes details about imaginary scientific developments. A romance novel is characterized by its emphasis on the romance relationship between two leading characters.

Forms and genres can be combined in various ways. For example, an epistolary novel, which is a novel written through a series of letters, uses the novel and the letter as forms. Such a novel could be written in any genre, and genres can be combined. A science fiction story might also be a romance, and a historical novel might also be a detective story. Also, elements of one genre are sometimes used in other genres.

There are many possible combinations of form and genre. The following chart contains examples of common text forms and genres.

<table>
<tr><th colspan="3">Examples of Forms</th><th>Examples of Genres</th></tr>
<tr><td rowspan="3">fiction</td><td>poetry</td><td>metrical
free verse
sonnet</td><td>epic
ballad
lyric</td></tr>
<tr><td rowspan="2">prose</td><td>play
musical
motion picture
Shakespearean
modern</td><td>tragedy
comedy</td></tr>
<tr><td>novel
novella
short story</td><td>historical
detective
fantasy
science fiction
realistic</td></tr>
</table>

non-fiction		history	political social military
		biography autobiography memoir	
		documentary film	
		essay	expository persuasive research
		letter	personal business letter to the editor
		diary	
		references	encyclopedia dictionary thesaurus atlas
		textbook manual	

The choice of form depends on the writer's purpose and intended audience.

11R2.2 identify a variety of text features and explain how they help communicate meaning

TEXT FEATURES

One of the formal elements to consider when rereading a text is its textual features. Textual features relate to the visual presentation of information and the ways in which it clarifies (or confuses) the meaning of the language. For example, the type of font, the thickness of the letters, and the size of the printing can all contribute to the reader's understanding of the meaning of the words spoken by a character in a graphic novel. You may feel confident in your ability to understand language on a semantic level, but the visual features of a text also contribute in important ways to your understanding of, and responses to, the text as a whole.

Font refers to a set of images (glyphs) representing the characters from a particular character set in a particular typeface. The words "font" and "typeface" are not interchangeable. Font refers to the size and design of the characters, for example, 10-point or 12-point Arial font.

When texts are being written, the font style, the layout of the text, and the spacing are all taken into consideration in order to enhance meaning and strengthen the impact of the text on the reader.

Science Texts

Textbooks, including science texts, use different sizes and types of font in order to help clarify explanations and organize content clearly. They often contain labelled diagrams and pictures or photographs that have captions. Italics are frequently used to set apart scientific words or to refer to figures. Make note of the font choice and size and the use of capitals, bolded text, and italics in the following biology text. Notice how the writers have varied the fonts and designed the layout of the pages in order to ensure maximum understanding of the information presented. The text is reader friendly in layout and word choice.

Example

Plants and other autotrophs are not able to metabolize these molecules until they have been nitrified into compounds that contain oxygen. Nitrification transforms the ammonia and ammonium ions into nitrates (NO_3) and nitrite ions (NO_2^-), which can be metabolized.

Abiotic factors can also transform free nitrogen into nitrogenous compounds. For example, lightning can convert nitrogen gas into nitrates, which can be washed into the soil through rainfall. Farmers often notice significant crop growth after a lightning storm as the root systems of the plants absorb the nitrogenous nutrients.

Plants can transform nitrogenous materials into a number of different important organic compounds, but the three most important categories are **amino acids, nucleotides**, and **adenosine triphosphate**. Since animals are unable to fix nitrogen themselves, they are dependent upon plants to form the foundation of the food chain, which eventually distributes these nutrients to all of the organisms in the biosphere.

The following diagram illustrates how nitrogen is removed from the atmosphere and directed into the lithosphere and hydrosphere.
It also shows how nitrogen migrates through the nitrogen cycle and back into the atmosphere.

The Nitrogen Cycle

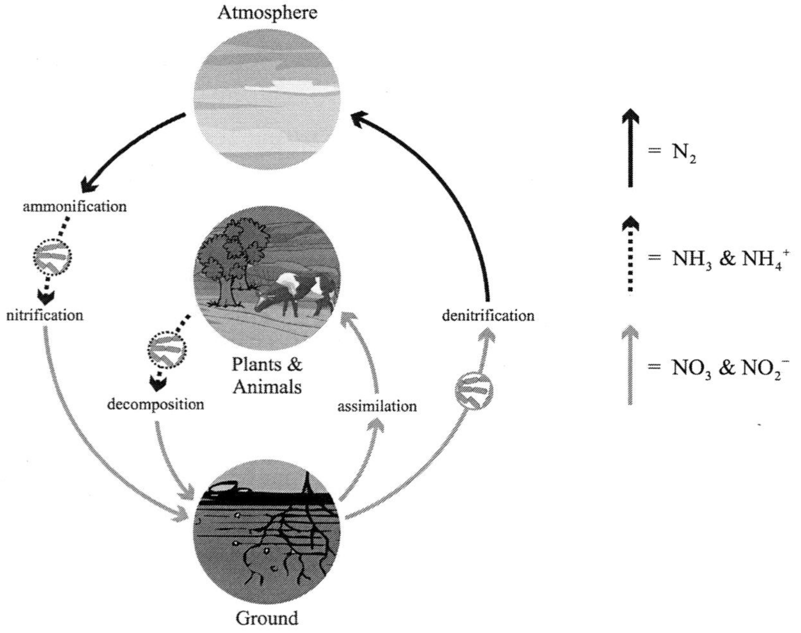

Animals are unable to store protein or other nitrogenous compounds in the same way as they store carbon compounds, such as glucose.
Therefore, excess metabolized nitrogen must be excreted as waste.
Digestive and urinary tracts function as means for the nitrogenous waste products to be returned to the nitrogen cycle.

NOTES

The three important types of nitrogenous compounds are **amino acids, nucleotides,** and **ATP**.

11R2.3 identify a variety of elements of style in texts and explain how they communicate meaning and enhance the effectiveness of the texts

Elements of Style

Language and syntax are used by writers in creative ways to manipulate mood, tone, suspense, and other elements of a text.

Sentence Variety

Sentence variety can refer to

- sentence length: a succession of short sentences can be used for strong effect after a series of longer
- sentence type: simple, compound, and compound-complex sentences can be used for variety or to control the development of ideas (transitional devices can be useful for this purpose).
- sentence order: the most important part can be emphasized by putting it first. NASA might note that "A meteorite hit a man in Whitehorse," while the *Whitehorse Star* might report, "Local Man Hit by Meteorite."
- word order is closely related to sentence order. For example, "accused mass murderer Goneril Brocadie" appears to be the same as "Goneril Brocadie, who is accused of mass murder," but the first phrase subtly suggests that Brocadie is actually guilty, not merely accused. The adjectives closest to the noun clearly imply the message *mass murderer Brocadie.*

Poetic Language

Poetic language includes such literary devices as

- **Onomatopoeia**: the use of words that suggest the sound of the thing they describe.
  - *Buzz*, *splash*, and *clash* sound like the sounds they describe.
- **Alliteration**: the repetition of first letters, often consonants.
  - "Dim drums throbbing in the hills half heard."
- **Assonance**: the repeated use of a vowel within successive words.
- **Consonance**: the repeated use of a consonant within successive words:
  - "The moan of doves in immemorial elms,
And murmuring of innumerable bees."

Word placement and sentence order can also be used to emphasize and suggest ideas or themes.

- **Parallelism**: the deliberate repetition of sentence elements or of some other structural pattern.
  - In Paul's letter to the Corinthians, he writes,
"Are they Hebrews? So am I. Are they Israelites? So am I. Are they Abraham's descendants? So am I."
- **Repetition**: similar to parallelism, although it may be on a smaller scale.
  - "Break, break, break,
On thy cold gray stones, O sea"

Figures of speech are used for effect and sometimes to convey information.

- **Simile**: a comparison that uses the words *like* or *as*.
  - "Her presence at the meeting was *like* a breath of fresh air."
- **Metaphor**: a comparison that does not use the words *like* or *as* and appears to be an actual statement of fact.
  - "He had the *eye of an eagle*."
- **Hyperbole**: deliberate exaggeration to make a point, but not to deceive.
  - "That joke is as *old as the hills*."
- **Synecdoche**: the naming of one part of something to stand for the whole thing, or of the whole thing to stand for a part.
  - "A fine herd of cattle you have there. About a hundred *head*, I guess?"
  - "Thirteen *sail* appeared on the horizon."
- **Metonymy**: the use of something associated with a second thing to stand for that second thing. The association can be arbitrary, as long as it is widely understood. Metonymy is often visual and is widely used in film as a visual shorthand. Rain falling at a funeral is a visual representation of grief because of its physical association with tears.
  - "The White House represents the American Government."
  - "An apple is often used to represent education."
- **Personification**: the attribution of human qualities or actions to something that is not human. Animals, inanimate objects, and ideas can all be personified.
  - "Life's but a walking shadow a poor player / That struts and frets his hour upon the stage."
- **Symbolism**: the use of something concrete to represent an abstract belief, feeling, idea, or attitude.
  - For example, a red rose is often used to symbolize love. Even certain colours can symbolize abstract ideas. Black, for example, often symbolizes death.
- **Oxymoron**: a two-or three-word phrase that contains opposite words or ideas.
  - "sweet sorrow"
  - "forward retreat"
- **Paradox**: an extended oxymoron that appears to present contradictory ideas.
  - "I must be cruel only to be kind."
- **Imagery**: words or phrases that appeal to the senses and help the reader imagine sights, sounds, smells, tastes, and touch.
  - "The children were nestled all snug in their beds."
  - "While visions of sugar plums danced in their heads."
  - "As dry leaves that before the wild hurricane fly."

- **Idiom**: an expression that means something other than what it actually says and is often associated with colloquialisms and proverbs.
  - "To make hay while the sun shines."

Literary Techniques

Literary techniques are the techniques and devices employed by a writer to make literature more effective and colourful. Literary techniques include

- **Dramatic irony**: when the audience knows something that the characters do not.
  - The audience watching *Oedipus Rex* knows that Oedipus is marrying his mother, but the characters do not know.
  - History produces dramatic irony. For example, in news footage shot in 1938, Prime Minister Neville Chamberlain proclaims to the British nation, "I believe it is peace in our time." Meanwhile, Chamberlain had actually condemned his nation and the world to five years of war.
  - Life produces dramatic irony. For example, for over 50 years after the end of the First World War, the bodies of men killed in France were recovered from excavations made for construction. It was not uncommon to find the last letter home perfectly preserved. In fact, it was common enough that there was a rule about handling them: letters to sweethearts were to be destroyed, letters to families were to be delivered. Imagine the bitter irony of receiving such a letter, written in the youthful voice and the forgotten slang of a time as dead as the writer—Dear All, I hope this finds you in the pink, as it leaves me.
- **Verbal irony**: when the true meaning of words is different from their surface meaning
  - If a politician praises his opponents for their honesty and integrity when he knows quite well that they are corrupt, he is speaking ironically.
- **Sarcasm**: similar to irony, except that it is directed at someone—usually in a sarcastic tone of voice—who knows that exactly the opposite of what is being said is what is meant.
  - The question "Well, you really are clever, aren't you?" stated in a sarcastic way actually means the contrary. A person may sometimes use sarcasm as a way of attacking someone without appearing completely nasty.
- **Satire**: when writing exposes the failings of individuals, institutions, or societies to ridicule or scorn. The purpose of satire is to correct or expose some evil or wrongdoing.
  - George Orwell's *Animal Farm* is a satire about life in Russia during the rise of Communism.
- **Allusion**: an indirect or passing reference to a person, place, or event. The writer relies on the reader's familiarity with the reference and does not explain it directly.
  - The line from Julius Caesar, "Why, man, he doth bestride the narrow world / Like a Colossus," alludes to the giant statue the Colossus of Rhodes.
- **Analogy**: a comparison between things intended to illustrate the similarities between them. Simile and analogy are alike, but analogy tends to be more extended.
  - "Knowledge always desires increase: it is like fire, which must first be kindled by some external agent, but which will after words propagate itself" (Samuel Johnson).

- **Cliché**: a phrase or opinion that is overused and betrays the lack of original thought.
  - Examples of clichéd phrases are "put all your eggs in one basket" and "don't count your chickens before they are hatched."
- **Juxtaposition**: exists when there is the deliberate contrast of characters, settings, or situations for effect.
  - "Nor did she look at the juxtaposition of cigar and finger, although she knew by the evidence of her rose that it still obtained."
- **Motif**: a recurring theme, situation, incident, image, or character type found in literature.
  - In Macbeth, blood is one of the major motifs. It is the outward sign of Macbeth's and Lady Macbeth's evil and is a continual reminder of the terrible acts that have been committed. The witches are also motifs representing the dark side of human behaviour.

Common Symbols in Literature

Some common symbols in literature include:

- Water: fertility, life-giving, rebirth, purification, and redemption
- Stagnant or polluted water: corruption, evil
- Fire: destruction, purification, passion, death
- Earth: baseness, fertility
- Air, wind: spirits, freedom, inspiration
- Sun: wisdom and vision, power, life-giving, regeneration
- Sunrise: birth, rebirth, joy, hope
- Sunset: death
- Mountains: obstacles, achievement, aspirations, awe, glory
- Storms: death, evil, inner turmoil
- Roads, ships, trains, railroads: journeys, changes
- Fork in the road, crossroads: choices, decisions
- Doors, gates, arches: escape, opportunities, utopias, fantasy worlds, freedom
- Bridges: transitions, crossing over
- Walls, fences, hedges: barriers, dividing lines, prisons
- Windows: freedom, longing, imprisonment
- Mirrors: illusion, unreality, passage to other worlds
- Birds, sky: freedom
- Circle: wholeness, unity
- Gardens: Eden, paradise, innocence, fertility
- Desert: spiritual aridity, death, hopelessness, sterility
- Lamb: innocence, Christ
- Sheep: conformity
- Black: evil, death, despair

- White: innocence, good, redemption
- Red: war, anger, blood, vengeance, love, passion
- Green: growth, renewal, life, nature, envy
- Yellow: sun, happiness, cowardice, betrayal

Effects of Literary Devices

When you read poetry, you expect to find figurative language that helps you see, hear, taste, touch, experience literature through your senses. Consider the following two poems:

FOG

The fog comes
on little cat feet.

It sits looking over harbor and city
on silent haunches
and then moves on.

—*by* Carl Sandburg

MOTHER TO SON

Well, son, I'll tell you:
Life for me ain't been no crystal stair.
It's had tacks in it,
And splinters,
And boards torn up,
And places with no carpet on the floor—
Bare.
But all the time
I'se been a-climbin' on,
And reachin' landin's,
And turnin' corners,
And sometimes goin' in the dark
Where there ain't been no light.
So boy, don't you turn back.
Don't you set down on the steps
'Cause you finds it's kinder hard.
Don't you fall now—
For I'se still goin', honey,
I'se still climbin',
And life for me ain't been no crystal stair.

—*by* Langston Hughes

When you read the poem "Fog," can you picture a stealthy grey fog creeping over the buildings and out to sea after lingering throughout the early morning over the harbour? Is a cat a good metaphor to provide readers with this mental image?

In "Mother to Son," "Life," for the mother "ain't been no crystal stair." Does this metaphor lead you to picture a smooth and glittering staircase, sparkling under the twinkling lights of a crystal chandelier? What the mother is trying to tell her son is that for her, life is tough and hard, like a neglected wooden staircase with threadbare carpeting, full of splinters and nasty surprises that she compares with "sometimes goin' in the dark." The speaker's references to "landin's," and "turnin' corners," are examples of symbolism. The "landin's" represent plateaus or small successes that the mother has achieved. The "corners" she turns could be new directions she has taken with her life. The mother ends her tale with words of encouragement: "So, boy, don't you turn back … Don't you fall now—for I'se still goin', honey." Basically, the mother is telling her son never to give up. What is notable is how beautiful and effective simple words of advice become when symbolism and metaphors replace plain language.

Reading with Fluency

11R3.1 automatically understand most words in a variety of reading contexts

Context and Background

Context provides perspective. A better understanding of the context of even a single word can help you better understand an entire text. For example, imagine that you were reading a book from the time of your great-grandparents, and you read a couple of lines at random. Most likely, you would be puzzled.

Example

- "Ah, poor Smythe. Both of his sons killed at Arras, you know. And he lost his wife in the last Zeppelin raid."

You might find this bit of dialogue hard to follow at first. Words and phrases like "Arras" and "Zeppelin raids" can seem foreign. At this stage, it is a good idea to slow down your reading. Take some time to analyse the text in smaller pieces. Among the unfamiliar phrases, you should be able to find some phrases that you can understand, such as "poor Smythe." You understand that someone is being referred to, and in this case, being pitied, so you can also infer that the speaker is expressing sympathy. In addition, the use of dialogue suggests that the book is a story.

If you read that the story takes place in the 1920s—not long after the First World War—you can use your general knowledge of that time to better understand the text. The context now suggests that the sons were soldiers and that Arras was a battle. The Zeppelin raids would have had something to do with civilian casualties, since Smythe's wife, as a woman in the time of the First World War, would not have been fighting. You can infer that she probably died as an innocent civilian. The context of only two sentences allows you to make numerous inferences. While these inferences do not make for a complete understanding, they help you develop a good beginning understanding, especially if the unfamiliar words initially confused you.

Why would a writer refer to details that might confuse the reader in the first place? Usually, a writer provides detail to make the story realistic. If a writer sets his or her story in a particular time and place, he or she will often refer to details that were part of the reality for that setting. Zeppelin raids would have been a reality for people living in Europe at the time of the First World War. When a writer refers to details of the world he or she is creating to make that world more realistic, the writer is using *verisimilitude*. For example, if a writer wanted to employ verisimilitude in a novel set in Canada in 2008, he or she might mention Prime Minister Harper, the war in Afghanistan, or describe the most common types of cars.

The Writer's Life and Context

Context includes background information, knowledge, ideas—anything that adds to the understanding of a text. Writers frequently draw on the experiences of their lives when they write. It makes sense, then, that finding out more about a writer's life will give you added insight into the themes and main ideas of a text. The following section touches on aspects of a text to consider when trying to understand the relationship between context and the writer.

Intended Audience

Who was originally meant to read the text?

- A poet might write for a small circle of friends—or for the whole world and for the coming centuries.
- A novel is generally written with the hope that it will be read by as many people as possible.
- Diaries are usually private, but some writers will journal their experiences with an eye on a potential future audience.
- E-mails and letters are usually written only for their recipients. Letters to the editor of a newspaper are written with the intention of reaching a larger audience.

Who is the intended audience?

- Shakespeare wrote for the Londoners who could make it to his theatre. It seems that the publication of his plays was an afterthought. The purpose of writing his plays was to attract more people to the theatre.
- Leonardo da Vinci wrote his famous notebooks for himself. He even wrote using a mirror, so that it would be more difficult for someone else to read what he wrote.

Purpose

- What did the writer intend to do?
- Some writers intend to persuade, spread ideas, and instruct.
- The purpose may be to move people to action.
- Some writers want to share personal thoughts and feelings.
- Sometimes, the writer writes simply for entertainment purposes.

Time

When was the work produced?

- Periods of war or upheaval may give a writer ideas or shape the writer's purpose.
- Peaceful and prosperous times also shape the writer's ideas and purpose, but neither the writer nor the audience may notice.

Place

Where did the writer live? Place can be just as relevant to the writer's life as the time in which he or she lived. Surroundings shape a writer's experiences and can also contribute to his or her material.

- Many people living in the 1930s shared a sense of insecurity and fear. Across the world, the Great Depression was affecting people's livelihoods and ability to survive. People everywhere were suffering from poverty and famine.

- North Americans of the past two generations have had their experiences shaped by years of peace and prosperity—across the world, however, people in countries plagued by poverty and war probably have a very different perspective on life. Because of this continent's relative stability and wealth, the suffering in other countries can be ignored or forgotten. Writers who tell stories of hardship in other countries bring to light the suffering that exists outside of North America.

Who Is Speaking?

Fictional characters can sometimes have a kind of real life. They can have their own thoughts, feelings, and opinions. Writers choose to create characters in different ways. Some characters are totally unique creations that do not express the viewpoints of the writer at all. Some characters are vehicles for the writer to make a point about something. When a writer feels strongly about something, he or she will often create a character who can express these opinions.

It is important to separate the writer from the characters he or she creates. Characters are not always reflections of the writer, nor are the opinions they express always those of the writer. Research about the writer's life and beliefs can sometimes help you figure out which type of character a writer has decided to create in a given text.

Writers often reveal themselves in their writing, but it is the reader's job to pay attention to the whole context of the work and decide when the writer is speaking and when the characters are speaking.

Diction = writers choice of words.

A writer's choice of words can affect the meaning and impact of the text. The following definitions deal with the different aspects of language a writer may change depending on the effect he or she wants to achieve in his or her writing.

- Diction is the choice of words and phrases.

- Register refers to the special features of speech or writing used by a particular group for a particular purpose. For example, newspaper reporters have a certain register, or common vocabulary, and established patterns of organization that they use in writing news stories.

- Jargon refers to specialized language that is used by the members of a particular group. Jargon has the advantage (for those who understand it) of shortening communication and sometimes of making communication more accurate. Jargon is like a set of tools: people who are not familiar with the jargon are lost, but those who do understand it can communicate more quickly.

The control of diction, the use of a certain register, and the use of jargon depend entirely on the intended audience.

Clichés

Clichés are overused, worn-out expressions that have lost their freshness and impact. You can generally convey meaning more concisely and with greater originality using your own words than by using clichés. For example, to "burn the midnight oil" simply means to work late and "as snug as a bug in a rug" means to be comfortable.

11R3.2 use decoding strategies effectively to read and understand unfamiliar words, including words of increasing difficulty

Word and Structural Analysis

It is not a bad idea to bring along a dictionary the next time you curl up with a good book in your favourite reading chair. You would not want to look up every word you do not know, or only know vaguely, because doing so would interrupt the flow of your reading and spoil the enjoyment of taking in someone else's ideas. But at some points, you might want to pause and look up a few words, even if just to confirm that your definition was correct. Not all new words are elevated and "smart"; many unfamiliar words you come across may be from a regional dialect or some slang or figure of speech you are not familiar with. Looking up the word gives you not only the definition of the term, but also some of the other ways in which it is used. Of course, another way to get pretty close to the definitions of new words is by considering the context of the sentences and paragraphs in which they appear. If you do not have time to look up words in a dictionary or only want to do so after reading the entire piece, determining the meaning of unfamiliar words based on their context is a reading skill you will continue to develop as you become more experienced with understanding a variety of texts.

Word analysis refers to the process of decoding unfamiliar words. It includes the ability to recognize spelling patterns; knowledge of the meanings of root words, prefixes, and suffixes; using word parts and determining pronunciation and meaning; and being able to use word-attack skills. If you are able to analyse everyday words, you will find it easier to attack unfamiliar technical and scientific terms.

Structural analysis is the process of using word parts to determine the meaning and pronunciation of unknown words. When you examine compound words, for example, focus on each part of the word and how each part contributes to the meaning of the word. Many scientific and technical English words consist of compound words composed from Latin or Greek root words. Examples of this include *thermometer*, *kilogram*, *centimetre*, and *astronaut*.

Communication Technology Terminology

Technological vocabulary is easier to understand if you are familiar with the meanings of the root words and affixes. The following prefixes and words are just a few examples of components of words that combine to form terms relating to computers and technology.

Example

Common Prefixes

kilo = a thousand = 1 000 = 10^3
mega = a million = 1 000 000 = 10^6
giga = a billion = 1 000 000 000 = 10^9

Common Root Words

byte = unit of measurement of information storage = 8 bits
hertz = unit of frequency = 1 per second
watt = unit of power = 1 per second

The technological terms are formed from the root words and prefixes to be *gigabyte*, *gigahertz*, *gigawatt*, *megabyte*, *megahertz*, *megawatt*, *kilobyte*, *kilohertz*, and *kilowatt*. From the definitions of the broken down parts of the word, you can determine the meaning of the whole word.

Example

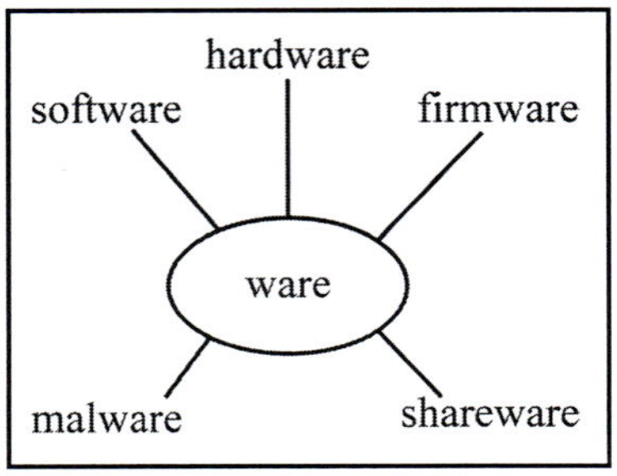

When you come across technical terms with which you are unfamiliar, remember to break them down into meaningful parts and look for the origins of the words.

General Scientific Term inology

Analysis of the affixes and root words in scientific terms can help you can find the meaning of the word.

Example

photo = light

synthesis = putting together (to synthesize is to create something new out of different parts)

photo + *synthesis* = photosynthesis = the process by which plants and some bacteria use chlorophyll to trap sunlight energy

Taking into consideration the meaning of the different components of the word *photosynthesis*, you could take a guess at what the word *chemosynthesis* means if you are told that the prefix *chemo* refers to chemicals.

Chemosynthesis refers to the formation of carbohydrates from energy resulting from the breakdown of inorganic substances. Was your guess at a definition close to the exact definition? Look at it this way:

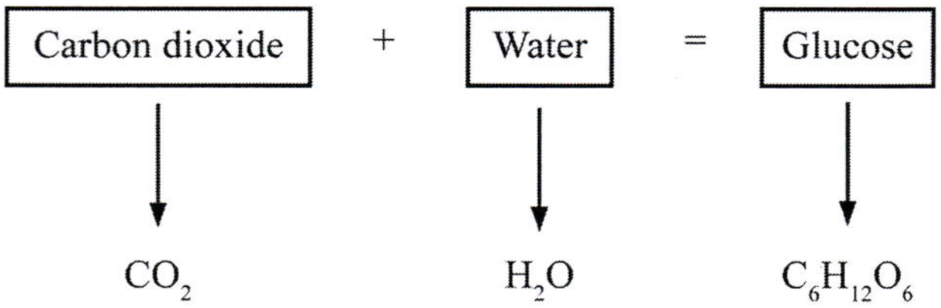

The following prefixes are examples of some common prefixes that are found in scientific terminology.

1. *Bio-* = life (Greek)

biology	biotechnology	biomass
biosphere	biography	biome
biologist	biotic	biological

2. *Hydro-* = water (Greek)

hydrogen	hydrothermal
hydrosphere	hydrologic
hydroponic	hydroelectricity
hydropower	hydroxide

3. *Trans-* = across (Latin)

transmission	translucence
transverse	transcription
transpiration	transmission
transforming	transposons

Understanding the components of words gives you access to understanding many more words. By paying attention to the different affixes that appear in words, you can make educated guesses at the meanings of other words.

11R3.3 use a variety of strategies, with increasing regularity, to explore and expand vocabulary, focusing on the precision with which words are used in the texts they are reading

Vocabulary

When you read, it is important to pay attention to the meaning of words, the writer's style, nuances (the subtle and slight differences in expressions and tone), and the diction used to describe characters and events. The different strategies you use to accomplish this will help you extend your own vocabulary usage.

Before reaching for the dictionary to find the definition of an unfamiliar word, try to figure out the meaning from the context. If a writer's style is unfamiliar, read carefully and focus your attention on the style. Are there patterns in the style? If the style makes frequent use of appositives, look for restatements of unfamiliar nouns.

Example

- She insisted on bringing her *Pomeranian*, a yappy, irritating little dog.
- Alcazar immediately *absconded*, slipping out of town one step ahead of the detectives.

Try reading slowly. Adjust your speed to the difficulty of the content and the complexity of the style. Reading aloud is often helpful, especially with poetry and plays, since they are usually meant to be heard, not read.

When reading a play, try to see the actors and hear the words. Read the directions and watch the characters move around the stage; hear and see their emotions. Reading aloud is helpful, but if that is not possible, try *subvocalizing*, or going through all the motions of speech without actually making any sounds.

Be prepared to reread several times. Remember that reading for information and understanding is different from reading for amusement and pleasure, although serious reading can often be both pleasant and amusing.

It is a good idea to start asking yourself questions as you read. It will soon become a natural part of your reading process. Questions such as "What is this about? Why did she do that? What will happen next? Will his words come back to haunt him? Why was this setting chosen?" can assist you in making inferences and in analysing the text on different levels.

Context gives life to the skeletons of structure and organization. Context requires understanding—you cannot read, write, or speak about something without understanding it—and understanding requires context.

PRACTICE QUESTIONS—READING

Read the following passage to answer questions 1 to 10.

BECAUSE I COULD NOT STOP FOR DEATH

Because I could not stop for Death-
He kindly stopped for me-
The Carriage held but just Ourselves-
And Immortality.

We slowly drove-He knew no haste
And I had put away
My labor and my leisure too,
For His Civility-

We passed the School, where Children strove
At Recess-in the Ring-
We passed the Fields of Gazing Grain-
We passed the Setting Sun-

Or rather-He passed Us-
The Dews drew quivering and chill-
For only Gossamer, my Gown-
My Tippet-only Tulle-

We paused before a House that seemed
A Swelling of the Ground-
The Roof was scarcely visible-
The Cornice-in the Ground-

Since then-'tis Centuries- and yet
Feels shorter than the Day
I first surmised the Horses' Heads
Were toward Eternity-

—*by* Emily Dickinson

1. The poetic technique of personification is used to portray the figure of Death in this poem by Emily Dickinson. The main purpose of this technique is to

A. show that Death is not scary

B. make the poem more interesting

C. give the idea of death a concrete form

D. present Dickinson's views about death

2. The **main** effect of beginning the poem with the pronoun "because" is to
   A. present the experience of dying as a reasonable one
   B. show the poet's poetic license with grammar
   C. give the reader more of a challenge
   D. start the poem with an abstraction

3. The presence of the third figure, "Immortality," in the carriage, **mainly** indicates that
   A. another abstract idea is being personified
   B. the speaker is going to live forever
   C. the carriage has at least three seats
   D. Death is not someone to fear

4. In this poem, the character of Death can **best** be described as
   A. cold
   B. spiteful
   C. grinning
   D. dignified

5. When the speaker says, "I had put away," she **most likely** means that
   A. she had finished packing
   B. the carriage was neat and tidy
   C. her feelings of fear had subsided
   D. she had given up her usual concerns

6. The beginning of the fourth stanza features a change in the pattern of movement that was established in the first three verses. This shift **most likely** indicates that
   A. the sun has moved faster than the carriage
   B. time and speed do not matter after death
   C. they have stopped to see the dew drops
   D. the speaker has entered her grave

7. Using the metaphor of a house in connection with the idea of death suggests that the poet believes that
   A. she cannot know what death will really be like
   B. dying will be a comfortable process
   C. after dying, one loses track of time
   D. the afterlife continues on forever

8. The **main** effect of the hyphens used throughout the poem is to

A. separate clauses into distinct segments

B. emphasize the leisurely pace of death

C. create visual space in the poem

D. make the reader slow down

9. As it is used in this poem, the word "strove" means

A. played

B. studied

C. worked

D. struggled

we passed the school were children strove - at recess in the ring.

Strive → struggle

10. Overall, this poem leaves the reader with a sense that the speaker is

A. accepting of her own death

B. reconciled to the events in her life

C. excited to be experiencing something new

D. anxious about riding with a figure like Death

was she anxious → poem was slow paced though

Read the following passage to answer questions 11 to 22.

A NICE PLACE TO VISIT

Having heard that Toronto was becoming one of the continent's noblest cities, we flew from New York to investigate. New Yorkers jealous of their city's reputation and concerned about challenges to its stature have little to worry about.

← No stress

After three days in residence, our delegation noted an absence of hysteria that was almost intolerable and took to consuming large portions of black coffee to maintain our normal state of irritability. The local people to whom we complained in hopes of provoking comfortably nasty confrontations declined to become bellicose. They would like to enjoy gratifying big-city hysteria, they said, but believed it would seem ill-mannered in front of strangers.

Extensive field studies—our stay lasted four weeks—persuaded us that this failure reflects the survival in Toronto of an ancient pattern of social conduct called "courtesy."

"Courtesy" manifests itself in many quaint forms appalling to the New Yorkers. Thus, for example, Yankee fans may be astonished to learn that at the Toronto baseball park it is considered bad form to heave rolls of toilet paper and beer cans at players on the field.

Official literature inside Toronto taxicabs includes a notification of the proper address to which riders may mail the authorities not only complaints but also compliments about the cabbie's behavior.

For a city that aspires to urban greatness, Toronto's entire taxi system has far to go. At present, it seems hopelessly bogged down in civilization. One day a member of our delegation listening to a radio conversation between a short-tempered cabbie and the dispatcher distinctly heard the dispatcher say, "As Shakespeare said, if music be the food of love, play on, give me excess of it."

This delegate became so unnerved by hearing Shakespeare quoted by a cab dispatcher that he fled immediately back to New York to have his nerves abraded and his spine rearranged in a real big-city taxi.

What was particularly distressing as the stay continued was the absence of shrieking police and fire sirens at 3 a.m.—or any other hour, for that matter. We spoke to the city authorities about this. What kind of city was it, we asked, that expected its citizens to sleep all night and rise refreshed in the morning? Where was the incentive to awaken gummy-eyed and exhausted, ready to scream at the first person one saw in the morning? How could Toronto possibly hope to maintain a robust urban divorce rate?

Our criticism went unheeded, such is the torpor with which Toronto pursues true urbanity. The fact appears to be that Toronto has very little grasp of what is required of a great city.

Consider the garbage picture. It seems never to have occurred to anybody in Toronto that garbage exists to be heaved into the streets. One can drive for miles without seeing so much as a banana peel in the gutter or a discarded newspaper whirling in the wind.

Nor has Toronto learned about dogs. A check with the authorities confirmed that, yes, there are indeed dogs resident in Toronto, but one would never realize it by walking the sidewalks. Our delegation was shocked by the presumption of a town's calling itself a city, much less a great city, when it obviously knows nothing of either garbage or dogs.

The subway, on which Toronto prides itself, was a laughable imitation of the real thing. The subway cars were not only spotlessly clean, but also fully illuminated. So were the stations. To New Yorkers, it was embarrassing, and we hadn't the heart to tell the subway authorities that they were light-years away from greatness.

We did, however, tell them about spray paints and how effectively a few hundred children equipped with spray-paint cans could at least give their subway the big-city look.

It seems doubtful they are ready to take such hints. There is a disturbing distaste for vandalism in Toronto which will make it hard for the city to enter wholeheartedly into the vigor of the late twentieth century.

A board fence surrounding a huge excavation for a new high-rise building in the downtown district offers depressing evidence of Toronto's lack of big-city impulse. Embedded in the fence at intervals of about fifty feet are loudspeakers that play recorded music for passing pedestrians.

Not a single one of these loudspeakers has been mutilated. What's worse, not a single one has been stolen.

It was good to get back to the Big Apple. My coat pocket was bulging with candy wrappers from Toronto and—such is the lingering power of Toronto—it took me two or three hours back in New York before it seemed natural again to toss them into the street.

—*by* Russell Baker

11. As it is used in the phrase "Toronto was becoming one of the continent's noblest cities," the word "noblest" means

A. richest

B. biggest

C. busiest

D. greatest

12. According to the speaker, what motivated the delegation to visit Toronto?

A. They wished to determine whether Toronto was a threat to New York's popularity. Jealous

B. The Canadian tourist industry requested the delegation's aid in promoting Canada.

C. The delegation was looking for an excuse to escape the stress of life in New York.

D. The people of Toronto had fascinated New Yorkers for quite some time.

13. The speaker suggests that the New York visitors consumed large quantities of black coffee in order to

A. calm their nerves in order to avoid arguments

B. shake off the fatigue accompanying a long trip

C. stay awake throughout a rather uninspiring visit

D. maintain a certain amount of New York "edginess"

maintare our normal state of irritability.

14. The phrase "comfortably nasty confrontations" contains an example of which of the following literary devices?

A. Pun

B. Metaphor

C. Oxymoron

D. Understatement

15. Which of the following words best expresses the meaning of the word "bellicose" as it is used in the sentence "The local people to whom we complained in hopes of provoking comfortably nasty confrontations declined to become bellicose"?

A. Timid

B. Hostile

C. Nervous

D. Embarrassed

16. Which of the following statements contains the clearest example of the writer's use of irony to create humour?

A. "It was good to get back to the Big Apple."

B. "One can drive for miles without seeing so much as a banana peel in the gutter"

C. "'As Shakespeare said, if music be the food of love, play on, give me excess of it.'"

D. "At present, it seems hopelessly bogged down in civilization."

17. According to the speaker, why did the Canadians refuse to become hysterical?

A. They knew their guests were teasing them.

B. They thought it would show poor manners.

C. They did not want to embarrass themselves.

D. They did not want to offend the American tourists.

18. The punctuation marks accompanying the phrase "—our stay lasted four weeks—" are used to signal

A. the addition of quoted material

B. a surprise or unexpected insight

C. an interruption in sentence structure

D. an emotional remark or exclamation

19. In the phrase "this failure reflects the survival in Toronto of an ancient pattern of social conduct," the word "failure" **most likely** refers to the speaker's belief that

A. Americans cannot understand Canadian customs

B. Torontonians are unable to reveal unpleasant emotions

C. Canadians do not appreciate frank and open conversation

D. Torontonians frequently display an inability to be courteous

20. The New York delegation found the Toronto subway system "embarrassing" because

A. it appeared to be better than theirs

B. many of the subway cars had been vandalized

C. spray-painted insults were commonly seen in stations

D. the subway cars were spotless and consistently well lit

21. From the point of view of the speaker, in the phrase "To New Yorkers, it was embarrassing, and we hadn't the heart to tell the subway authorities that they were light-years away from greatness" the word "greatness" means

A. fame

B. repair

C. appreciation

D. disintegration

22. The writer's main purpose in writing this passage was to

A. expose some of his concerns about living in New York

B. criticize the stuffy and smug attitudes of Canadians

C. encourage Torontonians to laugh at their mistakes

D. encourage the defacing of public property

Read the following passage to answer questions 23 to 45.

THE THRILL OF THE GRASS

1981: the summer the baseball players went on strike. The dull weeks drag by, the summer deepens, the strike is nearly a month old. Outside the city the corn rustles and ripens in the sun. Summer without baseball: a disruption to the psyche. An unexplainable aimlessness engulfs me. I stay later and later each evening in the small office at the rear of my shop. Now, driving home after work, the worst of the rush hour traffic over, it is the time of evening I would normally be heading for the stadium.

I enjoy arriving an hour early, parking in a far corner of the lot, walking slowly toward the stadium, rays of sun dropping softly over my shoulders like tangerine ropes, my shadow gliding with me, black as an umbrella. I like to watch young families beside their campers, the mother in shorts, grilling hamburgers, their men drinking beer. I enjoy seeing little boys dressed in the home team uniform, barely toddling, clutching hotdogs in upraised hands.

I am a failed shortstop. As a young man I saw myself diving to my left, graceful as a toppling tree, fielding high grounders like a cat leaping for butterflies, bracing my right foot and tossing to first, the throw true as if a steel ribbon connected my hand and the first baseman's glove. I dreamed of leading the American League in hitting—being inducted into the Hall of Fame…

I know the stadium will be deserted; nevertheless I wheel my car down off the freeway, park, and walk across the silent lot, my footsteps rasping and mournful. Strangle-grass and creeping charlie are already inching up through the gravel, surreptitious, surprised at their own ease… The whole place is silent as an empty classroom, like a house suddenly without children.

It is then that I spot the door-shape. I have to check twice to be sure it is there: a door cut in the deep green boards of the fence…. As I move closer, a golden circle of lock, like an acrimonious eye, establishes its certainty.

… My desire to be inside the ballpark is so great that for the first time in my life I commit a criminal act. I have been a locksmith for over forty years. I take the small tools from the pocket of my jacket, and in less time than it would take a speedy runner to circle the bases I am inside the stadium. Though the ballpark is open-air, it smells of abandonment; the walkways and seating areas are cold as basements. I breathe the odours of rancid popcorn and wilted cardboard.

The maintenance staff were laid off when the strike began. Synthetic grass does not need to be cut or watered. I stare down at the ball diamond, where just to the right of the pitcher's mound, a single weed, perhaps two inches high, stands defiant in the rain-pocked dirt.

The field sits breathless in the orangy glow of the evening sun. I stare at the potato-coloured earth of the infield, that wide, dun arc, surrounded by plastic grass. As I contemplate the prickly turf, which scorches the thighs and buttocks of a sliding player as if he were being seared by hot steel, it stares back in its uniform ugliness. The seams that send routinely hit ground balls veering at tortuous angles, are vivid, grey as scars.

I remember the ballfields of my childhood, the outfields full of soft hummocks and brown-eyed gopher holes.

… It was an evil day when they stripped the sod from this ballpark, cut it into yard-wide swathes, rolled it, memories and all, into great green-and-black cinnamonroll shapes, trucked it away, Nature temporarily defeated. But Nature is patient.

Over the next few days an idea forms within me, ripening, swelling, pushing, everything else into a corner. It is like knowing a new wonderful joke and not being able to share. I need an accomplice.

I go to see a man I don't know personally, though I have seen his face peering at me from the financial pages of the local newspaper, and the *Wall Street Journal*, and I have been watching his profile at the baseball stadium, two boxes to the right of me, for several years. He is a fan. Really a fan. When the weather is intemperate, or the game not close, the people around us disappear like flowers closing at sunset, but we are always there until the last pitch. I know he is a man who attends because of the beauty and mystery of the game, a man who can sit during the last of the ninth with the game decided innings ago, and draw joy from watching the first baseman adjust the angle of his glove as the pitcher goes into his windup….

"Tell him a baseball fan is here to see him," is all I will say to his secretary. His office is in a skyscraper, from which he can look out over the city to where the prairie rolls green as mountain water to the limits of the eye. I wait all afternoon in the artificially cool, glassy reception area with its yellow and mauve chairs, chrome and glass coffee tables. Finally, in the late afternoon, my message is passed along.

"I've seen you at the baseball stadium," I say, not introducing myself.

"Yes," he says. "I recognize you. Three rows back, about eight seats to my left…

… Now, what can I do for you?"

"I have an idea," I say. "One that's been creeping towards me like a first baseman when the bunt sign is on. What do you think about artificial turf?"

"Hmmmf," he snorts, "that's what the strike should be about. Baseball is meant to be played on summer evenings and Sunday afternoons, on grass just cut by a horse-drawn mower," and we smile as our eyes meet.

"I've discovered the ballpark is open, to me anyway," I go on. "There's no one there while the strike is on…. It's lonely as a ghost town."

"And what is it you do there, alone with the pigeons?"

"I dream."

"And where do I come in?"

"You've always struck me as man who dreams. I think we have things in common. I think you might like to come with me. I could show you what I dream, paint pictures, suggest what might happen …."

He studies me carefully for a moment….

"Tonight?" he says. "Would tonight be too soon?"

"Park in the northwest corner of the lot about 1:00 a.m. There is a door about fifty yards to the right of the main gate. I'll open it when I hear you."

He nods.

I turn and leave.

The night is clear and cotton warm when he arrives. "Oh, my," he says staring at the stadium turned chrome-blue by a full moon. "Oh, my," he says again, breathing in the faint odours of baseball, the reminder of fans and players not long gone.

"Let's go down to the field," I say. I am carrying a cardboard pizza box, holding it on the upturned palms of my hands, like an offering.

… "I think I know what you've brought," he says, gesturing toward the box, "but let me see anyway."

I open the box in which rests a square foot of sod, the grass smooth and pure, cool as a swatch of satin, fragile as baby's hair.

"Ohhh," the man says, reaching out a finger to test the moistness of it. "Oh, I see."

We walk across the field, the harsh, prickly turf making the bottoms of my feet tingle, to the left-field corner where, in the angle formed by the foul line and the warning track, I lay down the square foot of sod. "That's beautiful," my friend says, kneeling besides me, placing his hand, fingers spread wide, on the verdant square…

I take from my belt a sickle-shaped blade, the kind used for cutting carpet. I measure along the edge of the sod, dig the point in and pull carefully toward me. There is a ripping sound, like tearing an old bed sheet. I hold up the square of artificial turf like something freshly killed,

while all the time digging the sharp point into the packed earth I have exposed. I replace the sod lovingly, covering the newly bared surface.

"A protest," I say.

"But it could be more," the man replies.

"I hoped you'd say that. It could be. If you'd like to come back…"

"Tomorrow night?"

"Tomorrow night would be fine. But there will be an admission charge…"

"A square of sod?"

"A square of sod two inches thick…"

"Of the same grass?"

"Of the same grass. But there's more."

"I suspected as much."

"You must have a friend…"

"Who would join us?"

"Yes."

"I have two. Would that be all right?"

"I trust your judgment."

"My father. He's over eighty," my friend says. "You might have seen him with me once or twice. He lives over fifty miles from here, but if I call him he'll come. And my friend…"

"If they pay their admission they'll be welcome…"

"And they may have friends…"

"Indeed they may. But what will we do with this?" I say, holding up the sticky-backed square of turf, which smells of glue and fabric.

"We could mail them anonymously to baseball executives, politicians, clergymen."

"Gentle reminders not to tamper with Nature."

We dance toward the exit, rampant with excitement.

"You will come back? You'll bring the others?"

"Count on it," says my friend.

They do come, those trusted friends, and friends of friends, each making a live, green deposit. At first, a tiny row of sod squares begins to inch along toward left-centre field. The next night even more people arrive, the following night more again, and the night after there is positively a crowd. Those who come once seem always to return accompanied by friends, occasionally a son or young brother, but mostly men my age or older, for we are the ones who remember the grass.

Night after night the pilgrimage continues. The first night I stand inside the deep green door, listening…

During the nights that follow, I stand sentinel-like at the top of the grandstand, watching as my cohorts arrive. Old men walking across a parking lot in a row, in the dark, carrying coiled hoses, looking like the many wheels of a locomotive…. They move methodically toward the baseball stadium which hulks against the moon-blue sky like a small mountain. Beneath the tint of starlight, the tall light standards which rise above the fences and grandstand glow purple, necks bent forward, like sunflowers heavy with seed…

Night after night, virtually no words are spoken. Each man seems to know his assignment. Not all bring sod. Some carry rakes, some hoes, some hoses, which, when joined together, snake across the infield and outfield, dispensing the blessing of water. Others cradle in their arms bags of earth for building up the infield to meet the thick, living sod.

I often remain high in the stadium, looking down on the men moving over the earth, dark as ants, each sodding, cutting, watering, shaping. Occasionally the moon finds a knife blade as it trims the sod or slices away a chunk of artificial turf, and tosses the reflection skyward like a bright ball. My body tingles. There should be symphony music playing. Everyone should be humming "America The Beautiful."

Towards dawn, I watch the men walking away in groups, like small patrols or soldiers, carrying instead of arms, the tools and utensils which breathe life back into the arid ballfield.

Row by row, night by night, we lay the little squares of sod, moist as chocolate cake with green icing…

When the strike is over I know we will all be here to watch the workouts, to hear the recalcitrant joints crackling like twigs after the forced inactivity. We will sit in our regular seats, scattered like popcorn throughout the stadium, and we'll nod as we pass on the way to the exits, exchange secret smiles, proud as new fathers…

Players and management are meeting round the clock. A settlement is imminent. I have watched the stadium covered square foot by square foot until it looks like green graph paper. I have stood and felt the cool odours of the grass rise up and touch my face. I have studied the lines between each small square, watched those lines fade until they were visible to my eyes alone, then not even to them.

What will the players think, as they straggle into the stadium and find the miracle we have created? The old-timers will raise their heads like ponies, as far away as the parking lot, when the thrill of the grass reaches their nostrils. And as they dress, they'll recall sprawling in the lush outfields of childhood, the grass as cool as a mother's hand on a forehead.

"Goodbye, goodbye," we say at the gate, the smell of water, of sod, of sweat, small perfumes in the air. Our secrets are safe with each other. We go our separate ways…

—*by* W.P. Kinsella

23. The opening sentence of this passage contains which of the following language errors?

X **B.** Sentence fragment

A. Spelling error

C. Misplaced apostrophe

D. Incorrect use of a colon

24. Which of the following words **best** describes the mood of the opening paragraph?

A. Escape

B. Warmth

✓ **C.** Emptiness

D. Fulfillment

25. The main purpose of the second and third paragraphs is to provide the reader with

A. unnecessary historical background

✓ **B.** insight into the speaker's character

C. an understanding of the players' motives

D. a clearer description of the story's setting

2 = routine without baseball
3 = what baseball means to him

26. The phrase "rays of sun dropping softly over my shoulders like tangerine ropes" contains an example of which of the following literary devices?

A. Simile
B. Hyperbole
C. Onomatopoeia
D. Personification

27. Which of the following words best expresses the meaning of the word "acrimonious" as it is used in the quotation "a golden circle of lock, like an acrimonious eye"?

A. Welcoming
B. Unkind
C. Blind
D. Lazy

28. In the quotation "a golden circle of lock, like an acrimonious eye, establishes its certainty," the pronoun "its" refers back to which of the following antecedent nouns?

A. Eye
B. Door
C. Lock
D. Fence

29. The phrase "Strangle-grass and creeping charlie are already inching up through the gravel, surreptitious, surprised at their own ease" contains an example of which of the following literary devices?

A. Metaphor
B. Symbolism
C. Synecdoche
D. Personification

30. The speaker finds it easy to enter the ballpark for all of the following reasons **except**

A. it is late at night, and he is hidden by darkness
B. the speaker has the tools needed to open locks
C. a baseball strike is currently taking place
D. the maintenance crew has been laid off

31. Which of the following statements best explains the meaning of the quotation “it smells of abandonment”?

A. No one seems to care whether the stadium hosts games anymore.

B. The unpopular strike has created a stink amongst the avid baseball fans.

C. Being isolated on the field allows the speaker to sense his aloneness.

D. Common smells left over from previous games are left to linger alone.

32. Which of the following descriptions of artificial grass is the **least negative**?

A. “The prickly turf”

B. “Scorches the thighs”

C. “It stares back”

D. “Grey as scars”

33. Compared to the stadium ballfield, the ballfields of the speaker’s childhood are best described as

A. isolated but comfortable

B. natural but challenging

C. lush and well-kept

D. hard and weedy

34. Which of the following words is a synonym of the word *accomplice*?

A. Helper

B. Witness

C. Supplier

D. Counsellor

35. The speaker **most likely** chooses the businessman to help him because he

A. has a lot of influence

B. truly appreciates baseball

C. is a wealthy economic advisor

D. has been a friend of the speaker’s for years

36. Which of the following words best describes the businessman’s response to the speaker’s invitation to meet at the stadium?

A. Doubtful

B. Reluctant

C. Compliant

D. Instantaneous

37. When the businessman arrives at the stadium at night, he says, "Oh, my." This comment is best understood as an expression of

- **A.** shock
- **B.** surprise
- **C.** satisfaction
- **D.** disappointment

38. The description of the speaker holding the sod square "like an offering" suggests that he is

- **A.** hoping this gift will end the strike
- **B.** piously respectful of the box he carries
- **C.** afraid of the consequences of his actions
- **D.** wanting his friend to place the first square of sod

39. Which of the following statements **best** describes the type of people to whom the speaker and his friend wish to mail the discarded pieces of artificial turf?

- **A.** They are very influential individuals.
- **B.** They are all supporters of the natural order of things.
- **C.** They are keen baseball fans like the speaker and his friend.
- **D.** They are guilty of supporting materialism and all things artificial.

40. Which of the following words **best** describes the mood of the speaker and his fellow fan after they have planted the first square of grass and decided upon a plan?

- **A.** Smug
- **B.** Ecstatic
- **C.** Frustrated
- **D.** Apprehensive

41. According to the narrator, which of the following statements **best** explains why most of the sod contributors are older men?

- **A.** Gardening is a hobby usually associated with the elderly.
- **B.** Most young men do not have the spare time to take on such a huge task.
- **C.** Since baseball is a dying sport, the average "real fan" is of an older generation.
- **D.** Older men would have played on real grass before artificial turf became popular.

42. Which of the following descriptions is not used in the story to describe the speaker and his work crew?

A. A sentinel

B. Part of a train

C. Soldiers on patrol

D. Synchronized robots

43. The statement "There should be symphony music playing. Everyone should be humming 'America The Beautiful'" is **most likely** intended to reveal that the speaker

A. is overcome by a spirit of patriotism because baseball is an American game

B. believes classical music, like real sod, is a mark of good taste that only a few share

C. expects the strike to end soon, so he wants to celebrate his team's return to the field

D. is moved by the smooth unfolding of his turf replacement plan and wants to celebrate

44. In this passage, the narrative point of view is

A. objective

B. omniscient

C. first person uses I

D. limited omniscient

45. The writer's **main** purpose in writing this story was to illustrate

A. the power of the American people to initiate needed change

B. the changes that have taken place in American baseball

C. why real grass is important to the traditions of baseball

D. everything that makes baseball so popular

Read the following passage to answer questions 46 to 51.

THE TELL-TALE HEART

TRUE! nervous, very, very dreadfully nervous I had been and am; but why WILL you say that I am mad? The disease had sharpened my senses, not destroyed, not dulled them. Above all was the sense of hearing acute. I heard all things in the heaven and in the earth. I heard many things in hell. How then am I mad? Hearken! and observe how healthily, how calmly, I can tell you the whole story.

It is impossible to say how first the idea entered my brain, but, once conceived, it haunted me day and night. Object there was none. Passion there was none. I loved the old man. He had never wronged me. He had never given me insult. For his gold I had no desire. I think it was his eye! Yes, it was this! One of his eyes resembled that of a vulture—a pale blue eye with a film over it. Whenever it fell upon me my blood ran cold, and so by degrees, very gradually, I made up my mind to take the life of the old man, and thus rid myself of the eye for ever. he killed the old man.

Now this is the point. You fancy me mad. Madmen know nothing. But you should have seen me. You should have seen how wisely I proceeded—with what caution—with what foresight, with what dissimulation, I went to work! I was never kinder to the old man than during the whole week before I killed him. And every night about midnight I turned the latch of his door and opened it oh, so gently! And then, when I had made an opening sufficient for my head, I put in a dark lantern all closed, closed so that no light shone out, and then I thrust in my head. Oh, you would have laughed to see how cunningly I thrust it in! I moved it slowly, very, very slowly, so that I might not disturb the old man's sleep. It took me an hour to place my whole head within the opening so far that I could see him as he lay upon his bed. Ha! would a madman have been so wise as this? And then when my head was well in the room I undid the lantern cautiously—oh, so cautiously—cautiously (for the hinges creaked), I undid it just so much that a single thin ray fell upon the vulture eye. And this I did for seven long nights, every night just at midnight, but I found the eye always closed, and so it was impossible to do the work, for it was not the old man who vexed me but his Evil Eye. And every morning, when the day broke, I went boldly into the chamber and spoke courageously to him, calling him by name in a hearty tone, and inquiring how he had passed the night. So you see he would have been a very profound old man, indeed, to suspect that every night, just at twelve, I looked in upon him while he slept.

Upon the eighth night I was more than usually cautious in opening the door. A watch's minute hand moves more quickly than did mine. Never before that night had I felt the extent of my own powers, of my sagacity. I could scarcely contain my feelings of triumph. To think that there I was opening the door little by little, and he not even to dream of my secret deeds or thoughts. I fairly chuckled at the idea, and perhaps he heard me, for he moved on the bed suddenly as if startled. Now you may think that I drew back—but no. His room was as black as pitch with the thick darkness (for the shutters were close fastened through fear of robbers), and so I knew that he could not see the opening of the door, and I kept pushing it on steadily, steadily.

I had my head in, and was about to open the lantern, when my thumb slipped upon the tin fastening, and the old man sprang up in the bed, crying out, "Who's there?"

I kept quite still and said nothing. For a whole hour I did not move a muscle, and in the meantime I did not hear him lie down. He was still sitting up in the bed, listening; just as I have done night after night hearkening to the death watches in the wall.

Presently, I heard a slight groan, and I knew it was the groan of mortal terror. It was not a groan of pain or of grief—oh, no! It was the low stifled sound that arises from the bottom of the soul when over-charged with awe. I knew the sound well. Many a night, just at midnight, when all the world slept, it has welled up from my own bosom, deepening, with its dreadful echo, the terrors that distracted me. I say I knew it well. I knew what the old man felt, and pitied him although I chuckled at heart. I knew that he had been lying awake ever since the first slight noise when he had turned in the bed. His fears had been ever since growing upon him. He had been trying to fancy them causeless, but could not. He had been saying to himself, "It is nothing but the wind in the chimney, it is only a mouse crossing the floor," or, "It is merely a cricket which has made a single chirp." Yes he has been trying to comfort himself with these suppositions; but he had found all in vain. ALL IN VAIN, because Death in approaching him had stalked with his black shadow before him and enveloped the victim. And it was the mournful influence of the unperceived shadow that caused him to feel, although he neither saw nor heard, to feel the presence of my head within the room.

When I had waited a long time very patiently without hearing him lie down, I resolved to open a little—a very, very little crevice in the lantern. So I opened it—you cannot imagine how stealthily, stealthily—until at length a single dim ray like the thread of the spider shot out from the crevice and fell upon the vulture eye.

It was open, wide, wide open, and I grew furious as I gazed upon it. I saw it with perfect distinctness—all a dull blue with a hideous veil over it that chilled the very marrow in my bones, but I could see nothing else of the old man's face or person, for I had directed the ray as if by instinct precisely upon the damned spot. – on the eye

And now have I not told you that what you mistake for madness is but over-acuteness of the senses? now, I say, there came to my ears a low, dull, quick sound, such as a watch makes when enveloped in cotton. I knew that sound well too. It was the beating of the old man's heart. It increased my fury as the beating of a drum stimulates the soldier into courage.

But even yet I refrained and kept still. I scarcely breathed. I held the lantern motionless. I tried how steadily I could maintain the ray upon the eye. Meantime the hellish tattoo of the heart increased. It grew quicker and quicker, and louder and louder, every instant. The old man's terror must have been extreme! It grew louder, I say, louder every moment!—do you mark me well? I have told you that I am nervous: so I am. And now at the dead hour of the night, amid the dreadful silence of that old house, so strange a noise as this excited me to uncontrollable terror. Yet, for some minutes longer I refrained and stood still. But the beating grew louder, louder! I thought the heart must burst. And now a new anxiety seized me—the sound would be heard by a neighbour! The old man's hour had come! With a loud yell, I threw open the lantern and leaped into the room. He shrieked once—once only. In an instant I dragged him to the floor, and pulled the heavy bed over him. I then smiled gaily, to find the deed so far done. But for many minutes the heart beat on with a muffled sound. This, however, did not vex me; it would not be heard through the wall. At length it ceased. The old man was dead. I removed the bed and examined the corpse. Yes, he was stone, stone dead. I placed my hand upon the heart and held it there many minutes. There was no pulsation. He was stone dead. His eye would trouble me no more.

If still you think me mad, you will think so no longer when I describe the wise precautions I took for the concealment of the body. The night waned, and I worked hastily, but in silence. Cover the corpse

I took up three planks from the flooring of the chamber, and deposited all between the scantlings. I then replaced the boards so cleverly so cunningly, that no human eye—not even his—could have detected anything wrong. There was nothing to wash out—<u>no stain of any kind</u>—<u>no blood-spot whatever.</u> I had been too wary for that. Super precautions.

When I had made an end of these labours, it was four o'clock—still dark as midnight. As the bell sounded the hour, there came a knocking at the street door. I went down to open it with a light heart,—for what had I now to fear? There entered three men, who introduced themselves, with perfect suavity, as officers of the police. A shriek had been heard by a neighbour during the night; suspicion of foul play had been aroused; information had been lodged at the police office, and they (the officers) had been deputed to search the premises.

Police arrived at the house.

I smiled,—for what had I to fear? I bade the gentlemen welcome. The shriek, I said, was my own in a dream. The old man, I mentioned, was absent in the country. I took my visitors all over the house. I bade them search—search well. I led them, at length, to his chamber. I showed them his treasures, secure, undisturbed. In the enthusiasm of my confidence, I brought chairs into the room, and desired them here to rest from their fatigues, while I myself, in the wild audacity of my perfect triumph, placed my own seat upon the very spot beneath which reposed the corpse of the victim.

The officers were satisfied. My MANNER had convinced them. I was singularly at ease. They sat and while I answered cheerily, they chatted of familiar things. But, ere long, I felt myself getting pale and wished them gone. My head ached, and I fancied a ringing in my ears; but still they sat, and still chatted. The ringing became more distinct: I talked more freely to get rid of the feeling: but it continued and gained definitiveness—until, at length, I found that the noise was NOT within my ears. No doubt I now grew VERY pale; but I talked more fluently, and with a heightened voice. Yet the sound increased—and what could I do? It was A LOW, DULL, QUICK SOUND—MUCH SUCH A SOUND AS A WATCH MAKES WHEN ENVELOPED IN COTTON. I gasped for breath, and yet the officers heard it not. I talked more quickly, more vehemently but the noise steadily increased. I arose and argued about trifles, in a high key and with violent gesticulations; but the noise steadily increased. Why WOULD they not be gone? I paced the floor to and fro with heavy strides, as if excited to fury by the observations of the men, but the noise steadily increased. O God! what COULD I do? I foamed—I raved—I swore! I swung the chair upon which I had been sitting, and grated it upon the boards, but the noise arose over all and continually increased. It grew louder—louder—louder! And still the men chatted pleasantly, and smiled. Was it possible they heard not? Almighty God!—no, no? They heard!—they suspected!—they KNEW!—they were making a mockery of my horror!—this I thought, and this I think. But anything was better than this agony! Anything was more tolerable than this derision! I could bear those hypocritical smiles no longer! I felt that I must scream or die!—and now—again—hark! louder! louder! louder! LOUDER!—

"Villains!" I shrieked, "dissemble no more! I admit the deed!—tear up the planks!—here, here!—it is the beating of his hideous heart!" END.

—*by* Edgar Allan Poe

Down 4/1

46. The narrative of this story does not begin by describing how the old man died, but instead by revealing the narrator's concern with not being thought mad. The main effect of this introduction is to

A. confirm the possibility of his madness -> well simply he is mad.

B. indicate that the narrator is reasonable

C. implicate the readers in the crime that is committed

D. gain our sympathy for the narrator's nervous condition

47. The sequence of events leading up to the narrator's eventual capture helps to confirm the reader's doubts about his mental condition mainly because he

A. is able to tell the story so well

B. seems to live alone, without neighbours nearby

C. does not remember where the idea for murder came from

D. appeals so clearly to the principles of logic and careful planning

48. The tone of the narrator's statement "Now this is the point. You fancy me mad" suggests that he is

A. perfectly rational on some subjects

B. attempting to persuade himself of his innocence

C. making a convincing case about his mental condition

D. defending himself against the police who came to arrest him

49. One of the qualities that is evident in the narrator's telling of the story, if not in his committing of the crime, is that he is

A. dramatic

B. detailed

C. methodical -> a method to my madness

D. goal-oriented

50. At the end of the story, the narrator's guilt is confirmed by his sense of

A. vision

B. touch

C. hearing

D. humour

51. Near the end of the story, the narrator claims that his cheerful and friendly manner convinced the police of his innocence. This statement is ironic **mainly** because

A. he was not feeling so cheerful inside

B. it was his manner that finally gave him away

C. the police discovered where the body was hidden

D. the police would not leave because they so enjoyed his company

ANSWERS AND SOLUTIONS—PRACTICE QUESTIONS

1. A	12. A	23. B	34. A	45. C
2. A	13. D	24. C	35. B	46. A
3. D	14. C	25. B	36. C	47. C
4. D	15. B	26. A	37. C	48. C
5. D	16. D	27. B	38. B	49. C
6. D	17. B	28. B	39. A	50. C
7. B	18. C	29. D	40. B	51. B
8. B	19. B	30. A	41. D	
9. D	20. D	31. D	42. D	
10. A	21. D	32. C	43. D	
11. D	22. A	33. B	44. C	

1. A

One rule of thumb to keep in mind when answering multiple-choice questions in English is that the most specific answer is usually the best response. Therefore, although the poem does express something about Dickinson's views of death (**D**), stating that she views death as a friendly gentleman who is not frightening (**A**) is a better response because this answer provides more information about the poet's opinion about death.

2. A

Students are often taught not to begin sentences with the word "because" and may also think that starting the poem in this way presents a challenge to the reader, but the most successful response here is the answer that refers most directly to the meaning conveyed by the poet's use of the word "because." As you know, this word usually connects a reason with an event. Since death is typically perceived as a random and dreaded event, starting the poem in this way grabs the reader's attention by saying that Death's "stopping" for the poet was a reasonable and understandable event.

3. D

While it is true that the presence of the figure "Immortality" in the carriage does suggest that the speaker will live forever (**B**), the fourth answer (**D**) is the best response because it emphasizes one of the main themes of the poem, the idea that death is not a process that should be feared.

4. D

Death is commonly portrayed as a cold (**A**) and spiteful (**B**) reaper who does not wait for anyone, or as the symbol of a grinning skull with empty eye sockets (**C**). The speaker in this poem, however, describes Death as being kind and civil. Of the terms listed in the alternatives, the word *dignified* (**D**) best reflects the speaker's view of Death.

5. D

If you quickly reread the second stanza to refresh your memory about the meaning of this line, it becomes clear that the speaker is not referring to being neat and orderly (**A**, **B**), so these responses can be eliminated. Instead, when the speaker says, "And I had put away / My labor and my leisure too," she is referring to letting go of her usual preoccupations and concerns. The best response is the fourth one (**D**).

6. D

The description of the "House that seemed/A Swelling of the Ground" (17–18) provides the evidence needed to answer this question. The "house" here refers to the speaker's final resting place, a grave, and therefore the fourth answer (**D**) is the best one.

7. B

Although the final stanza of the poem emphasizes that the speaker experiences death as a timeless event (**C**, **D**), the metaphor of a house is not connected with the passage of time. Instead, the connection between the idea of home and a sense of comfort suggests that the speaker perceives dying to be a comfortable, non-frightening process (**B**).

8. B

The strongest answer from this list is the one that most accurately reflects the meaning of the poem. Since the speaker describes the leisurely yet methodical pace of Death, it can be said that the writing style—with its many pauses created by the inclusion of hyphens—reflects this leisurely pace. For this reason, the best answer is the second one (**B**).

9. D

The speaker says, "We passed the School, where Children strove/At Recess-in the Ring." In this phrase, the word "strove" is a form of the verb *to strive*, or *to struggle*, making the last answer (**D**) correct. Although children at school might study (**B**) or work (**C**), the speaker's mention of "the Ring" suggests a comparison between the children's experiences at school and a boxing match, which implies struggle.

10. A

The general impression conveyed by this poem is that the speaker's attitude is one of peaceful acceptance of the inevitability of death.

11. D

The word "noblest" suggests superiority, splendour, or greatness. Each of the other three alternatives, although positive in meaning, fails to convey this idea of superiority.

12. A

The answer is found in the first paragraph, in the statement, "New Yorkers jealous of their city's reputation and concerned about challenges to its stature have little to worry about."

13. D

The speaker makes it clear in the second paragraph that the delegation missed the combative atmosphere they had become used to in New York. The coffee was therefore consumed to "maintain our normal state of irritability" in the hopes of promoting familiar and presumably comforting confrontations in Toronto.

14. C

The use of the word "comfortably" to modify the word "nasty" creates an interesting conflict in logic because the word "nasty" is synonymous with offensive, injurious, or wicked. As a result, this contradiction is a clear example of an oxymoron: a figure of speech in which contradictory words or connotations are placed together.

15. B

The fact that Torontonians who were goaded by confrontational taunts declined to become "bellicose" suggests that they refused to do what one might expect in this situation: demonstrate a certain degree of hostility toward those set on badgering them. The meaning of the word "bellicose" is best expressed by the word *hostile*.

16. D

Stating that civilization is in any way a negative thing suggests a thought that is contrary to what would be expected; therefore, the expression "hopelessly bogged down in civilization" provides the best example of the writer's ironic wit.

17. B

According to the speaker, the Canadians refused to descend into "big-city hysteria" because "it would seem ill-mannered in front of strangers."

18. C

In this case, the interrupting phrase "our stay lasted four weeks" is not needed, nor does it fit grammatically with the rest of the sentence. Consequently, the dashes are used to signal this unnatural interruption.

19. B

The word "failure" in this phrase refers to the speaker's perception that Torontonians' unwillingness to engage in "bellicose" behaviour reflects their inability to reveal unpleasant emotions.

20. D

According to the speaker, the New York delegation found Toronto's "spotlessly clean" and "fully illuminated" subway system embarrassing because it did not possess that "big-city look" of filth, vandalism, and poor maintenance. Of course, the writer's comments are intended to be ironic, for any prudent reader will have understood by this point in the passage that all of the shortcomings cited by the writer are actually assets.

21. D

Given that, according to the speaker, vandalism, litter, and disrepair are what make New York's subway system great, in the context of this sentence, the word "greatness" refers to a state of disintegration that the Toronto subway system is "light-years away from."

22. A

This passage is an excellent example of irony employed for a satirical purpose. It is reasonable to assume that this writer's target is not Toronto and its varied amenities, but rather New York, with its long list of unpleasant traits. The title may very well be the only sincere statement in the passage. After all, the writer proves, in a satirical fashion, that Toronto is a nice place to visit, as opposed to New York.

23. B

The date, 1981, is not a full thought, and neither is the phrase that follows the colon. Consequently, this passage begins with a sentence fragment, which is most likely used to echo the incompleteness of the season in which the strike took place.

24. C

The writer's use of phrases such as "dull weeks drag by," " Summer without baseball," "a disruption," "unexplainable aimlessness," and the fact that he ends his opening paragraph by mentioning what the speaker would "normally be doing" but in fact is not suggests that something significant is missing from his life: baseball. The word that best captures the mood developed by such phrases is *emptiness*. Alternatives **B** and **D** are inappropriate, since they imply a positive mood, and alternative **A** is not well supported by text, since the speaker seems to be addressing his dissatisfaction with the lack of baseball rather than creating some kind of mental escape.

25. B

The second and third paragraphs provide insight about the speaker, such as what he enjoyed about his regular trips to the ballpark and the knowledge that he was once a capable player who dreamed of playing in the American League. From these two paragraphs, the reader learns that the speaker is a sentimental, sensitive, dedicated, and knowledgeable baseball fan. Alternative **B** is the correct answer.

26. A

Comparing the rays of the sun to "tangerine ropes" is an example of a simile. A simile is a literary device in which two unlike things are compared using the words *like* or *as*.

27. B

The word "acrimonious" means bitter or resentful. Of the given alternatives, the word *unkind* is closest in meaning. A lock of any kind would not bring to mind a sense of welcome; the words *blind* and *lazy* do not correspond to context clues or the definition of the word.

28. B

The speaker is looking for a way into the stadium when he comments, "It is then that I spot the door-shape." The door is "cut in the deep green boards of the fence," and as if to prove that it really exists as a possible entrance, the speaker notices that the door has a lock on it, which verifies its role as a lockable portal to the stadium. The phrase in question acknowledges this function when the speaker states that the lock, "like an acrimonious eye, establishes its [the door's] certainty."

29. D

The speaker gives two plants, "strangle-grass and creeping charlie," the ability to feel and think, since they are said to be "surprised at their own ease." The giving of human traits to inanimate or non-human things is defined as personification (alternative **D**).

30. A

Alternative **A** is correct. This alternative is not supported by the text, since, according to the speaker, the act of entering the stadium took place while the "field [sat] breathless in the orangy glow of the evening sun." There was evening light to see by, as is further attested to by the speaker's ease in noticing the "golden circle of lock," "a single weed" beside the pitcher's mound, and the "vivid, grey" seams of the artificial turf.

31. D

This quotation refers to the stadium and the lingering smells that haunt the walkways and seating areas. This is supported by the speaker's reference to the air when he points out, "Though the ballpark is open-air… I breathe the odours of rancid popcorn and wilted cardboard." These odours have remained from the last game played there almost a month previously, before the strike. Alternative **D** is correct.

32. C

Alternative **C** is the least negative description among the alternatives. The words "prickly" and "scorches" convey unpleasant or hurtful sensations, while the description "grey as scars" conveys lifelessness and injury.

33. B

According to the speaker, the ballfields of his childhood contained "outfields full of soft hummocks and brown-eyed gopher holes." Although only part of the ballfield is described, it can be assumed from this description that it is little more than pasture land being used as a baseball field. The reference to "soft hummocks" suggests a far more irregular but natural surface than the "uniform ugliness" of the stadium turf. The natural irregularities of real grass, including other anomalies such as gopher holes, makes grass more challenging than turf. The speaker does not describe the fields as being comfortable, isolated, lush, well kept, hard, or weedy.

34. A

The word appears in the story following the speaker's admission that an idea is evolving in his mind and that he needs "an accomplice" to help him with it. Soon after, the meeting at the stadium is arranged, and the speaker reveals his plan to replace the artificial turf with squares of real grass. He cannot accomplish this feat on his own, which is why he needs accomplices, or helpers.

35. B

The speaker goes to the businessman for help because "He is a fan. Really a fan." This statement implies that the speaker's chosen accomplice is very much like himself: someone who loves the game of baseball. Because he has a true appreciation for the game, the businessman is likely to be willing to help the speaker carry out his plan. Although alternatives **A** and **C** are likely true, they are not mentioned by the speaker as reasons for choosing to approach the businessman. Alternative **D** is incorrect; the speaker states that he does not know the man personally.

36. C

In response to the speaker's request, the businessman "studies [the speaker] carefully for a moment" and then asks, "Would tonight be too soon?" The word *compliant* best describes his reaction, since he goes along with the suggestion after only a moment's consideration and without further questions or doubts.

37. C

The comment in question, spoken by the businessman, occurs when he returns to the stadium and reacquaints himself with the sights and sounds of the ballfield. Immediately after this expression, the speaker describes the businessman as "breathing in the faint odours of baseball, the reminder of fans and players not long gone." A wave of satisfaction would likely sweep over a true fan who misses the sport. Shock and disappointment do not have positive connotations and are not well supported by the text. Alternative **C** is the correct answer.

38. B

The speaker is clear in his intent to place the first symbolic square, since he unhesitatingly cuts the artificial surface and lays the sod piece himself. Furthermore, he does not seem to be concerned about the consequences of his actions, since he agrees with his accomplice, who suggests, "it could be more." The speaker is hoping this one act will lead to more of the same when he responds, "I hoped you'd say that. It could be." In this quotation, the speaker's devotion in placing the sod is likened to that of a person participating in a religious ritual.

39. A

The speaker's friend makes this suggestion, and the speaker adds that such "gifts" could act as "gentle reminders not to tamper with Nature." With these comments in mind, it seems reasonable to eliminate alternatives **B** and **C**, since a supporter of Nature or the natural order of things would not need such a reminder, and there is no way that these gentlemen could know whether all executives, politicians, and clergymen are baseball fans. Consequently, his suggestion of mailing squares of artificial turf to the three groups listed would likely be an attempt to get the message out to as many people as possible.

40. B

The speaker and his friend are in high spirits when they leave the stadium. As they leave the stadium, the speaker remarks, "We dance toward the exit, rampant with excitement." The word that best captures this spirit is *ecstatic*.

41. D

The writer explains that "occasionally a son or young brother" might join the work party, but the dominant age group consisted of "mostly men my age or older, for we are the ones who remember the grass."

42. D

The speaker describes himself standing "sentinel-like" as he watches the sod planters arrive, "looking like the many wheels of a locomotive," and later leaving in small groups "like small patrols of soldiers." At no time does the speaker refer to the workers as synchronized robots.

43. D

Although these remarks are not linked to any specific antecedent, it is reasonable to assume that the speaker is motivated by what he sees when he looks down on the men at work. This is supported by the comment, "My body tingles" in response to his watching "the men moving over the earth… each sodding, cutting, watering, shaping."

44. C

The speaker begins his story by quickly establishing the setting and then stating, "An unexplainable aimlessness engulfs me. I stay later and later each evening." The speaker's thoughts and feelings are exclusively revealed from the beginning to the end of this passage. The story is told from the first-person point of view.

45. C

The title of this story gives the reader a good idea of the writer's intent. "The Thrill of the Grass" begins by criticizing the use of "plastic grass." The main body of the story deals with replacing Astroturf with real grass. The central focus of the story is on keeping traditional aspects of baseball intact, and how seemingly unimportant conventions, such as playing-field materials, can represent more to those who love the more abstract qualities of the sport. The speaker repeatedly calls up patriotic and sentimental images when referring to baseball: the fake grass is representative of the strike, which has, like the fake grass, impeded the sport for artificial reasons.

46. A

In order to introduce one of the main themes of the narrative beyond the narrator's own feelings of guilt, the story begins with him attempting to establish his own sound mental condition. His firm insistence that he is not "mad" leads the reader to suspect that he is in fact suffering from some form of mental unrest. For this reason, alternative **A** is the best answer.

47. C

The story is intentionally organized in such a way that clues undermining the credibility of the narrator intentionally encourage us to read the story ironically. One might expect that someone would remember where he or she got the cruel idea to kill an old man because of his glass eye. The most successful answer on this list is alternative **C** because only this one cites the evidence of the narrator's failing memory.

48. C

The next step in the organization of the story reinforces in the reader's mind that the narrator is attempting to use the tools of logic to defend himself against what he perceives to be our accusations: "You fancy me mad." In this way, "The Tell-Tale Heart" follows the form of an essay, because the narrator attempts to bring evidence in to support his main contention involving his sanity. For this reason the strongest answer from this list is alternative **C**.

49. C

The narrator's clear recounting of events and the careful, systematic way in which he committed the crime suggest that he is a highly methodical person.

50. C

The narrator's claim that he has an acute sense of hearing as a result of his mental condition leads the reader to suspect that this sense will undermine his efforts at concealing his crime. Indeed, hearing the heart beating increasingly loudly is what finally causes the narrator to declare his guilt, though the reader can be quite sure that the beating heart he hears at the very end is actually his own.

51. B

The concluding moments of the story connect the reader back to the beginning, since it is here that the reader begins to suspect that the police officers have recognized early on that the narrator is both mad and guilty, despite his claims of innocence. Of the alternatives listed, alternative **B** is the best answer because it is indeed the narrator's manner with the police that reveals his guilt.

UNIT TEST—READING

Read the following passage to answer questions 1 to 11.

A WORK OF ARTIFICE

The bonsai tree
in the attractive pot
could have grown eighty feet tall
on the side of a mountain
till split by lightning.
But a gardener
carefully pruned it.
It is nine inches high.
Every day as he
whittles back the branches
the gardener croons,
It is your nature
to be small and cozy,
domestic and weak;
how lucky, little tree,
to have a pot to grow in.
With living creatures
one must begin very early
to dwarf their growth:
the bound feet,
the crippled brain,
the hair in curlers,
the hands you
love to touch.

—*by* Marge Piercy

1. The central idea of this poem might be interpreted as

A. an indictment of the subordination of women

B. a celebration of the stately beauty afforded by trees

C. a protest against the unnatural restriction required to produce a bonsai tree

D. a condemnation of the practice of the ancient Chinese custom of binding women's feet

2. The character of the gardener is **most likely** intended to serve as a metaphor for

A. the destructive forces of nature

B. male-dominated society

C. a nurturing caregiver

D. a supportive parent

3. The word *prune* means to remove unwanted parts. In view of this definition, the allusion to the careful pruning done by the metaphorical gardener represents
   A. the artificial and unnatural expectations placed on women to live up to society's ideal image
   B. the sacrifices made by both people in a relationship to maintain its strength and solidity
   C. the rising popularity of plastic surgery to sustain the appearance of youth and beauty
   D. the gradual blurring of distinctions between the roles of men and women in society

4. In which line of the poem is the reader first made aware that the bonsai tree is a metaphor for a woman?
   A. Line 8
   B. Line 12
   C. Line 18
   D. Line 20 = crippled brain

5. The gardener's crooning to the bonsai tree contains an example of which of the following literary devices?
   A. Irony
   B. Allegory
   C. Metaphor
   D. Assonance

6. The best examples of lines from the poem that hint at social criticism are
   A. "The bonsai tree / in the attractive pot / could have grown eighty feet tall"
   B. "But a gardener / carefully pruned it"
   C. "to be small and cozy, / domestic and weak"
   D. "How lucky, little tree, / to have a pot to grow in"

7. An allusion to an unrealized promise of actualization is contained in
   A. lines 1 to 5
   B. lines 6 to 7
   C. lines 15 to 16
   D. lines 17 to 18

8. The rhythm of the poem changes in lines six through eight, as the poet shifts from the long sentence of the first five lines to two short, abrupt sentences in the next three lines. Which of the following statements offers the **best** explanation for this shift in structure?

- **A.** These lines refer to the protection that the gardener affords a small plant that would otherwise be destroyed by the forces of nature.
- **B.** The long initial sentence describes possibilities in a dreamlike fashion, but the next lines act as a wake-up call to the truth.
- **C.** The short, abrupt structure evokes the snipping and pruning the gardener performs to shape the tree.
- **D.** The bonsai tree is representative of East Asian culture, whose poetry is characterized by the simple, poetic structures emulated by the shorter, terser lines of poetry.

9. The paradox inherent in the metaphor of the gardener is that

- **A.** because the tree tends to grow wild and unruly by nature, it needs the pruning of a gardener to help it grow and survive
- **B.** a tree that would normally be considered undesirable can be moulded into an object of decoration and beauty
- **C.** in man's wish to make woman beautiful, he stunts the potential and growth of a lovely creature
- **D.** in order to be considered beautiful, a bonsai tree must be subjected to painful constrictions

10. The lines "But a gardener/carefully pruned it" and "It is your nature to be/small and cozy" are an example of

- **A.** masculine rhyme
- **B.** juxtaposition
- **C.** change of voice
- **D.** hyperbole

11. The choice of the word "artifice" in the title establishes that the poem will engage in criticism. A synonym of the word "artifice" is

- **A.** masterpiece
- **B.** splendour
- **C.** deception
- **D.** alteration

Read the following passage to answer questions 12 to 24.

THE EXPRESS

After the first powerful, plain manifesto
The black statement of pistons, without more fuss
But gliding like a queen, she leaves the station.
Without bowing and with restrained unconcern
She passes the houses which humbly crowd outside,
The gasworks, and at last the heavy page
Of death, printed by gravestones in the cemetery.
Beyond the town, there lies the open country
Where, gathering speed, she acquires mystery,
The luminous self-possession of ships on ocean.
It is now she begins to sing—at first quite low
Then loud, and at last with a jazzy madness—
The song of her whistle screaming at curves,
Of deafening tunnels, brakes, innumerable bolts.
And always light, aerial, underneath,
Retreats the elate metre of her wheels.
Steaming through metal landscape on her lines,
She plunges new eras of white happiness,
Where speed throws up strange shapes, broad curves
And parallels clean like trajectories from guns.
At last, further than Edinburgh or Rome,
Beyond the crest of the world, she reaches night
Where only a low stream-line brightness
Of phosphorus on the tossing hills is light.
Ah, like a comet through flame, she moves entranced,
Wrapt in her music no bird song, no, nor bough
Breaking with honey buds, shall ever equal.

—*by* Stephen Spender

12. In the quotation "After the first powerful, plain manifesto," the word "manifesto" refers to the

A. blowing of the steam whistle signalling the train's arrival at the station

B. conductor calling to straggling passengers to board the express quickly

C. engine idling quietly as it awaits its master's arrival and first command

D. loud spinning of piston-driven wheels announcing the train's departure

13. The phrase "gliding like a queen, she leaves the station" contains an example of which of the following literary devices?

A. Onomatopoeia

B. Hyperbole

C. Metaphor

D. Simile

14. In the first four lines of the poem, the train can best be described as

A. graceful and controlled

B. noisy and arrogant

C. plain and simple

D. fast and crazy

15. The phrase “She passes the houses which humbly crowd outside” contains an example of which of the following literary devices?

A. Personification

B. Oxymoron

C. Paradox

D. Simile

16. The phrase “the heavy page / Of death” contains an example of which of the following literary devices?

A. Pun

B. Metaphor

C. Oxymoron

D. Alliteration

17. By stating that the train acquires “the luminous self-possession of ships on ocean,” the poet **most strongly** suggests that trains and ships are both

A. independent and unruffled

B. vulnerable and isolated

C. large and cumbersome

D. metallic and swift

18. In the line “It is now she begins to sing,” the poet is **most likely** referring to the

A. sound of wind whistling past the train’s metallic sides

B. happy chorus of passengers finally on the move

C. musical sound of the speeding train’s whistle

D. personification of the train’s unleashed spirit

19. The poet **most likely** describes the tunnels as “deafening” because the

A. passengers’ momentary tunnel blindness also affects their hearing

B. earth-enclosed tunnel isolates the passengers from all outside noise

C. conversations within the passenger compartments are briefly suspended

D. noises made by the metal friction, brakes, and whistle blasts are amplified

20. In the quotation "the elate metre of her wheels," the description "elate metre" suggests that the sound is

A. quiet but irritating

B. heavy and intrusive

C. excited and rhythmic

D. irregular but comforting

21. The phrase "speed throws up strange shapes" most likely means that

A. recognizable shapes are blurred as they fly past

B. people experience travel sickness because of the speed

C. individuals react differently when confronted with speed

D. passengers are bounced about inside the train, blocking what others can see

22. The description "like trajectories from guns" **most strongly** creates an impression of

A. speed

B. power

C. emptiness

D. flawlessness

23. The quotation "At last, further than Edinburgh or Rome, / Beyond the crest of the world, she reaches night" contains an example of which of the following literary devices?

A. Simile

B. Hyperbole = exageration

C. Oxymoron

D. Apostrophe

24. Which of the following statements **best** supports the conclusion drawn in the last two lines of the poem?

A. The train has no time to pause and appreciate the wonders of nature.

B. The express will never match the beauty that is to be found in nature.

C. The sound of the train's "music" is as sweet as honey and fresh flowers.

D. Nothing in the natural world can compare with the magic of the express.

Read the following passage to answer questions 25 to 36.

SUITCASE LADY

Night after night, the woman with the red hair and the purple dress sits in the harsh light of a 24-hour doughnut shop on Queen Street West.

Somewhere in her bleary eyes and in the deep lines of her face is a story that probably no one will ever really know. She is taking pains to write something on a notepad and crying steadily.

She calls herself Vicomtesse Antonia The Linds'ays. She's the suitcase lady of Queen Street.

No one knows how many women there are like her in Toronto. They carry their belongings in shopping bags and spend their days and nights scrounging for food. They have no one and nowhere to go. This night, in a warm corner with a pot of tea and a pack of Player's, the Vicomtesse is in a mood to talk.

Out of her past come a few scraps: a mother named Savaria; the child of a poor family in Montreal; a brief marriage when she was 20; a son in Toronto who is now 40. "We never got along well because I didn't bring him up. I was too poor. He never called me mama."

She looks out the window. She's 60 years old.

With her words she spins herself a cocoon. She talks about drapes and carpets, castles and kings. She often lapses into French. She lets her tea get cold. Her hands are big, rough, farmer's hands. How she ended up in the doughnut shop remains a mystery, maybe even to her.

"Before, I had a kitchen and a room and my own furniture. I had to leave everything and go."

It's two years that she's been on the go, since the rooming houses stopping taking her. "I don't have no place to stay."

So she walks. A sturdy coat covers her dress and worn leather boots are on her feet. But her big legs are bare and chapped and she has a ragged cough.

Yes, she says, her legs get tired. She has swollen ankles and, with no socks in her boots, she has blisters. She says she has socks—in the suitcase—but they make her feet itch. As for money, "I bum on the street. I don't like it, but I have to. I have to survive. The only pleasure I got is my cigaret." She lights another one. "It's not a life." She recalls the Saturday, a long time ago, when she made $27, and laughs when she tells about how she had to make the money last through Sunday, too. Now she gets "maybe $7 or $8," and eats "very poor." When she is asked how people treat her, the answer is very matter-of-fact: "Some give money. Some are very polite and some are rude." In warm weather, she passes her time at the big square in front of City Hall. When it's cold she takes her suitcase west to the doughnut shop.

The waitresses who bring food to the woman look upon her with compassion. They persuaded their boss that her sitting does no harm.

Where does she sleep? "Any place I can find a place to sleep. In the park, in stores—like here I stay and sit, on Yonge Street." She shrugs. Sometimes she goes into an underground parking garage.

She doesn't look like she knows what sleep is. "This week I sleep three hours in four days. I feel tired but I wash my face with cold water and I feel okay." Some questions make her eyes turn from the window and stare hard. Then they well over with tears. Like the one about loneliness. "I don't talk much to people," she answers. "Just the elderly, sometimes, in the park."

Her suitcase is full of dreams.

Carefully, she unzips it and pull out a sheaf of papers—"my concertos." Each page is crammed with neatly written musical notes—the careful writing she does on the doughnut shop table—but the bar lines are missing. Questions about missing bar lines she tosses aside. Each "concerto" has a French name—Tresor, La Tempete, Le Retour—and each one bears the signature of the Vicomtesse. She smiles and points to one. "A very lovely piece of music. I like it." She digs in her suitcase again, almost shyly, and produces a round plastic box. Out of it emerges a tiara. Like a little girl, she smooths back her dirty hair and proudly puts it on. No one in the doughnut shop seems to notice.

She cares passionately about the young, the old and the ones who suffer. So who takes care of the suitcase lady?

"God takes care of me, that's for sure," she says, nodding thoughtfully. "But I'm not what you call crazy about religion. I believe always try to do the best to help people—the elderly, and kids, and my country, and my city of Toronto, Ontario."

—*by* Christie McLaren

25. In the opening sentence of this passage, the expression "harsh light" suggests that the light is

A. strangely coloured

B. constantly flashing

C. too weak to read by

D. uncomfortably bright

26. Which of the following quotation **least** contributes to the impression that the suitcase lady is unhealthy?

A. "Somewhere in her bleary eyes"

B. "The deep lines of her faces"

C. "And crying steadily"

D. "I wash my face with cold water"

27. In context, the quotation "Out of her past come a few scraps" (line 10) refers to the fact that the suitcase lady

A. remembers disjointed bits of her unhappy life

B. shows some of the items she has in her suitcase

C. has had many fights with formerly intimate friends

D. is an insignificant and discarded member of society

28. The **most likely** reason the lady's son never called her "mama" is that

A. others raised him because his mother was too poor to do so

B. when he was young, he constantly argued with his mother

C. he was embarrassed by his mother's wretched poverty

D. he never found out who his natural mother was

29. The phrase "With her words she spins herself a cocoon" contains which of the following figures of speech?

A. Pun

B. Metaphor

C. Hyperbole

D. Personification = not person

30. The most likely meaning of the quotation "With her words she spins herself a cocoon" is

A. a web of lies has been the cause of her wretched state

B. a maze of confusion is the result of her confused speech

C. she imagines that other people believe that she is royalty

D. she creates a closed and safe place of comforting thoughts

31. According to details in the passage, the suitcase lady's only pleasure is

A. smoking cigarettes

B. talking to older people she meets

C. writing interesting musical scores

D. sitting quietly in the doughnut shop

32. In the phrase "When she is asked how people treat her, the answer is very matter-of-fact," the description "matter-of-fact" suggests that she is

A. conversing confidently and optimistically

B. emotionally citing a string of troubling facts

C. calmly and unemotionally recalling experiences

D. listing details associated with a variety of themes

33. The use of the word "compassion" in the quotation "The waitresses…look upon her with compassion" (line 31) suggests that the waitresses are

A. shy

B. nervous

C. irritated

D. considerate

34. Which of the following character traits can be identified in the suitcase lady's remark "I feel tired but I wash my face with cold water and I feel okay"?

A. Naiveté

B. Courage

C. Foolishness

D. Cleanliness

35. The quotation "I don't have no place to stay" contains which of the following types of grammatical error?

A. Double negative

I don't have a place to stay

B. Sentence fragment

C. Misplaced modifier

D. Incorrect pronoun choice

36. The concluding paragraph of the passage contains several examples of which of the following literary techniques?

A. Irony

B. Paradox

C. Oxymoron

D. Onomatopoeia

37. The words "staggered," "ground," and "plodded" are **most likely** used to convey a feeling of

A. liberation

B. conviction

C. exhaustion

D. anticipation

38. In this passage, the narrative point of view is

A. objective

B. omniscient

C. first person

D. limited omniscient

Read the following passage to answer questions 37 to 51.

OLD MAN AT THE BRIDGE

An old man with steel rimmed spectacles and very dusty clothes sat by the side of the road. There was a pontoon bridge across the river and carts, trucks, and men, women and children were crossing it. The mule-drawn carts staggered up the steep bank from the bridge with soldiers helping push against the spokes of the wheels. The trucks ground up and away heading out of it all and the peasants plodded along in the ankle deep dust. But the old man sat there without moving. He was too tired to go any farther.

It was my business to cross the bridge, explore the bridgehead beyond and find out to what point the enemy had advanced. I did this and returned over the bridge. There were not so many carts now and very few people on foot, but the old man was still there.

"Where do you come from?" I asked him.

"From San Carlos," he said, and smiled.

That was his native town and so it gave him pleasure to mention it and he smiled.

"I was taking care of animals," he explained.

"Oh," I said, not quite understanding.

"Yes," he said, "I stayed, you see, taking care of animals. I was the last one to leave the town of San Carlos."

He did not look like a shepherd nor a herdsman and I looked at his dusty clothes and his gray dusty face and his steel rimmed spectacles and said. "What animals were they?"

"Various animals," he said, and shook his head. "I had to leave them."

I was watching the bridge and the African looking country of the Ebro Delta and wondering how long now it would be before we would see the enemy, and listening all the while for the first noises that would signal that ever mysterious event called contact, and the old man still sat there.

"What animals were they?" I asked.

"There were three animals altogether," he explained. "There were two goats and a cat and then there were four pairs of pigeons."

"And you had to leave them?" I asked.

"Yes. Because of the artillery. The captain told me to go because of the artillery."

"And you have no family?" I asked, watching the far end of the bridge where a few last carts were hurrying down the slope of the bank.

"No," he said "only the animals I stated. The cat, of course, will be all right. A cat can look out for itself, but I cannot think what will become of the others."

"What politics have you?" I asked.

"I am without politics," he said. "I am seventy-six years old. I have come twelve kilometers now and I think now I can go no further."

This is not a good place to stop," I said. "If you can make it, there are trucks up the road where it forks for Tortosa."

"I will wait a while," he said. "and then I will go. Where do the trucks go?"

"Towards Barcelona," I told him.

"I know no one in that direction," he said. "but thank you very much. Thank you again very much."

He looked at me very blankly and tiredly, then said, having to share his worry with some one. "The cat will be all right, I am sure. There is no need to be unquiet about the cat. But the others. Now what do you think about the others?"

"Why they'll probably come through it all right."

"You think so?"

"Why not," I said, watching the far bank where now there were no carts.

"But what will they do under the artillery when I was told to leave because of the artillery?"

"Did you leave the dove cage unlocked?" I asked.

"Yes."

"Then they'll fly."

"Yes, certainly they'll fly. But the others. It's better not to think about the others," he said.

"If you are rested I would go." I urged. "Get up and try to walk now."

"Thank you," he said and got to his feet, swayed from side to side and then sat down backwards in the dust.

"I was taking care of animals," he said dully, but no longer to me. "I was only taking care of animals."

There was nothing to do about him. It was Easter Sunday and the Fascists were advancing toward the Ebro. It was a gray overcast day with a low ceiling so their planes were not up. That and the fact that cats know how to look after themselves was all the good luck that old man would ever have.

—*by* Ernest Hemingway

37. The words "staggered", "ground," and "plodded" are **most likely** used to convey a feeling of

A. liberation

B. conviction

C. exhaustion

D. anticipation

38. In this passege, the narrative point of view is

A. objective

B. omniscient

C. first person

D. limited omniscient

39. Suspense is **most effectively** created by which of the following quotations?

A. "The mule-drawn carts staggered up the steep bank"

B. "listening all the while for the first noises"

C. "'The captain told me to go because of the artillery'"

D. "'I have come twelve kilometers now'"

40. According to the old man, which of the animals he left behind would be **least likely** to survive the expected military offensive?

A. The cat

B. The goats

C. The mules

D. The pigeons

41. Which of the following sentences best restates the question "What politics have you?"

A. "Are you a politician?"

B. "Who are your friends?"

C. "Are you carrying arms?"

D. "Which side do you support?"

42. The repetition of the statement "I was taking care of animals" is **most likely** intended to

A. reinforce the old man's love of animals

B. illustrate the old man's blind stubbornness

C. confirm the old man's commitment to duty

D. reveal the old man's distraught frame of mind

43. The fact that the fascist's attack was taking place on Easter Sunday is most likely intended to be

A. ironic

B. fortuitous

C. allegorical

D. coincidental

44. The old man can **best** be described as

A. isolated and pitiful

B. sensitive and caring

C. wilful but ineffectual

D. uninvolved but passionate

45. The old man and the animals are alike in all of the following ways **except** that they

A. provide each other with a kind of support

B. have an equal chance of survival

C. are residents of San Carlos

D. are affected by the war

46. The reference to the "gray overcast day" fulfills the literary task of

A. adding an element of contrast to the setting

B. signalling the climax and resulting turning point

C. supplying an element of suspense to the conflict

D. foreshadowing a possible dark ending to the plot

47. The concluding sentence to this story suggests that the old man will

A. remain where he is and consequently die

B. accept the soldier's offer of aid and go to Tortosa

C. return to San Carlos in order to care for his animals

D. gather his strength and follow the others to Barcelona

48. What is the central symbol in this story?

A. The cat

B. The bridge

C. Easter Sunday

D. An empty bird cage

49. The bridge is **most likely** a symbol of

A. a compromise between the two armies

B. the end of a long and trying journey

C. an escape from threats and violence

D. a crossing into an unfamiliar world

50. Which of the following words **best** captures the attitude of the soldier?

A. Sarcastic

B. Regretful

C. Indifferent

D. Compassionate

51. Which of the following statements best describes the central theme of this story?

A. With old age comes the inability to effectively deal with life's inevitable challenges.

B. The fortunes of human beings are determined as much by luck as by careful planning.

C. The timeless relationship between man and animal is a significant part of any society.

D. Although not directly involved, non-combatants are devastated by the effects of war.

Read the following passage to answer questions 52 to 59.

TO HIS COY MISTRESS

Had we but world enough, and time,
This coyness, lady, were no crime.
We would sit down, and think which way
To walk, and pass our long love's day.
Thou by the Indian Ganges' side
Shouldst rubies find; I by the tide
Of Humber would complain. I would
Love you ten years before the flood,
And you should, if you please, refuse
Till the conversion of the Jews.
My vegetable love should grow
Vaster than empires and more slow;
An hundred years should go to praise
Thine eyes, and on thy forehead gaze;
Two hundred to adore each breast,
But thirty thousand to the rest;
In age at least to every part,
And the last age should show your heart.
For lady, you deserve this state,
Nor would I love at lower rate.
But at my back I always hear
Time's wingèd chariot hurrying near;
And yonder all before us lie
Deserts of vast eternity.
Thy beauty shall no more be found,
Nor, in thy marble vault, shall sound
My echoing song; then worms shall try
That long-preserved virginity,

And your quaint honor turn to dust,
And into ashes all my lust:
The grave's a fine and private place,
But none, I think, do there embrace.
Now therefore, while the youthful hue
Sits on the skin like morning dew,
And while thy willing soul transpires
At every pore with instant fires,
Now let us sport us while we may,
And now, like amorous birds of prey,
Rather at once our time devour
Than languish in his slow-chapped power.
Let us roll all our strength and all
Our sweetness up into one ball,
And tear our pleasures with rough strife
Thorough the iron gates of life:
Thus, though we cannot make our sun
Stand still, yet we will make him run.

—*by* Andrew Marvell

52. The use of the word "thou" in this poem **mainly** indicates that the poet is

A. intentionally not using the woman's name at this point in the poem

B. using elevated language to demonstrate his love for his mistress

C. addressing his mistress directly through the poem

D. trying to disguise the woman's identity

53. The **main** reason the poet places his lady so far away from him, by the Indian Ganges river, is that

A. it is an exotic location compared with the poet's home in Britain

B. she is actually from India, and he is remembering their meeting

C. he would really rather dream about her than talk to her

D. he is trying to impress her with his words

54. The **main** effect that the poet is trying to achieve by referring to the Biblical flood is to

A. exaggerate the amount of time he wishes they had to get to know each other

B. influence her to decide to become more involved in a relationship with him

C. warn her about the possibility of a natural disaster like a flood

D. impress her with his knowledge of the Bible

55. The choice of the unusual adjective "vegetable" to modify the word "love" (line 11) **mainly** emphasizes that the poet's feelings of love for his mistress would

A. develop slowly

B. evolve naturally

C. be very healthy for her

D. involve some tending to

56. The word that best indicates a shift in the speaker's tone in this poem is

A. "nor"

B. "but"

C. "and"

D. "before"

57. Which of the following phrases best explains the reason for the speaker's fear that in the future his mistress's beauty will disappear?

A. "But at my back I always hear"

B. "Deserts of vast eternity" → nothingness

C. "My echoing song"

D. "then worms shall try"

58. The phrase "then worms shall try / That long-preserved virginity" attempts to convince the woman by creating a feeling of

A. pain

B. passion

C. aversion = avoid

D. curiosity

59. The final word of the poem, "run," **primarily** signifies that

A. their lives will end sooner

B. they will devour the time

C. she should decide sooner

D. time will move faster

ANSWERS AND SOLUTIONS—UNIT TEST

1. A	13. D	25. D	37. C	49. D
2. B	14. A	26. D	38. C	50. D
3. A	15. A	27. A	39. B	51. D
4. D	16. B	28. A	40. B	52. C
5. A	17. A	29. B	41. D	53. A
6. C	18. C	30. D	42. D	54. D
7. A	19. D	31. A	43. A	55. A
8. CC	20. C	32. C	44. A	56. B
9. C	21. A	33. D	45. B	57. B
10. C	22. D	34. B	46. D	58. C
11. C	23. B	35. A	47. A	59. D
12. D	24. D	36. A	48. B	

1. A

Alternative **A** is correct. The poem compares the societal pressures placed upon women to the practice of trimming bonsai trees to keep them small and contained. The poet suggests that women are trained and constrained so that they develop and display the characteristics society defines as beautiful.

2. B

Alternative **B** is correct. It is the gardener who decides which of the tree's attributes and characteristics should be encouraged or pruned. This is a criticism of society's image of the "perfect" woman and its beliefs about which characteristics should be encouraged or excised.

3. A

Alternative **A** is correct. Just as the metaphorical gardener snips off the branches and twigs he considers unattractive, society's expectations disallow any characteristics that are deemed "undesirable." Thus, a feminist critic might suggest that societal ideals demand women to adhere to a particular popular image and suppress any urge to grow in a manner unacceptable to the norm.

4. D

Alternative **D** is correct. The reader does not suspect that the bonsai tree is a metaphor for a woman until mention is made of "bound feet" in line 20. This is the first indication that the issue at hand is not merely an ornamental tree.

5. A

Alternative **A** is correct. The gardener is crooning to the tree, which is typically a soft, comforting manner of speaking; however, the content the gardener is expressing is actually quite negative. It is ironic that the gardener expects the little tree to be grateful to have the comfort of a container, when it is the container that confines the tree in an unnatural manner. This is a thinly-veiled allusion to the fact that a patriarchal society expects women to be grateful for their confinement to a role that restricts their freedom for intellectual and emotional growth.

6. C

Alternative **C** is correct. These lines refer, ironically, to characteristics deemed by society to be positive feminine attributes. Often, women are expected to create and preside over homes that conform to these standards, putting their own dreams and goals aside.

7. A

Alternative **A** is correct. These lines suggest the potential that might have been realized by the tree, had it not been placed in the pot and pruned by the gardener. Later in the poem, the poet explains what forces prevent this potential from being fulfilled: the metaphorical gardener who, under the guise of protection, hinders and stunts the growth of the tree.

8. C

Alternative C is correct. The short, decisive sentences of lines 6–8 serve to force the reader back to the reality of the situation.

9. C

Alternative **C** is correct. The gardener believes he is helping the little tree to grow and thrive by pruning out what he considers "undesirable" or "unattractive." In reality, he is cutting off those elements of the tree that would make it unique. According to some critics, this is a metaphor for the restrictions that are placed on women in our society. These critics would argue that society believes it is helping women achieve success according to ideal standards, when in reality it is placing restrictions on individual growth and intellectual expansion.

10. C

Alternative **C** is correct. The voice changes from third person to first person as the gardener addresses the tree he is pruning.

11. C

Alternative **C** is correct. The word "artifice" means a ruse or deceptive manoeuvre. The use of this term reflects an earnest criticism of the actions undertaken by gardeners (or society) to mould living things with great potential for growth into approved, confined beings.

12. D

As the poem begins, so does the train's journey. The statement in question begins in the first line of the poem and is not completed until part way through line two, where the poet directly reveals who or what has made the first "powerful, plain manifesto." It is the "statement of pistons," or the initial pumping of the pistons, that is needed to turn the heavy metal train wheels. Latent energy is converted to kinetic energy as the train slowly pulls out of the station. This is "plain" or easily seen, and requires much power.

13. D

In this phrase, the train is compared to a queen. A description that compares two unlike elements and links them with the words *like* or *as* is called a simile.

14. A

At the beginning of the poem, the train is compared to a queen, which immediately conveys a regal, graceful image. It is also made clear in a number of statements that the train is a controlled entity: "without more fuss," "without bowing," and "with restrained unconcern." Each of the incorrect alternatives contains at least one element that is not supported by the text.

15. A

In this sentence, the houses "humbly crowd outside," which means they are being given the ability to move, demonstrate free will, and express emotions. These are actions and feelings associated with human beings, not inanimate objects. Such an unrealistic endowment is identified as personification.

16. B

The comparison between the contents of a cemetery to a page is a direct comparison between two dissimilar elements. Such a comparison is identified as a metaphor.

17. A

Although both trains and ships are metallic and can at times be isolated, the only alternative that appropriately describes both modes of transportation is alternative **A**. Both types of vehicles experience periods of detachment from the world around them. Having to face the elements alone, they appear strong, independent, and queen-like: unruffled or self-possessed. They do not share vulnerability, speed, size, or awkwardness.

18. C

The poet states directly that "the song of her whistle screaming at curves" is the source of the "jazzy madness" given off by the train.

19. D

The enclosed space of the tunnel would act as an echo chamber, trapping any sounds made by the train, be they whistle noises, braking noises, or the grinding of "innumerable bolts." This sound would be extremely loud, momentarily deafening all who heard it.

20. C

The description "elate metre" suggests a sound that is excited and rhythmic. The word "elate," as in elation, conveys exhilaration or excitement, and the word "metre," as in poetic metre, suggests a repeated pattern or rhythm created by the motion of the wheels against the rails.

21. A

The key word in the phrase is "speed." The speaker establishes his point of view as that of one who is on the inside looking out. He notes the "broad curves / And parallels" of the tracks as one regains focus; however, if he were to look sideways as the express "screams" ahead with "jazzy madness," the view would certainly be blurred in such a way that familiar shapes would appear "strange" if not incomprehensible.

22. D

It is the "parallels" that are being compared to "trajectories from guns." Of the four alternatives, the word *flawlessness* best captures the image conveyed by this simile: that of the blurred parallel lines of fences or telephone wires as they would be seen through the window of an express train.

23. B

The train's ability to travel beyond Edinburgh, Scotland, and Rome, Italy, to the edge of the world in one trip exaggerates both the speed and the distance the train is capable of attaining. Such an exaggeration in literature is called hyperbole.

24. D

As the train races down the line "entranced," the poet endows this manmade creation with the kind of joy humans might express at a moment of accomplishment. This apparent delight in the speed and associated "music" of the journey are compared to two beautiful events in nature: the music of the songbird and the spring blossoming of honey buds. Of this comparison, the poet states that "no bird" and "no bough" can equal the beauty of the express.

25. D

The light in question is located inside a 24-hour doughnut shop. The suitcase lady frequents the shop, writing music by the light. One might reasonably assume that an interior light would not flash and would not be "strangely coloured." It can also be assumed that the light is not weak, as the adjective "harsh" connotes discomfort or unpleasantness.

26. D

The quotation "I wash my face with cold water" does not provide evidence that this woman has lived a hard life. Washing one's face with cold water is an act that many healthy people do to experience a refreshing or bracing sensation early in the morning.

27. A

In context, the phrase refers to the memories the suitcase lady is prepared to share. The speaker introduces the phrase by stating, "This night … the Vicomtesse is in a mood to talk." These memories or "scraps" include her mother's name and the facts that she had a brief marriage and has an estranged son.

28. A

The speaker states, "'We never got along well because I didn't bring him up. I was too poor.'"

29. B

The direct comparison between elements of a conversation and an insect's cocoon is a clear example of a metaphor, which is a figure of speech in which two unlike objects or elements are compared.

30. D

The phrase compares the woman's words with a cocoon: an enclosed, protective covering spun by many insects. The suitcase lady muses on memories of drapes, carpets, castles, and kings shortly after revealing the painful reality about her relationship with her son; this strongly suggests that she is escaping a negative memory by wrapping herself in a "cocoon" of positive or comforting thoughts.

31. A

According to the suitcase lady, her only pleasure in life is derived from her cigarettes.

32. C

The description "matter-of-fact" suggests relating or adhering to the facts. The calm resignation with which the woman recounts the grim facts of her life is evident as she "laughs when she tells about how she had to make the money last through Sunday." She is not optimistic or confident, neither troubled nor emotional.

33. D

The word "compassion" means sympathetic consciousness of others' distress and a desire to alleviate it. In context, the fact that the waitresses allow the suitcase lady to stay for extended periods of time and bring her food when she likely does not have the money to pay for it demonstrates sympathy and kindness. The fact that they negotiated with their boss on the woman's behalf to allow her to remain similarly shows compassion and consideration. The waitresses are considerate of her age, financial state, failing health, and her fragile state of mind.

34. B

The suitcase lady's attitude in spite of her conditions, her "shrugging off" of her destitute situation, and her willingness to splash her face with water and take on the world day after day demonstrates remarkable courage.

35. A

The repetition of negative expressions as in "I don't have no place to stay" cancels out the intended meaning: *I do not have any place to stay*. This type of unnecessary repetition is defined as a double negative.

36. A

Irony is prevalent throughout the last paragraph of the passage. For example, the statement "God takes care of me" is ironic, since from the perspective of others, it seems as though her basic needs are hardly met. She then contradicts her religious conviction somewhat by stating that she is "not what you call crazy about religion." Further irony is evident in the quotation "I believe always try to do the best to help people—the elderly, and kids, and my country, and my city of Toronto, Ontario." It is ironic, considering the juxtaposition of the suitcase lady's visions of philanthropy with her abject helplessness. It is also ironic that the suitcase lady exhibits pride for her country and city despite the fact that her homelessness and solitude suggest total isolation or lack of association with a society in which she is a pariah.

37. C

The verbs listed clearly suggest a loss of control ("staggered") and weariness ("plodded"). None of the other alternatives is consistent with the scene described, a scene in which non-combatants are fleeing for their lives.

38. C

The fact that the speaker is the only character whose thoughts and feelings are communicated in this short story indicates that the point of view is first person.

39. B

Suspense is defined as anxious uncertainty. With that in mind, alternative B provides the best example of suspense since it is the only alternative that features an individual actively awaiting an uncertain future. The speaker is listening for the noise of enemy aircraft or military bombardment. Either one would likely increase the watcher's level of anxiety. Although each of the other alternatives suggests struggle, sacrifice, and violence, there is no clear immediacy of threat and therefore no significant anxiety or suspense.

40. B

The old man believed that "a cat can look out for itself" and about the pigeons, he states, "certainly they'll fly." Although mules are mentioned in the passage, they are not among the few animals the old man left behind. Ruling out these other animals, it is clear that the old man is referring to the goats when he states, "It's better not to think about the others." This means that the man believes the goats will almost certainly be killed either incidentally in the line of fire or by soldiers passing through in search of food.

41. D

The soldier's question most likely means "Which side do you support?" This would be a logical question since the old man did not make any attempt to move from the bridge in spite of the fact that a hostile army was advancing towards him. Furthermore, the old man admits that he knows no one in Barcelona. If the old man were to claim to have no political affiliation as the innocent refugee that apparently he was, the soldier would consider it his duty to encourage the man to move from harm's way.

42. D

The old man is weak, isolated, and likely in shock. At 76 years of age, he has been forced to walk 12 kilometres, and he is obviously distraught at having to leave his animals in danger. His questionable state of mind and weakened physical condition are revealed when he agrees to leave, gets up, sways, and then sits down again. The soldier notices that he spoke "dully, but no longer to me." The old man's repetition combined with his physical condition and the situation in which he finds himself is far more likely a display of distress (alternative **D**) than any of the other alternatives.

43. A

Alternative **D** can be dismissed automatically since nothing in a piece of fiction is included coincidentally. Of the remaining alternatives, **B** is not supported by text, and alternative **C** suggests that the fact that it is Easter Sunday in some way imparts a lesson or moral, which does not seem to be the intention here. The more logical choice would be alternative **A**, since the attack takes place on the same day that Christians acknowledge the crucifixion of Jesus, an action which is a religious symbol for redemption and forgiveness. The cruel, retaliatory nature of warfare is ironic when juxtaposed with the message of forgiveness and peace that Easter Sunday is associated with.

44. A

Alternative **A** best captures the old man's character. He is isolated from his home, San Carlos, as a result of the military conflict, and he appears to be both disoriented and exhausted. The officer he talks with is sympathetic and encouraging, but his efforts are fruitless. The old man appears not to hear him, instead taking refuge in the recollection of a gentler time, as he says, "I was only taking care of animals." The soldier seems to pity him when he describes the old man as being luckless. Consequently, the old man appears isolated and pitiful. By comparison, the other alternatives each contain one descriptor that does not effectively describe the old man. For example, the adjectives *wilful* and *passionate* are inappropriate since the old man seems to lack any strength or drive. He repeatedly asks for reassurance ("what will become of the others" and "Where do the trucks go?"), and he lacks the strength to stand up and continue on. He is caring when it comes to his animals, but he appears numb as he struggles to hold on to reality.

45. B

Alternative **B** is the only answer that is clearly not supported by text. The conversation between the old man and the soldier reveals that the old man has doubts that the animals will survive an artillery attack ("But what will they do under the artillery when I was told to leave because of the artillery?"). The old man himself has a far better chance of survival because he is removed from the direct line of fire and has the potential to reason himself out of harm's way. The old man has a far better chance of survival than the animals.

46. D

The reference to the gray, overcast day comes near the end of the story. The reader does not know with any certainty how the characters will fare in the end, but it is reasonably certain that it will not be a happy ending. The old man's home of San Carlos is bound to sustain damage from artillery barrages, and it is quite possible that he and his animals will sustain injury or be killed. With that in mind, it is fair to assume that the writer describes the overcast day to foreshadow a negative end to the story (alternative **D**). It is less likely that the phrase in question is used to add conflict to the setting, since the setting is bleak throughout. The addition of suspense is also unlikely, since this story is not about action, but rather character. Furthermore, little suspense can be created in the second-to-last sentence of a story. The idea that the clouds signal the story's climax appears unlikely, since it is arguable that the climax has already occurred when the old man, immobile and in potential danger, is encouraged to move on.

47. A

Although the story does not offer an explicit explanation of the fate of the old man, the contents of the story support the prediction that he will remain where he is and die. This alternative is supported by descriptions of the old man's age and exhaustion. His motivation for survival was to see the animals in his care survive. The narrator adds strength to the conclusion that the old man will remain at the bridge and die when he remarks, "That and the fact that cats know how to look after themselves was all the good luck the old man would ever have." The word "ever" indicates that perhaps it is not just the man's luck but also his life that will soon end. Finally, the title of the story, "Old Man at the Bridge" further suggests a certain static permanence to the old man's position on the bridge.

48. B

The fact that the bridge is mentioned in the title strongly points to its significance in the story. Furthermore, all the action is focused around the old man who struggles with what he should do while remaining in a kind of suspended animation at the bridge. The bridge is also important to both sides in the conflict. The soldier has been sent to "explore the bridgehead beyond and find out to what point the enemy had advanced." One can assume that the bridge could be destroyed by either side if it aided an enemy force in gaining any military advantage. Each of the other alternatives is mentioned in the story and may well carry some symbolic significance: the open bird cage—freedom; the cat—independence; Easter Sunday—peace. However, the story is not primarily concerned with freedom, independence, or peace. It is obvious that the old man at the bridge is the focus of the story, and the bridge plays an important role in revealing aspects of the old man's character.

49. D

The fact that the bridge is mentioned in the title emphasizes its importance. It is the old man's hesitation to cross or leave the bridge that seems to be the writer's focus, for given the offer of help by the young soldier, the old man remains unable to move from the bridge. His focus is on what he has left behind: his animals. He hesitates to embrace what lies beyond. He is being asked to leave his past behind and enter the unknown. He remains at the bridge in spite of the fact that enemy troops are on their way. The young soldier reminds him, "This is not a good place to stop." It is unlikely that the old man sees the bridge as an end of a long journey, since he does ask about what lies beyond, and it is an unlikely escape from the violence if he refuses to leave it. After all, the enemy will arrive there shortly. The idea that it may be symbolic of a bridging of differences between the two enemy forces is not supported by the text; however, if it represents a point of crossing from past to future, known to unknown, life to death, one might well appreciate why the old man appears incapable of crossing it, since the fear of the unknown is a powerful emotion that frequently leads to inaction. With that in mind, alternative **D** is the alternative best supported by the text.

50. D

The tone of this passage is revealed through the speaker. The soldier, possibly the writer himself, views the old man and his situation with compassion. This is seen in the soldier's gentle encouragement and patience. He attempts to lessen the old man's concerns for the animals by downplaying the likelihood of their being caught in a dangerous situation. He also provides the distraught old man several avenues of escape. He takes the time to find out anything that may be used to help the old man: does he have any family, and does he support any political party? In the end, he warns the old man of the danger he would be in should he choose to stay at the bridge. The soldier is not regretful since he does not take upon himself any responsibility for the old man's situation, and he is not indifferent since he shows obvious concern. Lastly, the soldier is not sarcastic, for he does not seem to ridicule either the old man or the military involved.

51. D

As the title suggests, the narrator is most concerned with the fate of the old man at the bridge. The speaker clearly feels sympathy for this victim of war but can do little to aid him since the old man himself seems not to know where he wants to go. Once forced to move from his home, the old man is at a loss. He is representative of the many non-combatants who must endure the devastating effects of war. This plot has less to do with old age than it does with humanity in general trapped in an impossible situation. The old man's relationship with his animals is cited, but it is not the central theme of the story. The animals represent a reason for going back to San Carlos. The old man's pleasure in mentioning San Carlos suggests that he has lived a happy life.

52. C

Although the second-person singular pronoun "thou" is not in use today, in the 17th century, when the poet lived, this word was common. The poet uses the word "thou" because he is addressing his mistress directly.

53. A

The poet is trying to convince his mistress to be more involved in a relationship with him, and he has only has words at his disposal to create this effect. He is trying to impress her by placing her in an exotic location that contrasts with his rainy, British home.

54. D

The overall goal the poet is hoping to achieve with this poem is that the woman will decide to be his "mistress," and the poet does refer to the amount of time he wishes they had to begin their relationship, but the strongest response is the one that describes the specific effects the poet intends his Biblical allusion to have on the woman. In trying to persuade her to be with him, he attempts to impress her with his knowledge of geography and the Bible.

55. A

Alternative **A** is the strongest answer because it alludes to the specific issue, time, that the poet is taking up with his mistress. Although the word "vegetable" also alludes to the natural and organic quality of his feelings for her, this sense is not as strong as the one relating to the fact that he thinks they do not have "world enough, and time."

56. B

The use of the conjunction "but" indicates that the speaker is shifting from the amount of time he wishes they had to the amount of time he thinks they actually have. The other words do not perform this same function and therefore can be ruled out from consideration.

57. B

Here the argument the speaker uses to persuade the woman to become involved in a relationship with him does not involve that of advancing old age, but of death, or as he puts it, "Deserts of vast eternity." After trying earlier to impress her with his knowledge of the Bible and to flatter her with beautiful descriptions, in this section of the poem, the speaker appeals to her mind by mounting an argument about their mortality. The correct answer is alternative **B**.

58. C

Although the speaker might try to interest the woman by creating positive feelings involving passion (**B**) or curiosity (**D**), in this example, the feeling he creates is one of aversion. The vivid image is intended to get her to turn more directly to him, partly out of fear for what comes after death.

59. D

The irony in the final word of the poem, "run," is that, after complaining about how fast time is passing while his mistress decides whether or not to join him in tearing "pleasures with rough strife," the speaker says that their getting together will make the time go by even faster because of the fun they will have together.

NOTES

Writing

WRITING

Developing and Organizing Content

11W1.1 identify the topic, purpose, and audience for a variety of writing tasks

11W1.2 generate, expand, explore, and focus ideas for potential writing tasks, using a variety of strategies and print, electronic, and other resources, as appropriate

Developing Writing Tasks

By Grade 11, you should be confident using various forms of writing. The form of writing you choose will change according to your purpose for writing and your intended audience. These forms include analytic and argumentative essays, critical reviews, expressive works, such as narrative or dramatic scenes, and independent research essays and reports.

Recognizable Characters

- Picking *stock characters* that have been read or seen over and over again. The audience knows what to expect and can be immediately drawn into the story. It is then possible to move the character toward reality, or at least individuality.
- Assigning archetypal qualities to characters. One literary technique is the selection and emphasis of certain enduring character traits. These are archetypal qualities. Certain archetypes are instantly recognizable, such as the hero, the sidekick, and the foil (a character whose contrasts with the hero show off the hero's qualities). The reason stock characters work is that they share in the archetypes readers recognize and accept, and sometimes the distinction can be a matter of taste.

How Character is Revealed

In this context, *character* refers to qualities such as courage, honesty, generosity, and intelligence—and their opposites. *Character* also refers to fundamental ideas and beliefs held by the character, which can be revealed through

- actions
- dialogue
- thoughts revealed through internal dialogue or through other thought-revealing techniques, such as stream of consciousness narration
- the writer's narration

One limitation of film is the difficulty of revealing thoughts in any way other than action. Voice-over narration is one technique filmmakers use to get around this limitation.

Personality

Personality refers to things such as mannerisms, social skills, humour, and all traits that contribute to the words and actions of a person.

Motivation

Motivation is essential to character development and plot.

- Well-developed characters have believable motives—even multiple and conflicting motives.
- Motivation takes time to develop. That is one reason characters in movies often have simple motivation.

Appearance

Except in a movie, appearance is usually an unimportant part of character, unless the story is actually about appearance.

- Some writers do not describe their characters' appearance at all. A reader is left to imagine what the character looks like.
- When appearance is described, first-person narration and third-person limited narration can present problems as a result of subjectivity.

Understanding Character

Understanding fictional characters requires the same analytical, inferential, and interpretive skills that are used to judge people in real life. Conclusions are made by the reader's observations and through what is revealed by the narrator. It is possible to make supported assumptions and to draw logical conclusions about fictional characters.

People share human thoughts, emotions, and motives. Through an active and sympathetic imagination, it is possible to understand people who are genuinely different. Understanding is possible through one's own experiences and seeing something of oneself in a character's experiences. By coming to know or observing others, characters in fictional texts can be easier to understand. The better you know yourself and others, the better able you are to understand characters in fictional texts.

Skilful fiction and non-fiction storytellers can make feelings and motives so clear that the world and the individual have new meaning. Empathy—the sense of personal identification with the experiences of a character—develops when a reader can identify with or relate to a character's experiences.

Characterization

Everything that a writer does to portray characters is called characterization. Characters can be described directly or indirectly. The following chart contains examples of both types of characterization.

Direct characterization is received	Indirect characterization is inferred
• from what one character says or thinks about another character • from the writer's statements about a character. For example, "Jane was stubborn and persevering." • from "indirect characterization" that is obvious or contrived	• from what a character says—sometimes from what a character says about another character • from what a character thinks about his or herself, others, and the world • from what a character does, especially in small things or when under pressure • from other characters' reactions to a character

Direct = obvious
Indirect = reader has to infer.

One of the basic methods of characterization is to invent different kinds of characters that serve different purposes. Characters can be classified by type and function.

Types of Characters

flat	have only one quality or character trait; are one-sided; always act the same way
round	have different, even contradictory traits; are more like real people
stock	are like flat characters, except that stock characters have been used over and over and are instantly recognizable
archetypal	are like stock characters, except that archetypes are meant to be typical (even universal) examples of certain character traits
dynamic	change or grow in some way either for good or bad; are altered by events and by their own actions and choices
static	do not change; flat, round, stock, and archetypal characters can all be static
foil	used as a contrast to the main character or protagonist; the difference between the foil and the main character emphasizes the main character's qualities; the foil is used for indirect characterization side character.

Good storytellers use all of these types of characters. The most important character in a story is usually rounded and dynamic. The taxi driver whose only function is to delay the protagonist by taking a wrong turn is usually flat. In fact, some characters must be flat because there is no time or space to portray them as real people.

The amount of characterization that a character receives is generally controlled by the character's function in the story.

Characters Classified by Function

protagonist	the main character; often the hero, but not always, as sometimes the main character is a villain; often a dynamic character
antagonist	the character the protagonist struggles against; often but not always the villain
major	help move the plot forward in some way; they are often round and dynamic; the protagonist and antagonist are major characters
minor	have minor roles; they affect an event in the plot, but they do not move the whole plot forward; are often flat or stock because they do not appear long enough to be fully developed

Using a Model

If you have difficulty devising your own structure for essay writing, you may want to follow a straightforward structure, such as the one modelled here, that includes:

- an introductory paragraph that introduces your thesis and the text(s) that will be examined to support it
- three body paragraphs, each establishing and developing support for the thesis
- a concluding paragraph that unifies the writing

Essay Writing:

Creating a Thesis Statement

Your thesis statement often comes at the end of your introductory paragraph to provide guidance through the rest of your response. Your thesis statement contains the controlling idea for your essay.

This idea may be either implicit in your thesis statement or stated explicitly. Analysis of character, goal, conflict/obstacle, and realization/resolution should lead naturally to your thesis statement/controlling idea.

Introductory Paragraphs

If you have difficulty writing introductions, use some of the following tips to help make the process easier.

- Write a sentence that introduces the topic and text(s) you will be using.
- Write several sentences that explain the topic and present your thesis statement, including the order of the evidence you will be supporting.
- Explore alternative beginnings to find the one that works best for the idea you are developing. The first sentence is an important sentence because it introduces the mood and tone of your writing.

Developing Paragraphs

Developing paragraphs support your thesis. The first support for the main idea or the thesis is Body Paragraph A, the second support for the thesis is Body Paragraph B, and the third support for the thesis is Body Paragraph C. Body Paragraphs B and C follow the same pattern as Body Paragraph A.

Each developing paragraph contains the following elements:

- An effective introductory and topic sentence that focuses on the support for the thesis that you will develop in the paragraph.
- The development of the supporting idea through explanatory sentences. To bring power to your position, you must include concrete evidence from the text(s). Direct quotations are only useful if they precisely support your idea. Direct references to events, character traits, and literary symbols are all considered useful evidence.
- Explain your interpretation of the evidence in detail. Readers need to see evidence of your thinking. You need to demonstrate your intellect, your thinking, and your ability to interpret literature.
- Elaborate by specifically and overtly connecting the information in this paragraph to your thesis.
- A transition sentence must be considered. Transitions are necessary between paragraphs. They can happen at the end of paragraphs or in the introduction to a new paragraph.

Concluding Paragraph

In your concluding paragraph, you should always

- Generalize your thesis beyond the text—make your idea explicit
- Summarize your major points
- End with a strong sense of closure

End of Day 6

11W1.3 locate and select information to effectively support ideas for writing, using a variety of strategies and print, electronic, and other resources, as appropriate

Research

The Internet allows anyone to make information public, so you must be very careful when performing research using Internet resources. Not everything you read will be true, and if it is, it might not be totally accurate. Although you should be critical of any text you read, it is important to use critical reading more with Internet resources. Critical reading is especially necessary to check the quality and reliability of the information on the Internet.

How To Read a Website

Reading any text requires you to think critically and ask questions about the truth of the text. You should ask yourself some questions that will help you determine the validity and reliability of the information presented on a website.

Things to Consider During Internet Research

1. Take a look at the writer or editor of the website. Is it a professional academic journal or an amateur blog? How professional the writing sounds and how polished the site looks are factors that can help you determine how reliable the site is. Does the site post information about the writer of the materials found there? Does the writer have training or recognized expertise in the subject area dealt with on the site? Can you find any other sites that mention that particular writer? Well-known writers will usually be referred to on many sites.
2. What is the content like? Is the information consistent with information from other sources, such as books or other websites? Usually, academic publishers are reliable sources of information about a subject. Is the information easy to understand? Does the site present more than one side of an issue?
3. Who is the intended audience? Does the writer seem to have a specific audience in mind? Does the site have advertisements? At whom do you think the ads are targeted? How has the site been funded—through corporate sponsorships or through non-profit organizations?
4. How is the site structured? Is it easy to navigate? Can you exit at any time? Can you go back to a previous page without hitting the "Back" button on the browser? Are there links to other sites that give you additional information?

After you have analysed the different features of a site, it is time to evaluate the usefulness of the information on the site. Does it fit the topic of your research? Some sites may look great and have reliable information, but the information may not necessarily relate to your assignment. Make sure not to fill up a research paper with lots of citations from sites that do not have much to do with what you are writing about. More is not always better. You may find only a few websites that help you, but if they are large and comprehensive sites, you will only need a few Internet sources for your writing. Finally, remember that the Internet should not be the only resource you use. Books, newspapers, interviews, and academic journals are all excellent resources as well.

11W1.4 identify, sort, and order main ideas and supporting details for writing tasks, using a variety of strategies and selecting the organizational pattern best suited to the content and the purpose for writing

Organizing Ideas

When you consider the way ideas are organized and your own unique ways of presenting arguments that are important to you, you are beginning to think about your writing from a formal standpoint. Deciding what information should be presented first, second, and third, leading to the conclusion, is an important step in the early stages of writing your piece. Before beginning to compose your first paragraph, you should try to take a metaphorical step back from the information you have gleaned and the hard research you have done and think carefully about the order in which you want to present all this information. The organization of the discussion will not only enable your reader to follow your logic more easily, it will also be more effective in convincing him or her about the truth of your claiMs. As you become more skilled at writing arguments of your own, you also become a "writing reader," looking for the ways that other writers have organized arguments similar to your own and determining the strengths and weaknesses of their approaches to the topic.

Most forms of writing can be categorized according to how they are organized and developed. When you write about what you think, know, or feel about a subject, try to communicate in a unique and personal way. Even in unique and personalized writing, organizational patterns help your message have the most impact. The following organizational structures help ensure your ideas are presented in an interesting and original manner.

Inductive and Deductive Reasoning

Inductive reasoning consists of gathering facts and then using those facts to formulate a more general statement. It is important to have enough examples to justify your conclusion, but you also need to be prepared to review or alter your conclusions as new evidence comes to light.

Example

Specific fact	Shakespeare was a famous playwright
↓	
Specific fact	Shakespeare wrote numerous sonnets
↓	
Specific fact	Shakespeare wrote many monologues
↓	
General statement	Shakespeare was a versatile and prolific writer

Inductive

Deductive reasoning involves a different process. It begins with a generalization that you assume is true, and then specific facts are used to confirm that assumption.

Inductive = research summarized

Example

Generalization — All steel is attracted by a magnet

↓

Specific fact — This knife blade is made of steel

↓

Specific fact — This knife blade will be attracted by a magnet

Deductive

Analogy convey point by briefly comparing two things.

Analogy is reasoning by using a brief comparison; i.e., by reasoning that if two things are similar in one respect, they will be similar in other respects. For example, imagine you were outside one day and got a sunburn. If you did not know why you got a sunburn, you might try to think of reasons for it. Perhaps you would guess that it was because you were outside. If you thought this was the reason you got burned, through analogy you would guess that any time you were outside at all, even at night, you would get a sunburn. This is why analogies often do not make sense.

Process Analysis explains how something works = definition

Process analysis is used specifically in writing that informs or explains. Process analysis explains how something works, how it is defined, or how it has been made. In a process analysis, chronological order is the most common structure to use because it outlines the steps in which something occurs.

Example

How to program a VCR.

1. Turn on VCR
2. Set channel on VCR to match channel on TV from which show to be recorded will be on
3. Set timer on VCR to match time that show starts and finishes
4. Press record

Climactic Order = plot diagram

Climatic order is achieved by developing a sequence of events or conflicts that build toward a climax. A climatic order chart would look something like this:

Introduction of setting, characters, and conflict → Event 1 → Event 2 → Event 3

→ Climax → Resolution

Chronological Order

Chronological order is often used to organize ideas in narrative and descriptive writing. It is a good idea to use transitions, such as first, second, then, finally, next, and later to connect your ideas.

Example

One wintry day in 1926, as Lindbergh was flying his plane delivering mail, he was caught in a snowstorm. When his plane became unmanageable, he parachuted out. As he descended to Earth, he saw a barbed-wire fence below him, which he failed to miss—landing directly on top of it. Once he had untangled himself, he walked to the nearest farm to report the accident.

Cause and Effect

Cause and effect is frequently used in explanatory writing in order to present information clearly. It explains why something happened, what specific conditions exist, or what resulted from a certain action or condition. Cause and effect can be used in narrative writing to explain characters' actions, or it may be used in essays or reports to discuss how something progresses or the results of certain actions.

Cause-and-effect writing can be organized three ways:

Effect to Cause

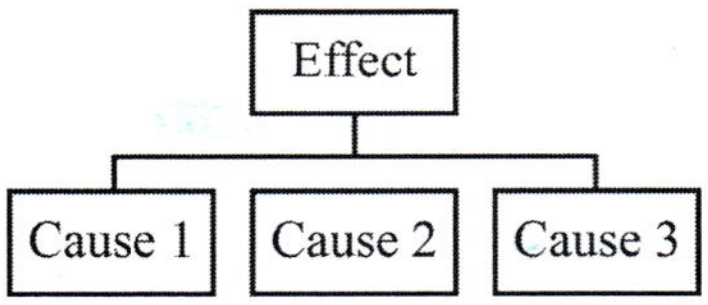

Cause to Effect

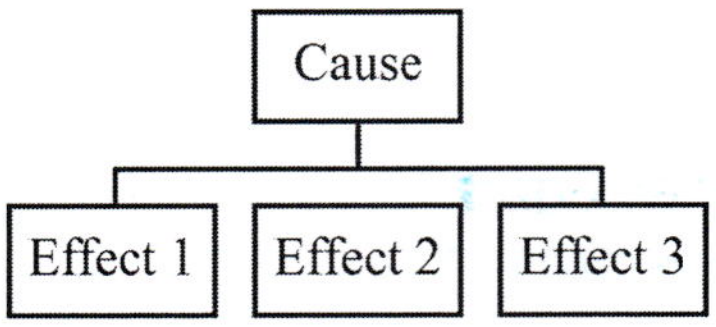

Cause and Effect Chain Reaction

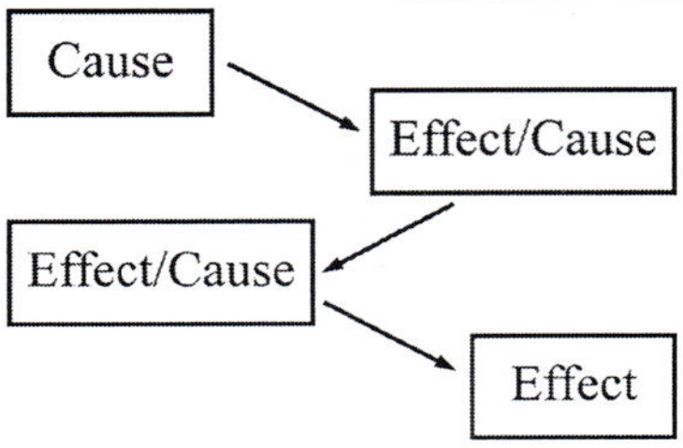

Regardless of the type of writing you are doing (narrative, essay, critical reviews, or reports), make sure you organize your writing well so that your ideas and information are logically presented. Logical organization gives your writing clarity. Experiment with different organizational methods to find the one that best suits the type of writing you are doing. An organizational structure gives you the skeleton upon which you can flesh out your ideas.

11W1.5 determine whether the ideas and information gathered are accurate and complete, interesting, and effectively meet the requirements of the writing task

Reviewing Content

Much of your writing at this stage of your life will be required writing, where you are given a set of topics that you must choose from. You then begin writing an essay that receives a grade and some feedback from your teacher. The first thing to keep in mind is that you should always choose a topic that seems interesting to you, for whatever reason. Even if most of the topics initially seem boring, you want to get through the assignment as successfully as possible, so it is a good idea to try to find one topic you think you could become interested in, even if you are not entirely interested at the beginning. Once you are underway, keeping a copy of the actual essay question somewhere nearby, if not actually printed out on top of the pages of your notes, will help keep your research and writing focused on the task at hand, and doing so will also help ensure that your final draft actually addresses

Using Knowledge of Form and Style

11W2.2 establish a distinctive voice in their writing, modifying language and tone skillfully and effectively to suit the form, audience, and purpose for writing Passive / Active

Voice Expressing your style in writing Formal / Informal

The term "voice" can have several meanings in the context of writing. This includes the passive and active voices of verbs that you may have heard about, where the action of an agent is either ahead of or behind the verb. The term "voice" also refers to your own distinctive writing style, your way of expressing yourself that is uniquely your own and that sets you apart from your fellow writers. Your personality shines through your writing to some extent, and this quality is called the "voice" of your writing. Some students might cleverly decide to call the spelling and grammatical errors they happen to make or the colloquialisms and slang they feel licensed to use their "voice." A good writer, however, keeps in mind the requirements of each writing occasion and tailors the tone voice of his or her voice accordingly. If you are writing a literary essay for school, your voice should be formal. If you are writing an anecdotal piece for a magazine, your voice could be more conversational, or informal. Either way, the basic rules of clear expression still apply, including those of spelling, grammar, and organization that are discussed in an English class. Over time, your own voice will emerge and become clearer as you continue to work at expressing your ideas effectively.

Voice refers to how the narrator or speaker of a text sounds to the reader. Using a voice and style appropriate to academic and personal writing and format is an important choice that should be evident in your writing. Depending on the formality of the occasion, for example, it would be more appropriate to write "Good Evening, Ladies and Gentlemen" than "It's great to see everyone here tonight" at the beginning of your banquet speech.

Expressive Writing

Your own expressive writing that responds to texts you read in class can help you understand those texts in greater detail. For example, an expressive poem or dramatic scene based on a novel can help you pinpoint the main themes or symbols within the novel. That is one reason your teacher may require students to adapt an episode in a novel to a different time period or setting, or to create a dramatic scene from a short story. For example, many students have recreated scenes from Shakespearean plays and put them into the language of modern English. Expressive writing is enjoyable, and it can teach you how to change the voice of your writing.the question initially presented by your teacher. Composing a brilliant essay that is off topic will not earn you the grade you deserve for your intelligence, effort, and otherwise excellent writing skills. So at each stage of the essay-writing process, you will want to double check your "answer" with the instructor's "question" and make sure that what you are writing actually lines up.

11W2.3 use appropriate descriptive and evocative words, phrases, and expressions imaginatively to make their writing clear, vivid, and interesting for their intended audience

Diction

= the author's/writter's choice of words.

As you might have guessed from its relation to the word *dictionary*, the word *diction* refers specifically to word choice. You can think of the words that hit the page as you write as the vehicles that carry along your thoughts and ideas to the minds of the readers who are going along with you for the ride. For this reason, you do not want to use words that will make understanding your smart ideas more challenging than is necessary. Instead, you should go for accuracy and precision in word choice, only turning to special terms when more commonly used words are not available to describe what you need to describe. Since diction is closely related to voice, the words you choose to express yourself also give readers an impression of where you are placing yourself in relation to them. If your writing contains many unnecessarily unusual or "big" words, some readers may feel put off by your diction and decide they would rather do something else with their time than read what you have written. If too many readers have that response, your time spent writing is being wasted. Instead of using fancy words, a good rule of thumb is to select common words, or the language of everyday speech, so that the reader's attention is not distracted from the interesting idea you are discussing to the individual words you are using.

11W2.4 write complete sentences that communicate their meaning clearly and effectively, skillfully varying sentence type, structure, and length to suit different purposes and making smooth and logical transitions between ideas

Sentence Craft and Fluency

Use of conjuctions -> help reader move along

Another aspect of your writing voice that will develop with time is that of crafting sentences that flow logically and pleasantly across the page. Although you want your reader to put in the effort of thinking along with you through the series of logical steps that lead you to conclusions he or she may or may not agree with, you do not want your reader to have put in too much effort struggling to follow what you have to say. Sometimes, students feel that a disorganized essay shows a higher level of complexity of thought, when in fact the opposite is true. Using conjunctions that guide the reader from one paragraph and idea to the next, various sentence lengths and types, and sequential markers such as "first" and "second," all help the reader move along with you from your introductory statements to your concluding assertions.

A sentence is a group of words that expresses a complete thought, begins with a capital letter, and ends with a period or other end punctuation. Every sentence contains at least a noun and a verb; a sentence must have a *subject* and a *predicate*. Parts of speech, which include nouns, pronouns, and verbs, are the building blocks of sentences.

Example

The *subject* is a noun and everything attached to that noun.	The **predicate** is a verb and everything attached to that verb.
Cattle **graze**	
A *tall girl* **ran** to the gate.	
Penelope, the faithful wife of Odysseus, slowly **wove** an intricate tapestry.	

Sometimes, a complete sentence seems to be missing a necessary part. “Stop!” is an example of a sentence that seems incomplete because it does not seem to have a subject. However, the subject, *you*, is implied and understood. Similarly, some sentences contain parts of speech that are understood and omitted:

- Here is a copy of the assignment I gave you. (*that* I gave to you)
- Write me when you find work. (write *to* me)

When you are editing your work, look for any incomplete sentences or fragments and be sure to rewrite them so that they are complete.

Sentence Variety

Sentence variety is a key element of efficient writing. It is a good idea to keep your ideas flowing smoothly using a mixture of long, short, and complex sentences.

Kinds of Sentences

There are different kinds of sentences:

- Declarative sentences are sentences that make statements
- Interrogative sentences are sentences that ask questions
- Exclamatory sentences are sentences that express strong emotion
- Imperative sentences are sentences that give instructions or commands

Remember that exclamation marks should rarely be used except in dialogue. Exclamation marks are not advisable in formal writing. If you want to stress a point, try using words that have intensity. It takes a lot more creativity and thought to emphasize using the best words possible than it does simply to conclude a sentence with an exclamation point when you want to show that you feel strongly about something.

Simple Sentences

Independent clauses that contain one subject and one verb make a simple sentence:

- The boy stood on the garden wall.

Sentence order can be altered for variety or for emphasis. The part to be emphasized usually comes first:

- On the garden wall stood the boy.

Compound Sentences

Two independent clauses that are joined by a coordinating conjunction make a compound sentence.

The two sentences "The boy stood on the garden wall" and "No one noticed him" are complete sentences on their own, but they can also be joined in a variety of ways:

- The boy stood on the garden wall, but no one noticed him.
- No one noticed the boy as he stood on the garden wall.

Complex

Two clauses joined by a subordinating conjunction make a complex sentence. One clause must be independent, and one clause must be dependent (subordinate):

- Although the boy stood on the garden wall, no one noticed him.
- No one noticed the boy, although he stood on the garden wall.
- While the firefighters were distracted by brush fires, three houses burned to the ground.
- Three houses burned to the ground while the firefighters were distracted by brush fires.

Changing the order of the sentence changes the emphasis. Compare the sentence "An actress who has won three Oscars will be present tonight" with the sentence "Present tonight will be an actress who has won three Oscars."

The order of the first sentence puts more stress on the accomplishments of the actress, whereas the second sentence puts more stress on the fact that the actress will be present.

Compound-Complex Sentences

A compound-complex sentence contains at least two independent clauses and one dependent clause:

- While I slept, the sun rose, and the birds began to sing.
- Although she did not win a medal, Janine competed at the Olympics, and she has never forgotten the wonderful experience.

When writing or editing your work, pay attention to how you structure your sentences. Consider varying sentence structure, length, and order for variety and emphasis. A succession of short sentences can be used for strong effect after a series of longer sentences. Use transitional devices (words like *although*, *next*, or *consequently*) to order and link ideas.

Transitions

Transitional words and phrases, which are used at the beginning of sentences or in the middle to join compound or compound-complex sentences, enhance sentence variety. The following chart contains examples of useful transition words and phrases.

Transitional phrases

Purpose	Transitional Words and Phrases
To show differences	On the other hand In contrast In opposition to Instead Unlike However In comparison
To show similarity	Just as important Not very different from In the same manner Similarly Hence Alike Also
To show preference	In preference to Preferred by more people However Nevertheless
To indicate time	At the same time A few days prior Following the completion of Next Soon In subsequent months
To indicate more	In addition to To add to On top of this Furthermore Moreover It is also true that Another example of

Conjunctive Adverbs

Conjunctive adverbs are used in compound sentences, while subordinate conjunctions introduce subordinate clauses in complex or compound-complex sentences.

Adverbs can be used with a semicolon to join independent clauses to compound sentences.

Example

- We have presented our case completely; on the other hand, there is no telling how the judge will respond.
- I like your pitch; however, it sounds too much like an *Indiana Jones* movie.

The following chart contains common conjunctive adverbs. Middle of the sentence

accordingly	as a result	at the same time
consequently	finally	for example
for instance	furthermore	hence
however	in fact	incidentally
indeed	instead	likewise
meanwhile	moreover	namely
nevertheless	next	nonetheless
of course	on the contrary	on the other hand
otherwise	similarly	so far
still	thereafter	therefore
thus	undoubtedly	

Subordinating conjunctions introduce a subordinate clause.

Example

- After the party, we will need to lock the hall.
- Unless you go, the party will be a bore.

The following chart contains common subordinating conjunctions. Starting the sentence

after	although	as
as if	because	before
even though	if	than
that	though	unless
until	when	where
whether	while	

Sentence Beginnings

The basic subject-verb construction that forms the primary English sentence pattern can be varied in a number of ways. The following section provides examples of different ways sentences can begin.

Basic Pattern

- The cowboy rode into the sunset.

Inverted Order

- Did the cowboy ride into the sunset?

Begin with a participle [verbal adjective]

- Sunburned and dejected, the cowboy rode into the sunset.

Begin with an adjective

- Victorious, the cowboy rode into the sunset.

Begin with an adverb

- Swiftly, the cowboy rode into the sunset.

Begin with a participial phrase

- Having delivered his message, the cowboy rode into the sunset.

Begin with a prepositional phrase

- Into the sunset rode the cowboy.

Begin with a subordinate clause

- Once he had delivered his message, the cowboy rode into the sunset.

Deliberate Sentence Fragments

Normally, a correct sentence requires a minimum of one main clause containing both a subject and a predicate. Occasionally, writers deliberately use sentence fragments as a part of their writing style.

- The last cowboy rode into the sunset. Alone. A solitary reminder of the relentless passage of time.

Fragment

Sentence and Word Order

The most important part of a sentence can be emphasized by using it to begin the sentence. NASA might note, "A meteorite hit a man in London," while the *London Star* might report, "London Man Hit by Meteorite."

Word order is closely related to sentence order. Word placement and sentence order can be used to emphasize and also to suggest things. For example, compare the quotations "accused mass murderer Goneril Brocadie" with "Goneril Brocadie, who is accused of mass murder." Because the first quotation has "mass murderer" so close to the man's name, it implies guilt more than the second quotation. The adjectives closest to the noun imply the message "mass-murderer-Brocadie."

11W2.6 revise drafts to improve the content, organization, clarity, and style of their written work, using a variety of teacher-modelled strategies

Revising Your Writing

One of the most important steps in the writing process is that of revision. Revising what you have already written requires entering a special frame of mind. You have to be able to appreciate the strengths in what you have already written (it will hardly ever be complete garbage) while at the same time recognizing areas of weakness that could be improved upon (even though you have worked hard at your writing, there is almost always something that can be further strengthened). One of the ingredients necessary for a useful revision session is time. Although students are almost always working on tight timelines, it is a good idea to give yourself a few days before the essay is due to set the essay aside and do other work before reading it again with a critical eye. Having this distance allows you to return to your work with a fresh point of view, and often areas of the argument that require more or less explanation will stand out for you. As well as revising the argument itself, you can reread the essay to evaluate the quality of the evidence you have supplied. You should ensure that you do not summarize the plot, but rather simply introduce evidence that directly supports the argument you are making. In this way, the final stages of the writing process can help elevate the final product you submit to your teacher.

When you are reviewing the first draft of your writing, make sure to focus on the following areas:

- The appropriateness and clarity of your controlling idea
- The evidence provided to support your arguments
- The clarity and effectiveness of the sentences and your use of vocabulary

Aplying Knowledge of Conventions

11W3.1 use knowledge of spelling rules and patterns, a variety of resources, and appropriate strategies to recognize and correct their own and others' spelling errors

Spelling Rules

One of the reasons most people do not become accomplished writers overnight is that writing requires so many levels of expression, from argument to organization, style, diction, grammar, and spelling. Spelling might seem like just a minor detail, but if you consider your own reaction to an e-mail, letter, or document that has spelling mistakes, you will begin to realize that providing clean copy, without spelling errors of any kind, is an important way to create a good impression with your writing. When your writing contains spelling errors, not only will your readers assume a weakness in your writing that they may link to your thinking, they may also assume that you do not care enough about your writing to tidy up the mistakes. Fixing spelling errors involves more than simply running the essay through a spell checker, since homonyms will not be flagged by this software. Instead, you must carefully and alertly reread your document, keeping an eye out for any spelling mistakes that may have slipped in.

You may have heard the complaint that there are always exceptions to spelling and grammar rules; however, spelling rules are still a good place to start. The rules take care of most cases and leave you free to pay attention to exceptions. The "*I* before *E*" rhyme is a good example:

- *I* before *E* except after *C* or when sounding like *A*, as in *neighbour* and *weigh*.

The rule this rhyme explains covers the majority of cases. It is possible to sort the common exceptions into groups:

- Words of foreign origin: German (*Geiger*, *stein*, *poltergeist*) or Greek (*protein*, *kaleidoscope*, *seismograph*)
- Words that have some connection: A group of words loosely connected with government, law, or property can be matched with reign, which does follow the rule. Then think of *reign*, *sovereign*, *foreign*, *heir*, *heiress*, *seize*, *counterfeit*, and *forfeit* as being a group.
- Words whose pattern matches a subset of words that follow the rule: *height* and *sleight* match *neighbour*, *weigh*, *weight*, and *freight*.
- A few more or less common words are left over. Simply pay attention to their spelling: *either*, *neither*, *leisure*, *weird*, *heifer*, *feisty*
- Words like *reinforce* can be ignored, since the pronunciation of the prefix makes it just about impossible to spell the *ei* incorrectly.

Use a writing guide or the Internet to look up a list of spelling rules for review.

Homonyms and Other Easily Confused Words

Words can be confused because they sound exactly the same (its, it's) or almost the same (insure, ensure). Certain contractions (when two words are combined with an apostrophe) and pronouns are also easily confused:

- "Your list is complete."
  "You're almost ready."
- "Their supper is ready."
  "They're about to sit down."
  "There is the book."
- "Its collar came off."
  "It's a great pity."

Remember that no possessive pronoun is ever written with an apostrophe. Because possessives written with apostrophes sound the same as plural forms when spoken, they are often confused when written.

- "The quarter's shape is distinctive."
- "I have four quarters in my pocket."

The complete list of homonyms, near-homonyms, and easily confused words is long. The following list provides some examples of commonly confused homonyms:

• allowed, aloud	• seen, scene
• bow, bough	• sight, site, cite
• not, knot	• sign, sine
• pore, pour, poor	• slight, sleight
• principal, principle	• sweet, suite
• prophet, profit	• there, their, they're
• red, read	• to, too, two
• waste, waist	

The following chart displays more examples of easily confused words that a computer spell check might not find.

all right, alright	In standard written English, only *all right* is recognized. Alright is strictly informal.
practice, practise	*Practice* is a noun (two hours of practice). *Practise* is a verb (He has been practising for two hours).
licence, license	*Licence* is a noun (driver's licence) and *license* is a verb (The state licenses us to drive).
stationary, stationery	*Stationary* means staying in one place; *stationery* is the writing materials sold by a *stationer*, originally a merchant who set up a station, or booth, to sell pens and paper.
a lot, allot	There is only one way to spell these two words when they are used together: *a lot*. The word *allot* means to allocate or give out.
it's, its	All the possessive pronouns are formed the same way: yours, his, hers, *its*, theirs, whose. Pronouns spelled with apostrophes are contractions: you're (you are), he's (he is), she's (she is), it's (it is), they're, (they are), who's (who is), *it's* (it is).

Frequently Misspelled Words

Certain words in the English language are frequently misspelled, even by people who see themselves as good spellers. Some of these words are listed below. Try to master them now. The tricky parts of these words have been underlined for you.

across	neighbour
argument	occasionally
calendar	possession
column	really
committed	relevant
conscience	restaurant
definitely	rhyme
discipline	rhythm
embarrass	schedule
equipment	separate
experience	until
foreign	weird
government	grateful
height	immediate
lightning	mischievous

Following are some examples of some frequently confused words:

- accept/except: Everyone was pleased to *accept* their reward, *except* Melody.
- a lot: Two words, as in "a lot of homework." This word gets confused with *allot*, which means to distribute a portion: Each child was *allotted* some personal space in the new classroom.
- believe/receive: These two words follow the *i* before *e* rule: "*i* before *e*, except after *c*."
- its/it's: *Its* without the apostrophe is a possessive pronoun, as in "The cat injured *its* tail." The word shows possession, just like the pronoun "yours." With the apostrophe, *it's* is a contraction of the phrase *it is*. The apostrophe is used to replace the missing letter.
- principal/principle: A principal is the headmaster of a school, as in "the *principal's* office." Principal also means main, as in "The *principal* reason I am moving is…" The word *principle*, however, refers to a belief or idea, as in "The school's anti-bullying policy is based on the *principle* that all children deserve to feel safe at school."
- their/there/they're: "*Their* new house," "*They* live over there," and "He said *they're* coming."
- to/too/two: *To* is a preposition, as in "*To* the track meet." *Too* means *also* or *in excess*, as in "She wants to go, *too*" and "He ate *too* much." *Two* represents a number, as in "He has *two* sisters."
- weather/whether: "Whether or not we attend the game depends on the weather."

Spelling and Proofreading

When you are proofreading for spelling, not every mistake will jump out at you. Look for mistakes like *vallies* (for valleys), *recieve* (for receive), or *resent* (for recent). Mistakes like these can be hard to catch. A good method for finding easy-to-miss mistakes is to read sentences backward. This allows each word to be seen as an individual item and not as part of a sentence. With the pattern of meaning removed, it is easier to find errors. The same method may help you to proofread your own work in the written-response questions on exams.

11W3.2 build vocabulary for writing by confirming word meaning(s) and reviewing and refining word choice, using a variety of resources and strategies, as appropriate for the purpose

Vocabulary

Expanding your vocabulary has everything to do with using it. The more you use the words you learn, the better they will stick in your head and become part of your everyday speech and writing. Like your reading vocabulary, your writing vocabulary should be a constantly growing body of words that you are incorporating into your writing with increasing confidence.

You should only use words you understand in your writing. If you are looking for a more precise word, check a thesaurus.

The words in a thesaurus are arranged in alphabetical order. Here is an example of an entry for the word "bright."

Example

Bright

Adj (adjectives/synonyms)

1. sunny, fair, mild, balmy; brilliant, vivid, resplendent
2. smart, brainy, brilliant, clever, gifted, talented, sharp, keen

Antonyms

1. dull, flat, dingy, cloudy, faded, leaden, dim, pale, weak, faint
2. slow-witted, dim, slow, thick-headed, bland, desensitized

Do you need a synonym or an antonym? Do you want the literal/denotative meaning ("sunny") or a more connotative (associated) meaning like "brainy?" The thesaurus helps you add variety to your writing, but avoid choosing words simply because they sound more elaborate. A simple word may be your best choice for the situation.

If you are using technical terms or "content" words in something like a research report, do not underestimate the dictionary as a useful reference.

Dictionaries are always a good place to start when you are looking for the meaning of a specialized term. Look for the meaning associated with the specific subject or content area.

Building Vocabulary

The following list describes different ways to build your vocabulary:

- extensive and varied personal reading
- personal lists of new words and phrases from texts you read
- lists of subject-related words and their definitions
- using new words in conversation
- word games
- classroom word walls

Classroom word walls are interactive and usually involve a weekly or monthly addition to the wall. Each student posts up words they have learned and want to share with the class. Even if word walls are not part of your classroom environment, you can create a mini word wall of your own in the back of your writing or English binder. Jotting down words from different sources in one easy-to-find location may encourage you to actually use the words in your writing.

Using New Vocabulary

It is a good idea to keep personal vocabulary lists at the backs of binders or in separate vocabulary binders. If you learn a new word in any content area, try to remember to add the word and its definition to your liSt. If the word is an adjective, for instance, record its other forms, too.

Example

- frugal (adjective), meaning “reluctant to spend”
- frugality (noun form), meaning “a reluctance to spend”

The best way to increase your vocabulary is to start using new words as often as you can after you learn them, in both speaking and writing. This helps you internalize both the words and their meanings.

11W3.3 use punctuation correctly and effectively to communicate their intended meaning

PUNCTUATION

Imagine if people never paused when they were speaking. It would be difficult to understand when thoughts started and ended, or if someone was asking a question. Punctuation translates many conventions of speech, such as pausing, into writing. It has its own set of rules that are necessary for clear writing.

Punctuation gives clarity and definition to your writing and can be used for a wide variety of rhetorical and stylistic effects.

Periods

The period is used at the end of most sentences and after fragments used as sentences:

- “I walked to the end of the world. And stopped.”

Do not use a period after a complete sentence that is contained by brackets or quotation marks within another sentence:

- “The company then sent him a registered letter (he was not answering e-mails or telephone messages) to explain the situation.”
- “That’s my friend Sonja (the Matchmaker).”
- “When she said, ‘Class dismissed,’ chaos erupted.”

Notice that the bracketed sentences in the first and second examples do not begin with a capital letter, but the quotation in the third example does. The quotation is also set off with both quotation marks and commas.

Punctuating Possessives

Most possessives are formed by adding an apostrophe and an *-s*:

- a girl’s smile
- one country’s history
- a coat’s buttons

The possessive of a noun that end in *-s* is generally formed with an apostrophe and an *-s*:

- the boss's car
- the countess's speech
- James's, Charles's, Alex's

Watch for the possessive of plurals. The rule is to add an apostrophe after the *-s* of the plural:

- five girls' smiles
- three countries' histories
- the actresses' Oscars
- the girls' car

Commas with Conjunctions

Coordinating conjunctions (*for*, *and*, *nor*, *but*, *or*, *yet*, *so*—think FANBOYS) are used with a comma if they join two independent clauses:

- "He will be late, *for* he must complete the game."
- "Go to the edge of the cliff, *and* tell me what you see there."
- "She will not learn from her failures, *nor* will she learn from her successes."

When a coordinate conjunction joins two short independent clauses, a comma may not be necessary:

- "She's late *and* she's tired."

When subordinating conjunctions (which include *after*, *because*, *although*, *before*, *since*, *though*, and *unless*) are used in an introductory clause, a comma follows the clause:

- "*Because* you have been elected, you must serve."
- "*Before* she leaves, she plans to write a note of farewell."

Do not use a semicolon to follow an introductory clause:

- "*Because* you have been elected; you must serve." (*incorrect*)

When the subordinate clause follows the independent clause, a comma is usually not used:

- "She plans to write a note of farewell *before* she leaves."
- "You must serve *because* you have been elected."

However, a comma should be used when it is necessary to avoid confusion:

- "He has done all his work since his failure last term threatened his final grade." (*unclear*)
- "He has done all his work, since his failure last term threatened his final grade." (*clear*)

The original sentence seems to mean that he has done all his work from the time that his failure threatened his final grade. It is only once you reach the end of the sentence that the meaning can be understood. A comma after "work" makes it clear that "since" is a subordinating conjunction and not a preposition.

Colons

When used in sentences, a colon can only follow an independent clause to introduce a list, explanation, or appositive:

- "You should bring the following items: a sleeping bag, a change of clothes, and matches."
- "There is only one honest thing to do: admit you made a mistake and apologize."
- "Everything about him was summed up in his nickname: Old Ornery."

When a list is set up in point form, the same rule applies:

- The introductory course will cover three topics:
  1. algebra
  2. geometry
  3. trigonometry

If a list does not follow an independent clause, no colon is used:

- "You must bring a sleeping bag, a change of clothes, and matches."

Similarly, the following list does not require a colon:

- The introductory course will cover
  1. algebra
  2. geometry
  3. trigonometry

A simple way of checking colon use is to cover up all the words after the colon. Can the first part of the sentence now stand alone as a sentence? If it can, use a colon. If it cannot, do not use a colon.

Quotation Marks

Use quotation marks at the beginning and end of all words in a direct quotation. Watch for the use of quotation marks before and after speech tags:

- Alfred said, "We are ready."
- "I'm finished the job," said Alfred. "We can go now."
- "When we are ready," said Alfred, "we will go."

Notice that the closing quotation mark is placed after a comma or a period and that a comma is used after a speech tag ("Alfred said,").

Closing quotation marks are also used with exclamation marks and question marks. When these punctuation marks belong to the sentence, they are placed outside the closing quotation marks:

- Didn't you hear him say, "I'm in trouble"?

If the quotation marks belong to the quotation, they are placed inside the quotation marks:

- He said sadly, "Why is it always me?"

The same rules apply to closing quotation marks used for other purposes. Periods and commas belong inside the quotation marks:

- You could say that her acting was "over the top."

Exclamation marks and question marks belong either outside or inside the quotation marks, depending on whether they belong to the sentence as a whole or to the words inside the quotation marks:

- She asked, "Are these seats taken?"
- I can't believe you call that dilapidated wreck a "car"!

Indirect quotations never require quotation marks:

- Alfred asked if we were ready.
- Alfred said that he had finished the job and we could go.
- Alfred said that when we were ready, we could go.

Quotation marks are also used for the titles of short stories and poems and to indicate that a word is being used in an unusual sense:

- "Housekeeping" on the space station is challenging.

Quotation marks can also indicate sarcasm or irony:

- The "suicide" of Jan Masaryk marked the end of democracy in Czechoslovakia.
- It seems that their "help" has put this project three weeks behind.

Punctuation for Effect

Consider the following examples, remembering that punctuation is your tool, not your taskmaster.

- John closes the door and asks Alice what is wrong.
- John closes the door and asks Alice, "What is wrong?"
- John closes the door and asks, "Alice, what is wrong?"
- We mustn't believe everything we hear is the truth.
- We mustn't! Believe! Everything we hear is the truth!
- Consider yourself one of the family.
- Consider yourself one of the family!
- Consider yourself one of the family? Never!
- Why? Because we can. Because we muSt. Because we care.

Sentence fragments can be used deliberately with sentence punctuation to create a rhetorical effect.

Italics and Underlining

For emphasis

Certain titles are printed in italic script. Italicize or underline the titles of all major works, such as books, long poems, newspapers, magazines, movies, and television series.

Example

- *A Tale of Two Cities*
- *Time Magazine*
- *The Times*
- *The Wizard of Oz*
- *Star Trek*

Italics are also used to indicate words and sometimes letters that are considered as objects rather than as structural parts of a sentence:

not an object but treated as one

- "The word *since* can be a subordinate conjunction or a preposition."
- "Add *-s* or *-es* to form the plural of a noun."

Italics should only be used sparingly for emphasis. It is more acceptable to use italics for emphasis in creative writing than it is for formal writing. Formal writing should use words and arguments so compelling that no extra emphasis is needed. In creative writing, for example, it can be useful to use italics for showing emphasis in the dialogue of characters.

Use quotation marks to set off shorter works or parts of works, such as chapters, short stories, short poems, songs, articles, and episodes in a television series.

11W3.4 use grammar conventions correctly and appropriately to communicate their intended meaning clearly and effectively

GRAMMAR

Grammar gives structure to language so that communication can be as clear as possible. Understanding grammar—the names of the parts of speech, kinds of sentences, rules for the agreement of sentence parts—gives you a common vocabulary so that you can speak about language. If your teacher gives you a comment on a paper such as, "use the objective case of that pronoun," it is helpful for you to understand the objective case.

Pronouns take the place of nouns: *I*, *she*, *it*, *we*, *that*, *all*, *whatever*, *some*. In your writing, ensure that there are no misunderstandings regarding the nouns to which your pronouns refer.

Example

> Both girls agreed that their projects had been prepared thoroughly. They were ready for the science fair. (What or who was ready? The girls? The projects?)
>
> When I got to the tax office, they told me they were closing for the day. (This sentence is fine for informal speech, but in written English, *they* can only refer to the tax office, and a tax office cannot be *they*.)

Ensure that your pronouns and their antecedents are clear.

The most basic group of pronouns is the personal pronouns. These pronouns replace persons or things and are used to identify point of view, particularly in narrative texts such as short stories, novels, and plays.

First Person:	I/Me	We/Us
Second Person:	You	
Third Person:	He/Him	They/Them
	She/Her	It

Using the Correct Case

For the most part, English is not inflected. This means that most words do not change their endings to show how they are used in sentences. Pronouns are one exception: they are inflected. Pronouns have three cases, as shown in the following chart. Whenever you use these pronouns, check the pronoun case and check for the correct spelling.

Subjective case is used for the subject of a sentence or clause and for the complement of a linking verb	**Objective case** is used for the object of a verb or preposition, gerund, participle, or infinitive	**Possessive case** is used to show ownership	
		Used as an adjective	**Used as a subject or as the complement of a linking verb**
I	Me	My	Mine
You	You	Your	Yours
He/she/it	Him/her/it	His/her/its	His/hers/its
We	Us	Our	Ours
You	You	Your	Yours
They	Them	Their	Theirs
Who	Whom	Whose	Whose

The possessive pronoun *its* follows the same pattern as *his*, *hers*, *yours*, and *theirs*. Remember that the possessive of pronouns is never formed with an apostrophe.

When the pronoun is the subject, use the subjective case:

- *You* have been elected.
- Despite the weather, *we* are certainly going.
- *He* and *she* ran the marathon.
- Even after a late start, *they* still won the marathon.

If the pronoun is the subject and a possessive, use the second form of the possessive case:

- *Mine* is nearly ready.
- *Yours* is already finished, but theirs is not ready.

When the pronoun is the object (either direct or indirect), use the objective case:

Give it to her

- The government mailed *me* a letter.
- The fall smashed *it* to pieces.
- When the paper is ready, give it to *her* and *me*.

A pronoun following a linking verb is a noun complement (or predicate nominative or subject completion), and it is in the subjective case:

- It is *he*.
- Yes, I've seen Miss Jones. It was *she* who walked past just now.
- I am *he*.
- It is *I*.

When writing comparisons using *than* or *as*, use the objective case:

- He likes me more than *him*.
- Evan can type as accurately as *her*.

These examples illustrate the problem of different levels of language in different situations. Consider the sentence “It is I.” The sentence is grammatically correct, but it may appear to be stuffy, even pretentious. However, in a formal or solemn context, such sentences are not only correct, they are suitable. On the other hand, in everyday life, few would complain about, “It’s me.” Sometimes the pronoun agreements cause trouble. The following is a useful rule of thumb:

> Most of those who might say *Him and me did it* would never say *Me did it* or *Him did it*. Whenever you have more than one pronoun, try the sentence with one of the pronouns at a time. *He* did it + *I* did it = *He* and *I* did it.

When the pronoun that follows a linking verb is a possessive, use the form of the possessive case that would be used for the subject of a sentence:

- The red one is *mine*. Did you hear me? *Mine* is the red one.
- This car is *hers*—or is it *theirs*? No, *theirs* is the car on the right.

Note the difference when a pronoun is used as an adjective and when it is used as a predicate complement:

- *Their* win was amazing.
- The win was *theirs*.

You would not want to memorize all the pronouns, but it is a good idea to be aware of them and of their uses.

Kinds of Pronouns	**Examples**
Demonstrative I want to enter *this* in the exhibition.	This, that, these, those
Interrogative *Who* said that?	Who, whom, which, what, whoever, whomever, whichever, whatever
Relative Choose *whichever* you like.	Who, whom, that, which, whoever, whomever, whichever
Indefinite *Many* have asked that question.	All, another, any, anybody, anyone, anything, each, everybody, everyone, everything, few, many, nobody, none, one, several, some, somebody, someone
Reflexive She did the job *herself*.	Myself, yourself, herself, himself, itself, ourselves, yourselves, themselves
Intensive The professor *himself* was not sure of the answer.	Myself, yourself, herself, himself, itself, ourselves, yourselves, themselves

Notice the reflexive and intensive pronouns, which are often used incorrectly as a compromise: “Give it to myself.” The examples given in the chart show the only correct uses of the reflexive pronoun. Notice that when the reflexive is used immediately after the noun, it is an intensifier.

What about the pronouns *who* and *whom*? Although the distinction between these two pronouns may be disappearing in spoken English, you should be able to use both of them in formal writing. *Who* is an interrogative subjective pronoun. Use it whenever the pronoun is the subject of a sentence or a clause:

- Who are you?
- Who is going?
- The candidate who should be elected is Julia.

Whom is an interrogative objective pronoun. Use it whenever the pronoun is the object of a predicate or a preposition:

- The prize will be given to whom?
- Whom did you tell?
- To whom did they refer?

A simple mnemonic for remembering the difference is "he/who" and "him/whom."

If the sentence could use *he*, then use *who*; if the sentence could use *him*, then use *whom*:

- He will win. Who will win?
- Give it to him. Give it to whom?
- The crowd followed after him. The crowd followed after whom?
- The robbers left him for dead. The robbers left whom for dead?
- For him, we would do anything. For whom would we do anything?
- Yes, it is he that won. Who was it that won?

Of course, there is an extra mental step if the pronoun is not masculine:

- Give it to her. Give it to whom?
- For her, we would do anything. For whom would we do anything?
- Yes, it is she that won. Who was it that won?

Verbs: Voice and Mood

The mood and voice you choose for the verbs you use in your writing makes a difference. The following section describes different voices and the subjunctive mood in writing.

Active = requires an object -> subject does action
Passive = theres no object -> subject recieves action

Active and Passive Voice

The active voice is transitive, which means it requires an object. The active voice is stronger and more direct than the passive voice, and it usually makes your writing more effective. A sentence is written in the active voice when the subject clearly *does* the action; a sentence is written in the passive voice when the subject of the sentence *receives* the action. The following examples will help you to understand how much stronger and more direct the active voice is than the passive voice.

- "John completed his exam."

The active voice emphasizes the "doer" of the action. This makes a stronger statement and helps the writer avoid dangling or misplaced modifiers:

- "Her dog was walked in a bright orange skirt." (incorrect)
- "In a bright orange skirt, she walked her dog." (correct)

The placement of the modifier in the first sentence makes it seem that the dog is wearing the skirt.

The passive voice is intransitive, which means there is no object. The action is implied:

- "The exam was completed early."

The passive voice emphasizes the receiver of the action and minimizes the importance of the doer.

Example

*Active Voice*My dad packed the car for the trip.

Passive Voice The car was packed for the trip by my dad.

*Active Voice*Sue ate her birthday cake.

Passive Voice The birthday cake was eaten by Sue.

Passive Voice in Writing

The passive voice can come across as unnecessarily wordy. The passive voice is a form of the verb where who or what is doing the action is implied but never actually stated. The active voice is preferred over the passive voice for clear, engaging writing. The active voice indicates the agent who performs the action.

Politicians often use the passive voice because they do not want to identify a specific individual responsible for some problem in government. They may say, "There has recently been a decline in economic activity." The passive voice does not state who or what is responsible for this economic decline. Critics of government, on the other hand, use the active voice because they do want to identify who is responsible for some government problem. They may say, "The finance minister's recent budget has caused a decline in economic activity." The active voice, "The new budget has caused…," offers an agent that the critics feel is to blame for the economic decline.

In the active voice, the subject of each sentence is placed before the object. Active language conveys the same ideas in fewer words.

Subjunctive Mood condition that is not actually true.

The subjunctive mood expresses a wish or condition that is not actually true. Verbs such as *could*, *would*, and *should* are commonly used in the subjunctive mood.

Example

- If I *were* prime minister, I *would* allow everyone to work a four-day week.
- If Colin *could* take his dream vacation, he *would* spend it in Antarctica.

11W3.5 regularly proofread and correct their writing

PROOFREADING

Proofreading to edit your writing is a crucial stage of the writing process. Do not underestimate the power of using correct English. While the content of your ideas may be substantial, it is the clarity achieved through correct expression that often persuades or impresses your reader. Careless usage, spelling, and punctuation, on the other hand, tend to produce the opposite effect. You do not want your ideas being dismissed or missed altogether because you did not edit or proofread carefully.

The following information provides you with some specific areas to be aware of when you are proofreading your writing.

Grammar

- Verb Tense
- Subject/Verb Agreement
- Complete Sentences
- Comparative and Superlative Forms of Adjectives and Adverbs
- Subordinate Clauses and Coordinating Conjunctions
- Modifier Placement
- Correct Word Usage

Verb Tense

The tense of a verb tells the reader when the action happens. The most common verb tenses you will use in your writing are the past tense (before), the present tense (now), and the future tense (later).

Here is an example of three tenses of the verb to work.

Past tense	Present tense	Future tense
He worked.	He works.	He will work.

When planning a story, think about when your story will take place: the past, the present, the future, or some combination of these time frames. You may decide to begin your story in the present but include flashback sequences. Make sure that when you are writing in the present, your verbs reflect the present tense. When you use a flashback sequence, make sure that the verbs are written in the past tense. Whatever you decide, make sure you use consistent verb tenses in your narrative writing.

Example

- Consistent: Her uncle often *came* to visit her. One day he *asked* her …
- Inconsistent: Her uncle often *comes* to visit her. One day he *asked* her …

Subject-Verb Agreement

Most of the difficulties in subject-verb agreement are caused by difficulties in recognizing singular and plural subjects.

When subjects are joined by or or nor, the verb agrees with the nearest subject:

- "Either Miller *or* Smith *is* guilty."
- "Neither Miller *nor* Smith *wants* to confess."
- "Neither the *speaker* nor the *listeners are* aware of the irony."

When one part of the verb is singular and the other part is plural, write the sentence so that the plural part is nearest the verb:

- "Neither the *band members* nor the *conductor* is satisfied." (*weak*)
- "Neither the *conductor* nor the *band members* are satisfied." (*better*)

Nothing that comes between a singular subject and its verb can make that subject plural. Students should not make the verb agree with the nearest noun:

- "Our school basketball *team*, the Gerbils, *is* victorious again."
- "The *prime minister*, accompanied by several cabinet ministers, *arrives* at the airport."
- "*Either* Miller or Jones—both are suspects—*is* guilty."
- "The *contestant* with the most votes *is* now on stage."
- "*One* of the girls *sings* better."
- "The *ringleader* of the rebellious miners *is* sorry."

Indefinite pronouns, such as *each*, *each one*, *either*, *neither*, *everyone*, *everybody*, *anybody*, *anyone*, *nobody*, *somebody*, *someone*, and *no one* are singular:

- "*Each* of the contestants *wins* a prize."
- "E*verybody* near the river *is* in danger."
- "*No one* who wants to be successful in the exams *is* likely to be late."

Collective nouns are singular unless there is a reason to consider them as plurals:

- "The *group works* well."
- "The *company is* bankrupt."
- "The *jury is* deliberating its verdict."
- "The *jury are* arguing among themselves."

Using the correct pronoun is often a problem because the form of a pronoun varies depending on how the pronoun is used. Use *I*, *you*, *he/she/it*, *we*, *you*, *they*, and *who* as the subject of a sentence or clause and for the complement of a linking verb:

- "*You* have been chosen."
- "*We* will be the last of the contestants."
- "*Who* is going to be next?"
- "It is *she* who will be chosen."

Use *me*, *you*, *him/her/it*, *us*, *you*, *them*, and *whom* as direct or indirect objects of verbs or as objects of prepositions:

- "Give it to *me*."
- "Hit the ball to *them*."
- "Ask *them* the time."
- "The child next to *him* laughed suddenly."

Use *my*, *your*, *his/her/its*, *our*, *their*, and *whose* as adjectives:

- "*my* car"
- "*your* umbrella"
- "*its* fur"

Use *mine*, *yours*, *his/hers/its*, *ours*, *theirs*, and *whose* as subjects of sentences or as the complement of a linking verb:

- "*Yours* is the one on the left."
- "This is *mine*."

The possessive pronouns *my*, *your*, *his*, *hers*, *its*, *our*, *yours*, *theirs*, and *whose* never use apostrophes to show possession.

Complete Sentences

As a general rule, all sentences should be complete sentences:

- "He went ahead with his plan. Even though it was faulty." (*incorrect*)
- "He went ahead with his plan, even though it was faulty." (*correct*)

Occasionally, an incomplete sentence is used deliberately for effect. Fragments that are used deliberately are sometimes called minor sentences:

- "Is anyone in favour of dictatorship? No? Well, of course not." (*correct*)

Dialogue and reported speech are exceptions to the rule about fragments:

- "Ready yet?"
- "Not yet."
- "Well then—!"

The opposite error exists in run-on sentences and with comma splices when punctuation between sentences is omitted or a comma is used to join two sentences.

- "We went to Toronto we decided to visit the zoo." (*run-on sentence*)
- "We went to Toronto, we decided to visit the zoo." (*comma splice*)

These errors can be fixed by correcting the punctuation or by rewriting:

- "We went to Toronto. We decided to visit the zoo."
- "We went to Toronto. Then, we decided to visit the zoo."
- "After we went to Toronto, we decided to visit the zoo."
- "We went to Toronto, and then we decided to visit the zoo."

Comparative and Superlative Form s of Adjectives and Adverbs

Comparatives and superlatives are special forms of adjectives and adverbs. They are used to compare things. When comparing two things, use the comparative form:

- "A car is much *more* expensive than a lollipop."
- "Five plus five is *greater* than four plus four."

When comparing more than two things, use the superlative form:

- "That was the *best* movie I have ever seen."
- "I wanted to buy the *largest* dog in the window."

The following chart provides some examples that compare the base form of an adjective or adverb with the comparative and superlative forms of the same word.

Comparative = A is faster than B
Superlative = A is the fastest amongst all.

Base	Comparative	Superlative
fast	faster	fastest
good	better	best
wide	wider	widest
bad	worse	worst
quickly	more quickly	most quickly
harmful	more harmful	most harmful

Subordinate Clauses and Coordinating Conjunctions

A clause is a group of words containing a subject and a predicate. A subordinate clause is a group of words that cannot stand alone as a sentence. Using subordinate clauses allows you to create interesting sentences by combining ideas:

Words that cannot stand alone as a sentence.

- "My sister, *who is a doctor*, has four children."
- "*While I clean my room*, I like to listen to music."

The clauses *who is a doctor* and *while I clean my room* cannot stand alone as sentences and are therefore called subordinate clauses. Subordinate clauses add information to a sentence but are not complete ideas on their own.

Coordinating conjunctions are words used to join two clauses together. Some examples of coordinating conjunctions are *for*, *and*, *not*, *but*, *or*, *yet*, and *so*. These simple words can be used to join ideas and create complex sentences:

- "Wendy loved to read books *but* did not enjoy magazines."
- "John heard the weather report *and* hurried home."
- "The sun was shining brightly, *yet* the air was still cold."

Modifier Placement

As a general rule, a modifier, which is usually an adjective or an adverb, should be placed as closely as possible to the word being modified.

Example

- Vague: Entering the room, the door was shut by mother.
  Clear: Entering the room, mother shut the door.
- Vague: At six years of age, my parents started me in piano.
  Clear: At six years of age, I started taking piano lessons.

Correct Word Usage

The following words are easily confused:

Lie, which means "to recline"

Lay, which means "to place"

- Father would *lie* down for a 10-minute nap after lunch.
- We were asked to *lay* our uniforms neatly on the shelf.

Accept, which means "to receive"

Except, which means "with the exception of"

- Jeremy will *accept* the reward on behalf of his brother.
- Everyone in the family *except* Nolan came down with the flu.

Borrow, which means "to have borrowed from"

Lend, which means "to lend to"

- May I *borrow* your baseball glove?
- Could you *lend* me your textbook?

Their, which is a possessive adjective, means "it belongs to them"

There, which is an adverb denoting a place, position, or existence

They're, which is a contraction of "they are"

- The students will take *their* final exam on Friday morning.
- We decided *there* were enough people present to take a vote.
- The Smith family lived *there* for eight years.
- If *they're* arriving Tuesday, someone should meet them at the airport.

Its, which is a possessive pronoun

It's, which is a contraction of "it is" or "it has"

- The cat injured *its* front paw.
- *It's* been snowing for three days.

Lose, which is a verb that means to be deprived of something

Loose, which is an adjective that refers to something that is not tightly in place

- Try not to *lose* your backpack.
- Our mechanic discovered that a *loose* bolt caused the problem.

Can, which means "are able to"

May, which means "are allowed to"

- Most children *can* print their own name.
- You *may* watch a movie on Saturday.

In, which is a preposition that expresses a situation

Into, which is a preposition that expresses movement or action

- The key is *in* the mailbox.
- Sara needs the key to get *into* her house.

Whose, which means "belonging to whom"

Who's, which is a contraction of "who is"

- I don't know *whose* wallet is missing.
- *Who's* willing to help pick up this litter?

Good, which is an adjective

Well, which is an adverb that means "in a satisfactory way"

- It seemed like a *good* idea.
- Terri didn't feel *well* after her game.

Could have, *should have*, and *would have* are correct usages:

- I could have spelled that word correctly.
- I should have spelled that word correctly.
- I would have spelled that word correctly had I been paying attention.

Using *of* with these verbs (*could of*, *should of*, *would of*) is always incorrect.

Different from is correct usage: Cabbage is *different from* lettuce. Using *different than* is always incorrect.

Capitalization

Although there are many special rules for capitalization, the following rules are the most important to practise for now.

- Capitalize the first words of sentence, including sentences used in quotations.
- Capitalize proper nouns, including any specific person or place (Jon Doe, Calgary, December).
- Always capitalize the word "I."
- Capitalize some abbreviations. For example, R.S.V.P. (please respond), WWF (World Wildlife Federation), Ave. (Avenue), Dr. (Doctor).
- Capitalize the main words in a title, such as The Cat in the Hat or My Summer in Mexico.

The following proofreading checklist will help you make sure your revised draft is ready for publishing or handing in. Always save your working draft on the computer in case you have to make changes after proofreading. Proofread both silently and out loud, if possible.

Check for smooth flow of ideas, with all of your revisions made to the draft.

- Sentences: varied lengths, beginnings, types, and no run-ons or fragments
- Punctuation: all end marks, commas, and quotation marks
- Capitalization
- Spelling: use your computer's spell check and a dictionary
- Check for agreement in subject, verb, pronoun, and antecedent
- Check with your "personal alert" list from your writing binder:
  - your most frequent usage errors; for example, run-ons or verb agreement
  - your most frequent punctuation and capitalization errors
  - words you have misspelled this year

- Print or write your final edited copy

Peer Conferences

Peer conferences can be helpful both at the revision and at the proofreading stages of your writing. At a peer conference, always read your work out loud. Peer conferences often work best as partner situations.

Tips for Readers	Tips for Listeners
1. Show your punctuation through pauses.	**1.** Listen carefully and pay attention to your reader's ideas.
2. Do not rush your reading.	**2.** Make sure to tell the reader what they have done well.
3. Be open to suggestions.	**3.** Be specific in criticism: "That sentence is confusing," "you need a stronger verb there."
4. Jot notes for changes on your draft.	**4.** Try to be constructive: "What if you switched those two ideas to make the argument more clear?"
5. Clarify your partner's comments with questions as needed.	**5.** Remember that you are only trying to help. The writer may choose not to follow some of your suggestions.
6. Thank your partner.	
7. Appreciate that your peer is trying to help you improve your writing.	

Appropriate Modifiers

Adjectives modify nouns by telling what kind of person, place, or thing they are.

Example

- *Wild* geese, *high-flying* geese, *honking* geese, *southbound* geese, *excited* geese; *those* geese, *that* goose, *my* geese, *six* geese, *some* geese, *your* goose

Adverbs modify verbs or other modifiers by telling when, where, how, or how much.

Example

- The wild geese flew *south* yesterday.
- The wild geese flew *noisily* and *swiftly in a 'V' shape.*

Modifiers can also be phrases that do the work of a single adverb.

Example

- The geese flew *toward the south.*
- *With loud honking and flapping of wings*, the geese flew south.

This section is intended to help you develop vocabulary and grammar skills. Remember that careful reading and writing will help you better understand how proper grammar works and help you expand your vocabulary. The rules and guidelines you have learned in this section of your ***KEY*** offer tools that are meant to be used when you are reading and writing. After you have finished reading something, take another look at the text for grammar and vocabulary. Notice how sentences are constructed, which words are being used, and how they are being used. Remember that your vocabulary and grammar will improve not only through knowing and following grammar rules and guidelines, but also through being curious and observant in your reading.

11W3.7 produce pieces of published work to meet criteria identified by the teacher, based on the curriculum expectations

Producing Finished Works

A finished work should be neat, well-organized, and polished. The final stages of writing involve double-checking your work for spelling, grammar, and punctuation. During the revision and editing stages of the writing process, grammar, style, and format should be checked with a recognized print or electronic style guide. The following list of recognized style guides may be helpful. Your teacher may also recommend a style guide.

RECOGNIZED STYLE GUIDES

Publication Manual of the American Psychological Association. Fifth Edition. Washington, DC: American Psychological Association, 2001.

Rozakis, Laurie. The Complete Idiot's Guide to Grammar and Style. New York: Alpha Books, 2003.

Sabin, William; Millar, Wilma; Sine, Sharon; Strashok, G. Wendy. The Gregg Reference Manual. Toronto: McGraw-Hill Ryerson, 2006.

Tasko, Patti, Editor. The Canadian Press Stylebook. Toronto: The Canadian Press, 2006.

Troyka, Lynn. Simon and Schuster Handbook for Writers. New Jersey: Prentice Hall, 1990.

Style Information Online

If you do an Online search for English language conventions, your results will provide links to websites where you can purchase guides. Others provide information electronically. You could vary your search according to the specific style information you are seeking.

PRACTICE QUESTION—WRITING

Writing Task

Throughout your life, certain people have influenced your development in positive ways. Think about someone who has been a particularly significant role model for you. What caused you to look up to this individual?

Write an essay in which you discuss a person who has been a positive role model for you. Explain what has made this person such a meaningful influence. Use details and examples to support your ideas.

ANSWERS AND SOLUTIONS—PRACTICE QUESTION

Score Point 4

Student Response

The most significant role model in my life has been my mother's older sister, Aunt Ena. Aunt Ena was consistently fashionable, a stylish person who taught me that you don't have to be a celebrity to look your best for your audience. With her globe-trotting confidence, she inspired me to be a world traveller. Aunt Ena was a family leader in cultural sophistication. To her dying day, though, my Aunt's greatest gift was the importance she placed on family.

As a grade one teacher for more than 40 years, Aunt Ena once told me that she dressed up for her students. "The children are just learning their primary colors. When I dress in bold red and black, with shiny red earrings and matching beads, they just stare! Then we talk about all the red things in the classroom, at home, and the red apples in their lunch kits. They love it!" Even when she was finally in a wheelchair, Aunt Ena and I were still shopping for a yellow blouse to wear with her wide-brimmed yellow hat and navy suit.

Aunt Ena also inspired me to become a seasoned world traveller, to explore those magic kingdoms and exotic places she first saw in her *National Geographic* magazine. Every summer brought a new trip—by air, by land, by sea. Walking along the Great Wall of China, relaxing in a gondola on the canals of Venice, marvelling at the treasures of the Louvre, or lingering in the factory that produced her favourite English bone china, Aunt Ena was a lifelong learner who brought home pictures, experiences, and mementos we could share through the winter at one of her lively dinner parties. When I finger the sparkling stones of an Austrian Crystal necklace she left me, or walk past a small Japanese print on my guest bedroom wall, I remember those times.

Probably because she had travelled so extensively, Aunt Ena loved culture. Whether it was attending Agatha Christie's *The Mousetrap* in London or a performance by our hometown symphony orchestra, my aunt basked in the riches of art, music, literature, and theatre. If a show came to town, Aunt Ena bought tickets. Well into her eighties, she could join in a knowledgeable discussion of cultural experiences and trends.

Lastly, and most importantly, Aunt Ena taught me to celebrate family. She kept in touch, by letter and phone, across the country, with loved ones near and far. Aunt Ena was the driving force behind her father's 100th birthday party. In a well-guarded journal, she kept track of birthdays, marriages, births, deaths, and milestones. We were a large and extended family, and postage kept going up, but, as well as I can remember, there were always cards in the mail for those special occasions. Single by choice all her life, she hosted grand games nights at Christmas, where we shouted at boisterous games of Rook and devoured abundant plates of Christmas goodies.

A wonderful fashion sense, love of the world's unexplored corners, passion for culture, and devotion to family live on in my memories of Aunt Ena. To be seen as "a bit like your Aunt Ena" is the ultimate compliment for me. The giant atlas she once used lies open on a table in my home, to a map of Italy … where my travels will take me this fall. Where I would take her, if only I could.

- In this response, the writer responds to the writing task meaningfully with a thesis that directly addresses the prompt to write about a significant role model.
- The thesis is supported by four main ideas: the aunt is a role model in fashion, in travelling, in appreciating culture, and in making family a priority. These ideas are elaborated on throughout the essay with specific examples and details from the writer's memory.
- The organization is purposefully controlled by following the order established in the opening paragraph. The focus on the "role model" is maintained throughout by using a personal tone ("Aunt Ena once told me") that reminds the reader that this role model was an important part of the writer's life. The writer seems to have a clear sense of a comfortable, accepting audience that is receptive to the writer's ideas and memories.
- There are a variety of sentence types: "The most significant…," "As a grade one teacher…," "They love it!" The writer tries to use precise, descriptive language. Examples of this are "Shiny red earrings," "wide-brimmed yellow hat," and "gondola on the canals of Venice."
- The essay shows some signs of being a first draft piece of writing. Some of the wording, for instance, could be rearranged or tightened, but it is essentially error-free. The essay is an example of a 4-point response.

Score Point 3

Student Response

Throughout your life, several people will have influenced you as a positive role model. My Aunt Ena was one of those people. She influenced me in her role as an educator and also as a person.

As an educator, my aunt was quite remarkable. She taught children their primary colors by modelling bright clothing with colour-matching jewellery. She designed picture flashcards at home and made learning numbers into a game. She brought a friend who was an author to class to inspire her students to read good books.

I absorbed my aunt's love of reading, but she was more than an educator. Aunt Ena was also an amazing human being. She loved departing on trips, but after all the sightseeing was done, arriving home beat out the Eiffel Tower. Her love of family was legendary. Here was a woman who never forgot a birthday or special occasion.

I miss her, & I miss her extraordinary influence in my life, I hope & pray that I may be more like her as I grow older. Role models are great!

- In this response, the writer adequately responds to the prompt—to write about a role model with a thesis paragraph that introduces the aunt's two main roles that influenced the writer's life: her role as an educator and as a fine human being.
- The writer is able to support the main ideas introduced with somewhat general details and examples such as "modelled bright clothing" and "loved departing on trips."

- The focus on the aunt as a role model is consistent throughout the essay, as is the tone of summarizing for the reader the key influences in the writer's life. There is a general sense of writing for an unknown audience, although it lapses somewhat in the impulsive-sounding outburst at the end: "Role models are great!"
- The writer does endeavour to provide some variety in sentence types: "Throughout your life," and "I absorbed." The essay also includes some descriptive language such as "my aunt was quite remarkable" and "her extraordinary influence."
- The essay contains a few errors in conventions (such as using the symbol "&" in the last paragraph), but the errors do not interfere with the reader's understanding of the essay. The response is characteristic of a 3-point essay.

Score Point 2

Student Response

In my life I have had a lot of role models and I learnt a lot from them, but my best role model was probally my aunt, I learnt a lot from her.

My aunt was a great person. When I saw the question I knew she would be the one, cause her role is more clear than anyone els. I did love her, I realy did, cuz she always sent us kids gifts & cards, rain or shine. She was a great teacher too, the little kids loved her bright cloths.

Well anyway, that's about all there is to say on this topic. I think we shuld all have a role model. All's well that ends well, as they say. Thanks for the Canct to write about my aunt. She was a great lady.

- This response does provide a thesis that is related to the writing task: "my best role model was probally my aunt, I learnt a lot from her." The somewhat brief response includes some limited details/examples such as "always sent us kids gifts & cards" and "kids loved her bright clothes."
- The focus on the aunt is inconsistent with unrelated statements such as "All's well that ends well." This also makes the tone inconsistent—at times, the writer is enthusiastic about the subject ("I did love her"), and at other times vague and dismissive ("Well anyway, that's about all there is to say on this topic"). The inconsistent focus and tone contribute to a rambling style that demonstrates little or no sense of audience. There are few types of sentences—most are simple subject/verb patterns or run-ons. The language is basic and predictable: "learnt a lot," "us kids," "great teacher," "great lady." The writer makes fairly frequent errors in conventions. The spelling errors in particular may interfere with the reader's understanding of the response. Generally, this response contains characteristics typical of a 2-point essay.

Score Point 1

Student Response

> Role models are very important in are lif. Gud stuff to learn. Gud people to think about. I no a lot of role models, cuz role models are all around. Some gud, some bad. I ask you, who is yore role model? Think about it. Write it down, cuz you want to remember them.

- The writer of this extremely short, one-paragraph response does attempt to address the prompt ("Role models are very important"), but fails to provide an example as requested. The haphazard comments and questions about role models suggest that the writer is confused about the writing task except that it somehow involves role models. There is no clear thesis established, and none of the ideas presented are developed with details and/or examples.
- Because of the writer's apparent confusion, no tone, focus, or audience awareness is established. The paragraph lacks organization in that the only phrase linking the rambling ideas is the phrase borrowed from the prompt "role models." There is one question, which varies the sentence structure a little, but the number of fragments suggests that the writer has limited understanding of sentence patterns. The vocabulary is limited, repetitive, and often riddled with errors: "cuz," "role models," "gud." The many errors in conventions throughout the paragraph interfere with the clarity of the response. The many problems and limitations make this response an example of a 1-point essay.

NOTES

Reflecting on Skills and Strategies

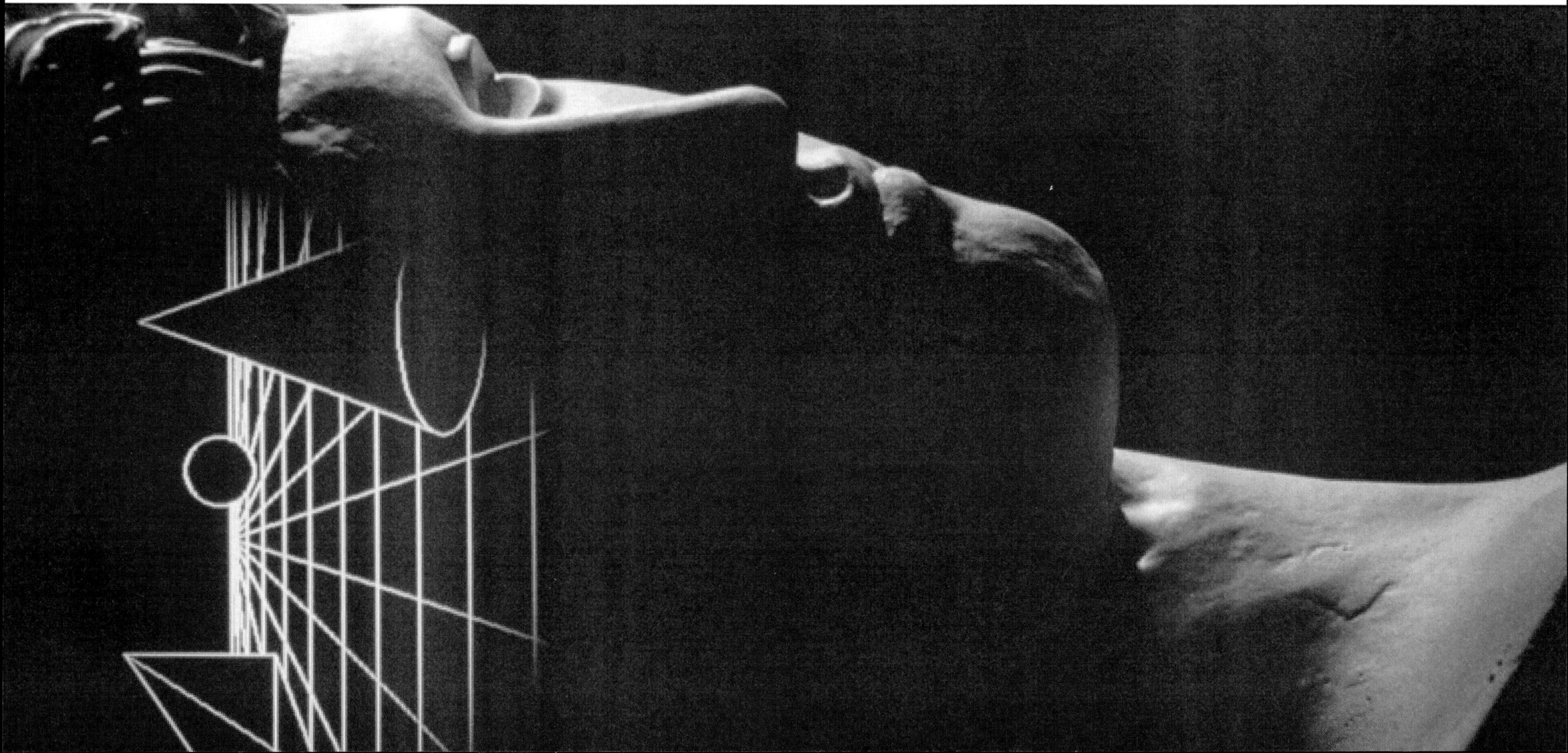

REFLECTING ON SKILLS AND STRATEGIES

METACOGNITION

11R4.1 explain which of a variety of strategies they found most helpful before, during, and after reading, then evaluate their strengths and weaknesses as readers to help identify the steps they can take to improve their skills

11W4.1 explain which of a variety of strategies they found most helpful before, during, and after writing, then evaluate their strengths and weaknesses as writers to help identify the steps they can take to improve their skills

11M4.1 explain which of a variety of strategies they found most helpful in interpreting and creating media texts, then evaluate their strengths and weaknesses as media interpreters and producers to help identify the steps they can take to improve their skills

The word metacognition refers to thinking about how you think; this process includes thinking about how you learn. As you discover and think about strategies that work best with your individual learning style, you will become a more confident and productive learner. It is important to think about your learning style and to ask yourself questions about how it works for you. Do you work better in groups or on your own? Do you memorize things visually? What kind of reading do you like to do best? The more time you spend analysing how you think, the better able you will be to pinpoint the areas in which you excel and the areas in which you have trouble.

The following section of your ***KEY*** provides examples and guidelines on metacognition. These examples are designed to illustrate how an individual student performs metacognition activities. Keep in mind that the way you think and learn is unique, so different methods may appeal to you more than others. Learning what appeals to you is also part of metacognition.

SETTING GOALS

One of the keys to improving your English skills is to set personal goals for language growth. You may wish to use the following rubric that identifies some of the major English skills in order to identify your strengths and areas for growth. Reviewing assignments and assessment rubrics from your current or past English courses will help you to assess your strengths and the areas that need improvement.

Skill	Yes	Needs Improvement
Read regularly		✓
Predict and ask questions while reading, discuss unfamiliar concepts with others	✓	
Take note of words I am not sure of and use context or references to find meanings	✓	
Reread passages to clarify meaning	✓	
Use visualizing and graphic organizers as aids to analysing text and planning for communicating ideas	✓	
Connect what I am reading to what I know about and to other texts I have read		✓

Understand symbols, archetypes, and literary devices and use them to enhance understanding of texts	✓	
Use ideas in texts to better understand and communicate understandings of self and the world around	✓	
Know how to effectively introduce and conclude topics in writing or oral presentations	✓	
Connect all ideas to a controlling idea	✓	
Fully support ideas with explanations and examples	✓	
Identify when ideas are not communicated clearly	✓	
Use a variety of sentences and precise diction for effect	✓	
Find and correct errors in spelling, usage, and punctuation	✓	
Understand oral instructions	✓	
Listen carefully, build on the ideas of others, and ask questions to help others clarify ideas	✓	
Comfortable making formal presentations	✓	
Use voice effectively: volume, rate, tone, and pacing, to communicate effectively and convey emotion	✓	
Use eye contact and gestures for emphasis	✓	
Use charts, graphs, and visual aids to contribute to presentations	✓	
Know how to find resources, effectively record information, and correctly reference sources	✓	

11R4.2 identify a variety of their skills in listening, speaking, writing, viewing, and representing and explain how the skills help them read more effectively

11W4.2 identify a variety of skills they have in listening, speaking, reading, viewing, and representing, and explain how these skills help them write more effectively

11M4.2 explain how their skills in listening, speaking, reading, and writing help them interpret and produce media text

Interconnected Skills

Using the Checklist

Put checkmarks in the "Most Effective for Me" column next to the five strategies in the checklist that work best for you.

- Write a number beside each checkmark showing how effective the strategy is for you (1 is most effective, 5 is least effective).
- Think of logical reasons for the order you have chosen.
- Discuss and compare your top five most effective strategies with a peer.
- Collaborate to identify the top five strategies for you and your peer and describe the best uses for each strategy.
- List five ways that you and your peer can become better readers.

Reading Metacognition Checklist

The following questions are examples of how you can use metacognition to examine your learning style.

What is the best way to approach this learning task?

- At this point, how well do I understand the information, concepts, and characters?
- How can I maintain my motivation to complete what I have started?
- Am I using the best tools for this learning task?

The following checklist shows different strategies you can use to get the most out of your reading. More importantly, it helps you to think about how you approach various reading tasks. You could use this checklist several times during the school year to help you understand or change your approach.

Thinking About My Reading Strategies	**Most Effective for Me**	**Use Most Often**	**Use Sometimes**	**Should Try**
Before Reading I *preview* (look over exams, texts, stories, articles, and assignments) to determine: • What is involved in this text? • What is my purpose for reading? • How should I approach this? • How should I read (speed, etc.)?				
I think about my *prior knowledge*—what I already know that might be relevant to the topic or task in front of me.				
I *visualize* or try to picture the characters, setting, what I hope to find out, etc.				
While Reading I *check back* to verify a definition, information about a character, etc.				
I use *vocabulary strategies*, such as context clues, root words, prefixes, and suffixes, to understand unfamiliar words and phrases.				
I make point-form notes or use *graphic organizers* when I need to remember plots, key ideas, etc.				
I pause while reading and *predict* what I think will happen next in the story.				
I *tag text* with sticky notes or mark parts I find confusing, so I can ask about them later.				
I use a *highlighter*—when I am allowed—to mark the text (notes, handouts, etc.) for key phrases and important ideas.				

Thinking About My Reading Strategies	**Most Effective for Me**	**Use Most Often**	**Use Sometimes**	**Should Try**
I write *notes*, *questions*, and *comments* in margins if I am allowed. Sometimes, I use these later on to clarify information.				
I ask questions to *monitor my understanding* of what I read: • Does this make sense to me? • What exactly is the writer saying? • What is the narrator's point of view? • Do I agree? Why or why not?				
When the text does not state something directly, I make *inferences* and draw *conclusions* from my reading.				
I deliberately use *skimming* and *scanning* skills when appropriate, such as to locate a specific answer or idea in the text.				
I *adjust my reading rate* as needed, slowing down for detailed information, etc.				
I *pay attention* to diagrams, pictures, charts, and graphs—anything that may help me make more sense of the text.				
After Reading I *summarize*, using notes or a graphic organizer.				
I write my thoughts, questions, and reactions in a *personal response journal*.				
I *share with a peer* in the following ways: • in written form, such as a double-response journal, in which we write back and forth • by discussing informally within a share-pair or small group • by explaining a newly learned concept I try to *support my own opinions* and to *show respect* for the opinions of others.				
I write *critical responses* to text when invited to do so. I try to include comments on the form, purpose, writer's viewpoint, historical context, mood, imagery, etc. When possible, I *make comparisons* with other texts or draw from my personal experiences to deepen my response.				

Sample Applications of Metacognition

The following section shows you some strategies that involve metacognition. Journals, visual charts, and literature circles and book clubs are all great methods of making yourself more aware of how you read. Some of these may be more useful to you than others. Figuring out which methods work best for you will give you insight into your learning style.

Personal Response Journal

A personal response journal can be a great record of what you read. A journal can also be a good starting point to get ideas for homework assignments. A journal entry should include the date, title, and name of the work that you describe. The entry should express your connections with the text. How does the work connect to your experiences? How does it relate to your opinions?

The following example shows a poem and one student's personal response journal entry regarding that poem. The personal response describes that student's individual experience with the poem. To practise metacognition, try writing your own response to this poem.

DRAGON NIGHT

Little flame mouths,
Cool your tongues.
Dreamtime starts,
My furnace-lungs.

Rest your wings now,
Little flappers,
Cave mouth calls
To dragon nappers.

Night is coming,
Bank your fire.
Time for dragons
To retire.

Hiss.
Hush.
Sleep.

—*by* Jane Yolen

PERSONAL RESPONSE JOURNAL ENTRY: "DRAGON NIGHT" BY JANE YOLEN

February 27, 2008

Although this poem seems to be written as a lullaby for baby dragons, it means something different and very personal to me. Of all the poems we studied in our September poetry unit, this is my absolute favourite. It brought back lots of memories of the summer, sitting with my family on the deck of our cottage at Muskoka Lake, relaxing and looking at the lake. As I read the poem, I thought of tiny flashes of light down by the lakeshore—fireflies flicking their mini-lanterns on and off. The poem has lots of summer and evening imagery. I felt quiet and relaxed by the end of the poem.

The great thing about journal entries is that you do not have to worry that you are being too casual with your language. Even though the entry may be casual and talk about your own life experience, the information about your opinions can be used to write something more formal later on. Keeping a journal about what you read is a great tool for keeping track of your learning.

Literature Circles and Book Clubs

A literature circle or book club may help you to better understand a novel. They can also be fun ways to talk with classmates about literature in a more casual way than in the classroom. Everyone interprets literary works a little differently. By talking freely to others about your impressions of a text, you can learn about different ways of looking at it. You also gain a better understanding of your own opinions by having to express them to others.

Skills That Aid Reading

Now that you are in Grade 11, you have developed a variety of communication skills that will help you as a reader. As your reading improves, for example, your ability to state your opinions out loud also improves. Honing your skills in presenting ideas in different media, such as plays or poster art, can improve your skills in summarizing or understanding concepts as you read.

Communication Tools

Being able to communicate using one tool will boost your ability to communicate using another tool. The following examples show different communication tools and how improving your use of them will improve your overall reading.

Listening and Reading

When good readers read out loud, they use several tools to make their reading effective: clear articulation, appropriate tone and expression, pacing, rate of reading, and pauses. As you acquire these skills through listening, you can use them when you read out loud.

When you listen to peers in a small group setting, you should

- clarify things you missed or misunderstood
- hear a description of an experience that you might not have known or thought about
- discuss views and opinions arising from the same text and learn to use text to support your own viewpoint
- consider the viewpoint of a peer, which could be just as well supported in the text as your own opinion

Speaking and Reading

As you share your insights and viewpoints, you will

- improve your reading comprehension
- learn to support your viewpoint using text statements and inferences
- improve your oral reading skills as you read out loud

In a pair or a small group, comfortably express your ideas from your reading. In a peer group, there is no pressure to use precise or formal language. You can feel free to explain your ideas in a more casual setting. Discussion is used to shape your ideas, so they do not have to be perfectly formed at this time.

Writing and Reading

When you write a response to your reading, you can craft a thoughtful response using words you have taken time to decide upon. Written responses are also an efficient way for you to answer questions from a text and to reread parts of a text. Effective readers use both of these strategies.

Viewing and Reading

Viewing material can enrich your reading experience. In a film, characterization, costumes, and settings enhance the descriptions in the book on which it is based, and the stories can come to life in a new way. Viewing a film version of a book may help you better identify with the characters in the book. Sometimes, you might find that the film version is not how you imagined it when you read the book. Perhaps the actors do not look the way you imagined the characters or the setting is different than you pictured it. Readers can become resentful if a movie does not seem true to a novel.

It is important to keep in mind that the film version of a novel is based on how the people who made the film interpreted the novel. One of the best things about reading is that in a sense you have the power to create the same visuals in your mind that a director does when making a movie. You direct the movement and appearance of a book in the same way that a director might. In order to understand your interpretation of a novel, you could adapt portions of a story to a dramatic form. This will enhance your effectiveness as a reader as you review the story for accurate dialogue and consistent character portrayal.

Presenting Ideas Using Different Media

Taking ideas from a text and using them in a different medium can aid your understanding of the text. After reading a book, taking ideas from it and addressing them in a play or on a poster can give you a better understanding of the book's focus and themes. Presenting a text in a new way can highlight aspects of a book's theme, mood, character qualities, or symbolism that you might not have thought about otherwise. For example, a poster or a collage could be used to show the dominant theme in a novel using nothing but pictures cut from magazines.

Applying Your Skills

The following section provides a few examples to demonstrate more specific learning situations in which interconnected skills are used to understand text more effectively. A single work is shown to be presented in different media. This can give you ideas as to how you can do a similar project with texts that you have read.

Presenting a Work Using Different Forms

After reading the legend "The Fork in the Graveyard," two students are asked to dramatize some of the dialogue from the story and use it to share with the class how this project helped them better understand Peter, the main character.

"The Fork in the Graveyard" is an exciting a story of the supernatural, and as such is still retold by the people of Tracadie who, to this day, puzzle over the truth of the episode. The tale is originally written in the form of a short story.

THE FORK IN THE GRAVEYARD

The spirit, or ghost, of a dead man is said to have committed the dastardly deed of murdering Peter, a Scottish settler, who arrived in the area on the good ship *Alexander* in 1773.

The scene is set [with] men relaxing around the warmth of a stove, chatting of mysterious events. When Peter arrives, room is made for him in the warmth, and conversation continues until one Ben Peters mentions having seen a light in the old French burying place at Scotch Fort. He describes a huge ball of fire dancing across the graves, lighting up the whole cemetery.

Peter, the newcomer, scoffs at the idea, boasting that such exaggerations will not keep him from walking through any churchyard, even the Scotch Fort one, on that very night.

There are, he claims, more devils to fear among his mortal companions than in the resting place of the dead.

His boasting, of course, is quickly taken up on, and the challenge thrown out to do more than brag by the comfort of the fire.

"It's all very well to put on a brave front when yer in the company of humans," pipes a fellow lounger. "But going to a graveyard that's haunted in the dead of night, and alone, is a horse of another colour. Why, man, you must be clear off your beam to even suggest such a thing let alone go through with it. That old cemetery may be full of dead men's bones, but it's also full of dead men's spirits."

Peter takes offense at the remarks, shrugging off superstitious talk as nonsense. The ire is up in his companions who are slighted by his attitude and quickly a bet is made that Peter should go to the old cemetery and plant a hay-fork in a grave to prove he has been there. Should he succeed, a pound of tobacco will be his.

Peter accepts the challenge, and with a jaunty air leaves the cabin, telling them to have his tobacco ready on the morn. "I don't expect to be detained by the dead," he says. "I've never known dead people to harm anyone."

As it is midnight, all file from the store. Peter, in a long black rain slicker, is given the hay-fork and bid on his way to Scotch Fort, while the others scuttle for the dry warmth of their own beds.

Come dawn, all are seeking Peter, who it seems has disappeared. His cabin is empty and cold, obviously vacant for some time. More ominous, his livestock is bleating with hunger. With the realization that Peter is not to be found comes fear, fear for the fate of a man brazen enough to risk defying the very spirits of the dead at the witching hour on a night that seems to portray the very depths of Hell itself.

The men arm themselves, justifying their actions by expressing a concern about bears in the vicinity, and set out to solve the mystery.

The cemetery is a small clearing in the heart of the forest, reached by means of a narrow footpath, permitting not more than two persons to walk abreast. Every now and then the search party stop to peer through the braches of the trees, their voices never above a whisper. Finally they are out of the woods and stare in amazement at the sight that meets their eyes.

The handle of a hay-fork shows plainly above a grave situated right in the centre of the graveyard. A large black object is curled up on the ground beside it.

Cautiously the party press forward, and, as they near the spot, the black object begins to take shape. A few more steps and they raise their voices in unison, "Peter! Can't you speak to us?"

There is no answer save the echo of their own voices. MacIntyre's body lies across the grave, his face turned toward them. It is a face frozen in agony, a haunted, fear-crazed face that makes the living tremble and wish they'd never seen it.

A hand reaches out and grabs the dead man's collar. The hand pulls hard on the collar but the body won't come loose.

A second hand reaches out and grasps the fork. It has been driven into the grave with a powerful thrust and right through the tail of Peter MacIntyre's long black coat.

—*retold by* Julie V. Watson

The following passage is a dramatization of the story you just read. As you read this rewritten dramatic dialogue, think about what has changed from the original form and what has stayed the same. Think about why certain changes are made when a different form of writing is used. Think about some of the works you have read that might make exciting plays or movies.

Rewriting as Dramatic Dialogue

DRAMATIC DIALOGUE VERSION OF "THE FORK IN THE GRAVEYARD"

CHARACTERS

Middle-aged men, dressed in casual shirts and pants:

BEN PETERS

JOHN SMITH

MIKE HOLLAND

DAN ELLIOTT

Younger than the others:

PETER MACINTYRE

Setting: A smallish cabin with a large stove in the middle of the room. The men are sitting around the stove warming themselves. The sounds of a wintry storm outside can be heard. Peter enters. He takes off his rain slicker and hangs it on a hook beside the door. The men greet Peter as they make room for him in the warmth.

BEN: I saw a light tonight at the old French burying place at Scotch Fort. The light looked like a huge ball of fire dancing around and over the graves, and it lit up the whole cemetery.

PETER: Must have been your imagination. There is nothing to light up that old cemetery. Cemeteries don't bother me by day or by night, and even your ball of fire wouldn't scare me away from Scotch Fort tonight or any other night. I fear mortal people more than any dead man.

JOHN: Oh, come on. You're boasting!

MIKE: It's alright to talk like that when you are sitting here keeping warm by the fire. Midnight in a cemetery is scary enough for me.

DAN: It's all very well to put on a brave front when yer in the company of humans. But going to a graveyard that's haunted in the dead of night, and alone, is a horse of another colour. Why, man, you must be clear off your beam to even suggest such a thing, let alone go through with it. That old cemetery may be full of dead men's bones, but it's also full of dead men's spirits.

PETER: Yer all just a bunch of superstitious old codgers. The very idea of dead men's spirits makes me laugh.

BEN: You haven't seen the light. I have and you don't know what yer talkin' about. It was scary.

JOHN: I bet you wouldn't go right now in this awful weather to the cemetery.

PETER: Yes I would. Superstition doesn't scare me.

MIKE: Rising and fetching a hay-fork that was propped up by the door. All right, then. You take this hay-fork and plant it in a grave in the middle of the cemetery. You come back to us and a pound of tobacco is yours.

DAN: Great idea. The hay-fork will be the proof you have been to the cemetery.

PETER: I could do with a pound of tobacco—get it ready, mates. I don't expect to be detained by the dead. I've never known dead people to harm anyone.

MIKE: Handing the hay-fork to Peter. Off you go, then. Visit the dead. We're off to our beds. [*Exits*]

PETER puts on his black rain slicker, takes the hay-fork, and exits.

DAN: Good night. See you in the morn.

BEN: See you.

JOHN: Goodnight.

All exit.

Following their brief dramatic presentation, the two students share their comments about how they adapted the story:

Student A: I didn't really like Peter when we first read the story. I thought he was kind of stupid and gullible to fall for such an obvious trick to scare him. Why didn't he just walk out of the cabin and leave the old guys to their stories? He probably came to the area to work, not to listen to stories. But when we turned the story into spoken words, my opinion changed. He was a newcomer, and probably terrified of failure. He had to make a good impression on people who had lived in the area longer. He wanted to be accepted. I decided that his boasting was really just being brave because he wanted to look confident to the men.

Student B: We talked about Peter a lot while we were writing the play. We decided he was kind of a victim. Ben, John, and Mike were like students who go on a power trip to show off to a new guy at school. We saw them as bullies. We are pretty sure Peter jabbed the fork by accident through his own cloak, which was dragging on the ground. When he thought a ghost was grabbing on to his cloak, he literally was scared to death. Those three men must have felt awful when they found him the next day. No one ever expects their pranks to go wrong, but sometimes they do. You may not agree with our interpretation, but that's how we saw it.

As you can see from the students' remarks, they developed empathy and understanding for the characters during the process of changing the text into another form. An important skill the students used in this assignment was drawing inferences that they could logically support. Working with and changing a text can help you understand the original work better than you did previously.

Applying Skills: Using Research in Projects

Research is a vital part of writing formal papers. Metacognition can be applied to your research in order to see where you can improve your researching techniques. In the following fictional account, two students were given a news article about a local issue and were asked to use research to clarify and extend their understanding of the article and the issues it presents. As you read about their assignment, try and think about how you might go about researching this issue if it were your own assignment. How might the techniques you would use be different from the ones used by the fictional students in the following example?

The students are given two weeks to work on a project about current events. They are asked to identify an issue raised in a news article that they are given, track the issue for two weeks, consider perspectives and possible outcomes, and afterwards engage their classmates in a discussion about the issue.

The article is about an airport safety issue arising from a recent crash landing at Pearson International Airport in Toronto that could have resulted in a tragic loss of lives. According to the news item, an Air France jet carrying 309 passengers and crew landed halfway down the runway during a summer rainstorm. Overshooting the 90-metre buffer zone at the end of the runway, the plane careened over a bank and finally came to a stop. Fortunately, before the damaged aircraft burst into flames, everyone on board was safely evacuated and removed from danger. The accident was caused by human error, but the issue arising from this incident involved passenger safety and accident prevention. After reading the information, the students felt that the runway buffer zone should be extended to 300 metres, the required length at most major European airports.

The students decided to use a kind of tracking log to record what they did to clarify or extend their understanding of this story and the issues it raised. This is what they recorded over their two-week assignment.

CLASS PROJECT: THE PEARSON AIRPORT

1. We collected stories on the topic from the newspaper, television, and Internet for about two weeks. We ended up with a total of 21 news items.
2. We recorded facts or messages common to all of the stories, such as:
   - the Pearson runway has a 90-metre buffer zone
   - the weather conditions were severe
   - the pilot landed halfway down the runway
   - incidents such as this happen more frequently than is commonly believed
3. We looked for public reactions in the newspaper, on television, and on websites and recorded repeated responses, such as:
   - safety is of major concern
   - the expense of extending the runway is worth possibly saving lives
   - Pearson airport should have the same standards as the rest of the world
4. We watched for different opinions on the issue and found opinion articles from:
   - the Airline Pilots' Association
   - the Ontario Department of Tourism
   - city and provincial governments (about who would bear the cost of the runway upgrade)
5. Based on all that we found, we tried to predict an outcome:
   - the runway extension would be built over the next two years, funded by the province
6. We watched to see if the issue was resolved in two weeks. It was not, but the matter was under review by a transportation committee.
7. We summarized our findings and prepared our class presentation.
8. After our presentation, we will allow a brief time for discussion on our issue. We will then ask Miss Fergusen to review business letter format and take us to the computer lab to write letters to the Transportation Safety Board of Canada to be forwarded to the Honourable Lawrence Cannon, Minister of Transport, Ottawa. The purpose of the letters will be to request mandatory lengthened buffer zones for major Canadian airport runways by 2010.

Our Concluding Comments:

Through reading, research, and discussion, we clarified and extended our understanding of an important and newsworthy safety issue. We came to have a strong personal interest in the outcome of this issue because, like most Canadians, we will use air travel throughout our lives. If a short-sighted decision is made, we ourselves could someday be victims.

Research is critical to writing non-fiction text. The more you learn about an issue, the better able you will be to form an opinion that is informed and balanced. Finding information that is accurate and that does not have a bias can be difficult. As you become a better researcher, understanding information and how to find good information will become easier.

Use metacognition the next time you are researching for a project. Think about areas of research you may have missed and how you could effectively use your research.

Evaluating Your Process

Metacognition consists of two processes occurring at the same time: monitoring your progress as you learn, and changing and adapting your strategies if necessary. In writing, this involves identifying what strategies you found most helpful before, during, and after writing and what steps you can take to improve as a writer. After you have finished a writing project, think back to how you developed your ideas for writing, the research you did, and how you sorted and organized it. This will help you to identify the strategies you used. Next time you do similar writing, use the strategies that worked the best for you and reconsider the others.

For example, a Grade 11 student came up with the following examples of strategies he used during the first half of the year.

Example

MY WRITING STRATEGIES

Before Writing

- Went online to find information about topics when I could, like the natural disaster topic after we read the short story "The Worst Day Ever."
- Jotted down the titles of books, TV shows, and music related to the topic
- Talked with mom about topic choice
- Wrote down purpose and audience
- Made a web plan and outline

During Writing

- Spread out notes and outlines
- Tried to follow outlines
- Checked with assignment criteria
- Tried to write correctly
- Tried to use good transitions
- Tried to include things teacher was emphasizing, like different sentence openers and replacements

After Writing

- Labelled my revisions to make sure I was intentionally including the teacher's suggestions.
- Read drafts aloud from computer screen while revising and editing.
- Paid attention to my peer partner so we could help each other improve.

Next, the student explained the strategy he found the most helpful. The strategy he chose was the idea of labelling revisions to require thinking specifically about what he was changing and why. Since the students were sharing their metacognition activities with the teacher, he submitted the following paragraph:

> [Sometimes, (transition)] Groups of large ocean waves [caused by a storm] ~~may~~ slam into [a powerful] ~~an~~ ocean current passing in the [opposite] ~~other~~ direction. [When this happens,] ~~S~~several storm waves pile up to form freak waves. These waves [can (consistent tense)] ~~could~~ be more than 100 feet tall and can sink cargo ships beneath the [sea] ~~water~~. [Rogue (more precise)] ~~The~~ waves are most common off the coasts of Japan, Florida, and Alaska. Over the next few years, oceanographers hope to [analyze (more precise)] study these satellite images to help them better understand why such waves occur. [Switch the last two sentences around for better organization] Currently a project known as WaveAtlas [monitors (more precise)] ~~studies~~ the oceans with satellites.

Finally, the student identified several steps he could take to improve as a writer. His list included the following ideas:

1. Keep a writing log with sections: Spelling Errors, Writing Errors, Story Ideas
2. Start a list of words I want to use in my writing
3. Look online for sites where I can share some of my writing

After collecting the class's reflections, Ms. Harmon gave the students two 4 × 6 cards to tape inside their writing logs. The cards contained reminders to help the students think about each piece of writing.

This Piece

- What is best?
- What could I improve?
- What stage was smoothest?
- What ideas could I use for new writing?

Learning from this Piece

- Have I learned any new techniques?
- Did I try something new?
- Have I eliminated personal errors I have commonly made in the past, such as sentence fragments?

Writer's Reflection

Reflecting on your writing is something you probably have to do in class. The following passage is an example of a fictional student's response to metacognition questions from his or her class. You may have to answer questions similar to these about your own writing and language skills. See if you can answer the following questions yourself.

Example

Before Grade 11, what did you know or understand to be your strengths as a writer? Has this changed?

I always thought that my greatest strength was writing humour. It was because I found it easy to remember the punch line of a good joke, and I could always seem to make my friends laugh. Sometimes at the wrong time, like in the middle of your class on sentence fragments! When you asked us to think hard about our strengths in September, and to think of ways to branch out from those strengths, I realized that one reason I can describe things in a humorous way is that I am a people watcher. I am always watching what people do, how they react, and what they say in certain situations. I used that strength to branch out when I wrote my one-act play on peer pressure. With realistic sounding dialogue and characters based on what I had really seen around me, I think I was able to get some serious points across using humour. During your comments after my group presented my play, you said our dialogue was convincing and real.

What did you learn about yourself as a writer as a result of the group writing experience?

You mean the short story project. The truth is, I wasn't too happy at first. I actually like writing independent stories from my own head, so it was annoying to have to stop and pay attention to the other two guys in my group. One hated writing, period, and the other didn't want to write anything but fantasy, which I have never read. We wasted a bit of time in the beginning, but when you started posting deadlines on the board we had to think of something. We had just learned about parodies, so we decided to write a modernized parody of a well known fairy tale. The partner who hated writing didn't mind working from a basic plot we all knew—"Little Red Riding Hood." He even started to contribute a few ideas. My other partner added some twists, I added some ideas for humour, and we all liked the result, because it turned out like a bit of a fantasy. What I learned about myself as a writer was that

- I am more creative than I realized
- Sometimes other points of view can improve writing
- I can motivate a peer who thinks writing is an unpleasant chore

How do you determine whether the peer feedback you receive is valid?

I pay the closest attention to revision ideas. I figure if my ideas are boring or confusing to any reader, especially a peer, I need to fix that. Sometimes it's just the organization that is confusing, so I make it more chronological, or use better transitions. When a peer suggests different spelling or punctuation, I look at it, but not as hard unless the peer is a classmate I know to be a strong speller or one who makes very few errors in their own writing. Even when I don't agree with the peer feedback, it does force me to take another look at my writing before publishing the final draft.

How you learn matters. Keeping track of what has affected your language skills is important. How easy was it to answer the three questions in the example? Could you think of any other questions that might be good to ask about your learning? Metacognition means thinking about your learning while you are learning. The more you ask yourself questions like the ones in the given example, the more aware you will become of your learning.

Interconnected Skills

Learning to be a good writer does not happen in isolation. What you hear, speak, and see influences what you write. Many of the skills you practise every day help you develop as a writer. In fact, everything you do and experience can become part of your writing experience, if you take time to reflect on it. To start thinking about how language skills are connected, consider the following questions.

- What do you know about different media texts that might help when you are writing? Media texts are found in newspapers and magazines as well as in advertising, posters, and leaflets.
- In what ways do you think the reading you do helps you as a writer? Can you give an example?
- What do you listen to that might help you as a writer?
- Have you ever seen a picture or a movie that made you think of a story? Or, have you ever written a story based on something you saw?

To understand more about how different skills interact, read the following fictional experience of Timothy, a Grade 12 student. His experiences describe how interconnected skills played a part in his learning to write more effectively. As you read, think about how your own experiences in English class can be improved by using a variety of skills.

Listening

Timothy is sitting with his friends in a Grade 11 assembly. He does not know what to expect as his English teacher, Mr. Kennedy, introduces the guest speaker:

"Ladies and gentlemen, our guest today was once a teacher like myself. Like me, he too wracked his brains on a daily basis, trying to think of ways to encourage his students to write, to get them excited about writing. He came up with the idea of writing a novel for them. The novel, *Stand Your Ground*, was set in the school where he worked. The setting was his community. Many of the characters had the same names as his students. That novel came out in 1993. It was a big hit, especially with the students who found their names in the book.

Since 1993, our guest has given up his teaching career to become a full-time writer of over 45 novels, with more on the way. He has won more than 30 awards, including the Ontario Library Association Silver Birch Award, three times. The selection panel was made up of over 750 000 young people like yourselves, country-wide, who voted for Mr. Eric Walters. It is my honour to present him to you today. Eric Walters is a man who loves a great story and who knows how to turn young people into fans of his books."

As the author approaches the podium, Timothy starts to pay attention, especially when Mr. Walters launches into the dramatic reading of a chapter from his novel called *Shattered*. The chapter is about a 15-year-old boy, Ian, starting to work as a volunteer in a soup kitchen as part of a social studies project. After a near mugging, in which Ian is saved by a homeless man, Ian later spots the man at the soup kitchen. It turns out he is a returned member of the Canadian Armed Forces whose last tour involved peacekeeping duties in Rwanda.

Mr. Walters also reads a foreword from the novel by Canadian General Romeo Dallaire, Force Commander for the United Nations Mission to Rwanda.

The rest of the presentation is a blur. Mr. Walters calls up a couple of students who have prepared some interview questions. He is both entertaining and serious. He talks about writing and about researching historical events in Canada to get ideas for writing. All Timothy can think about is getting his hands on that first novel. Timothy is not from Rwanda, but his parents came to Canada from Zaire before it was renamed Congo. He was too young to remember, but he wants to find out about why his parents ended up in a refugee camp for a year before they emigrated.

Reading and Viewing

Timothy signs out the novel *Shattered* from the school library. The librarian suggests that he might also like to watch the movie Hotel Rwanda, which is about a courageous hotel manager who saved people from being caught in a tribal massacre during the Rwandan crisis. Timothy rents the movie after he finishes the book.

Writing

The teacher, Mr. Kennedy, has encouraged his students to try writing some form of historical fiction, using suggestions from Eric Walters. Timothy decides to create five journal entries written by a fictional character, Akunda, who lives with his parents in a refugee camp in Congo. They are hoping to immigrate to Canada.

Speaking

Timothy records his journal entries to play for his writing group. He uses his older brother to be the voice of Akunda, and he reads the part of the narrator. As a writer, Timothy is supposed to use the group's suggestions to help him revise his writing.

Reflection

Mr. Kennedy poses the following two questions to his student writers, which they are to attach to the final draft of their writing before handing it in. You can read Timothy's answers to both questions:

How did listening to the taped reading of your writing help you to revise it?

One of my peer listeners suggested that I write two more entries to show the contrast when Akunda started his new life in Canada. He said the journal ended too abruptly. I thought that was a good idea, so I added those to my assignment. They also thought I could make the African entries a bit more realistic if I used actual places, so I looked up a map of the Congo on the Internet when I went home and changed a couple of location names.

What did you discover from reading Young Adult fiction that you could apply to your own story?

After Mr. Walters spoke to us a month ago, I read his novel Shattered. I tried to make my character, Akunda, seem as real as Ian seemed to me when I read the book. I also did some research on the Congo and talked to my parents about their experiences to make the journal entries as authentic as I could. I went on Eric Walters' website for more ideas, but what I learned from that one novel was to

- Use real places and events
- Make the main character have the same worries and concerns as young people all over the world—with dreams of a better life, a successful future, and solid friendships

The great thing about all your language skills being connected is that you can tailor your learning to how you learn best. If you learn better by talking to others or by speaking out loud about your ideas, do that. Your writing will improve if your ideas come to you more easily through verbal communication. Maybe you need to write out what you think before you prepare a formal essay. Some people learn better by reading, some by listening to others speak, and others by watching visual demonstrations.

It is important to remember that related skills in listening, speaking, reading, viewing, and representing contribute to improving your proficiency as a writer. The more you are able to recognize these connections, the better your writing will become.

NOTES

Key Strategies for Success on Tests

KEY STRATEGIES FOR SUCCESS ON TESTS

THINGS TO CONSIDER WHEN TAKING A TEST

It is normal to feel anxious before you write a test. You can manage this anxiety by using the following strategies:

- Think positive thoughts. Imagine yourself doing well on the test.
- Make a conscious effort to relax by taking several slow, deep, controlled breaths. Concentrate on the air going in and out of your body.
- Before you begin the test, ask questions if you are unsure of anything.
- Jot down key words or phrases from any instructions your teacher gives you.
- Look over the entire test to find out the number and kinds of questions on the test.
- Read each question closely, and reread if necessary.
- Pay close attention to key vocabulary words. Sometimes, these words are **bolded** or *italicized*, and they are usually important words in the question.
- If you are putting your answers on an answer sheet, mark your answers carefully. Always print clearly. If you wish to change an answer, erase the mark completely, and ensure that your final answer is darker than the one you have erased.
- Use highlighting to note directions, key words, and vocabulary that you find confusing or that are important to answering the question.
- Double-check to make sure you have answered everything before handing in your test.
- When taking tests, students often overlook the easy words. Failure to pay close attention to these words can result in an incorrect answer. One way to avoid this is to be aware of these words and to underline, circle, or highlight them while you are taking the test.
- Even though some words are easy to understand, they can change the meaning of the entire question, so it is important that you pay attention to them. Here are some examples.

all	always	most likely	probably	best	not
difference	usually	except	most	unlikely	likely

Example

1. Which of the following expressions is **incorrect**?

A. $3 + 2 \geq 5$

B. $4 - 3 < 2$

C. $5 \times 4 < 15$

D. $6 \times 3 \geq 18$

Test Preparation and Test-Taking Skills

Helpful Strategies for Answering Multiple-Choice Questions

A multiple-choice question gives you some information and then asks you to select an answer from four choices. Each question has one correct answer. The other choices are distractors, which are incorrect.

The following strategies can help you when answering multiple-choice questions:

- Quickly skim through the entire test. Find out how many questions there are, and plan your time accordingly.

- Read and reread questions carefully. Underline key words, and try to think of an answer before looking at the choices.
- If there is a graphic, look at the graphic, read the question, and go back to the graphic. Then, you may want to underline the important information from the question.
- Carefully read the choices. Read the question first and then each choice that goes with it.
- When choosing an answer, try to eliminate those choices that are clearly wrong or do not make sense.
- Some questions may ask you to select the best answer. These questions will always include words like *best*, *most appropriate*, or *most likely*. All of the choices will be correct to some degree, but one of the choices will be better than the others in some way. Carefully read all four choices before choosing the answer you think is the best.
- If you do not know the answer, or if the question does not make sense to you, it is better to guess than to leave it blank.
- Do not spend too much time on any one question. Make a mark (*) beside a difficult question, and come back to it later. If you are leaving a question to come back to later, make sure you also leave the space on the answer sheet, if you are using one.
- Remember to go back to the difficult questions at the end of the test; sometimes, clues are given throughout the test that will provide you with answers.

- Note any negative words like *no* or *not*, and be sure your answer fits the question.
- Before changing an answer, be sure you have a very good reason to do so.
- Do not look for patterns on your answer sheet, if you are using one.

HELPFUL STRATEGIES FOR ANSWERING WRITTEN-RESPONSE QUESTIONS

A written response requires you to respond to a question or directive indicated by words such as explain, predict, list, describe, show your work, solve, or calculate. The following strategies can help you when answering written-response questions:

- Read and reread the question carefully.
- Recognize and pay close attention to directing words such as *explain*, *show your work*, and *describe.*
- Underline key words and phrases that indicate what is required in your answer, such as *explain*, *estimate*, *answer*, *calculate*, or *show your work.*
- Write down rough, point-form notes regarding the information you want to include in your answer.
- Think about what you want to say, and organize information and ideas in a coherent and concise manner within the time limit you have for the question.
- Be sure to answer every part of the question that is asked.
- Include as much information as you can when you are asked to explain your thinking.
- Include a picture or diagram if it will help to explain your thinking.
- Try to put your final answer to a problem in a complete sentence to be sure it is reasonable.
- Reread your response to ensure you have answered the question.
- Ask yourself if your answer makes sense.
- Ask yourself if your answer sounds right.
- Use appropriate subject vocabulary and terms in your response.

TEST PREPARATION COUNTDOWN

If you develop a plan for studying and test preparation, you will perform well on tests.
Here is a general plan to follow seven days before you write a test.

COUNTDOWN: 7 DAYS BEFORE THE TEST

1. Use "Finding Out about the Test" to help you make your own personal test preparation plan.
2. Review the following information:
   - Areas to be included on the test
   - Types of test items
   - General and specific test tips
3. Start preparing for the test at least seven days before the test. Develop your test preparation plan, and set time aside to prepare and study.

COUNTDOWN: 6, 5, 4, 3, 2 DAYS BEFORE THE TEST

1. Review old homework assignments, quizzes, and tests.
2. Rework problems on quizzes and tests to make sure you still know how to solve them.
3. Correct any errors made on quizzes and tests.
4. Review key concepts, processes, formulas, and vocabulary.
5. Create practice test questions for yourself, and answer them. Work out many sample problems.

COUNTDOWN: THE NIGHT BEFORE THE TEST

1. Use the night before the test for final preparation, which includes reviewing and gathering materials needed for the test before going to bed.
2. Most importantly, get a good night's rest, and know you have done everything possible to do well on the test.

TEST DAY

1. Eat a healthy and nutritious breakfast.
2. Ensure you have all the necessary materials.
3. Think positive thoughts, such as "I can do this," "I am ready," and "I know I can do well."
4. Arrive at your school early, so you are not rushing, which can cause you anxiety and stress.

Summary of How to Be Successful during a Test

You may find some of the following strategies useful for writing a test:

- Take two or three deep breaths to help you relax.
- Read the directions carefully, and underline, circle, or highlight any important words.
- Look over the entire test to understand what you will need to do.
- Budget your time.
- Begin with an easy question or a question you know you can answer correctly rather than follow the numerical question order of the test.
- If you cannot remember how to answer a question, try repeating the deep breathing and physical relaxation activities. Then, move on to visualization and positive self-talk to get yourself going.
- When answering questions with graphics (pictures, diagrams, tables, or graphs), look at the question carefully, and use the following steps:
    1. Read the title of the graphic and any key words.
    2. Read the test question carefully to figure out what information you need to find in the graphic.
    3. Go back to the graphic to find the information you need.
- Write down anything you remember about the subject on the reverse side of your test paper. This activity sometimes helps to remind you that you do know something and are capable of writing the test.
- Look over your test when you have finished, and double-check your answers to be sure you did not forget anything.

Practice Tests

PRACTICE TESTS

Table of Correlations

Specific Expectation		Practice Test 1	Practice Test 2
Students are expected to:			
11R1.0	*read and demonstrate an understanding of a variety of literary, informational, and graphic texts, using a range of strategies to construct meaning; (Reading for Meaning)*		
11R1.3	*identify the most important ideas and supporting details in texts, including increasingly complex or difficult texts*	8, 14, 16, 21, 25, 26, 3, 7, 51, 54	7, 12, 20, 24, 28, 34, 38, 47, 56, 61
11R1.4	*make and explain inferences of increasing subtlety about texts, including increasingly complex or difficult texts, supporting their explanations with well-chosen stated and implied ideas from the texts*	4, 10, 11, 12, 13, 17, 23, 38, 43, 47, 59, 63	1, 4, 6, 10, 11, 17, 25, 29, 37, 42, 45, 48, 50, 59, 60
11R1.5	*extend understanding of texts, including increasingly complex or difficult texts, by making appropriate and increasingly rich connections between the ideas in them and personal knowledge, experience, and insights; other texts; and the world around them*	39, 53, 61	5, 9, 18, 30, 39, 43, 49, 55, 57
11R1.6	*analyse texts in terms of the information, ideas, issues, or themes they explore, examining how various aspects of the texts contribute to the presentation or development of these elements*	1, 7, 15, 32, 34, 40, 48	2, 8, 41, 52
11R1.8	*identify and analyse the perspectives and/or biases evident in texts, including increasingly complex or difficult texts, commenting with growing understanding on any questions they may raise about beliefs, values, identity, and power*	6, 33	15, 23, 33
11R2.0	*recognize a variety of text forms, text features, and stylistic elements and demonstrate understanding of how they help communicate meaning*		
11R2.1	*identify a variety of elements of style in texts and explain how they help communicate meaning and enhance the effectiveness of the texts*	20, 64	3, 46
11R2.2	*identify a variety of text features and explain how they help communicate meaning*	3, 36	
11R2.3	*identify a variety of elements of style in texts and explain how they help communicate meaning and enhance the effectiveness of the texts*	2, 5, 18, 22, 24, 28, 31, 41, 46, 55, 58, 60, 62	14, 16, 21, 26, 31, 35, 40, 44, 51, 58
11R3.0	*IS MISSING*		
11R3.1	*automatically understand most words in a variety of reading contexts*	9, 19, 27	22, 27, 36
11R3.2	*use decoding strategies effectively to read and understand unfamiliar words, including words of increasing difficulty*	49, 50, 52	13, 19, 53
11R3.3	*use a variety of strategies, with increasing regularity, to explore and expand vocabulary, focusing on the precision with which words are used in the texts they are reading*		Writing Prompt
11W1.0	*IS MISSING*		
11W1.1	*identify the topic, purpose, and audience for a variety of writing tasks*	Writing Prompt	Writing Prompt
11W1.2	*generate, expand, explore, and focus ideas for potential writing tasks, using a variety of strategies and print, electronic, and other resources, as appropriate*	Writing Prompt	Writing Prompt

11W1.3 locate and select information to effectively support ideas for writing, using a variety of strategies and print, electronic, and other resources, as appropriate	Writing Prompt	Writing Prompt
11W1.4 identify, sort, and order main ideas and supporting details for writing tasks, using a variety of strategies and selecting the organizational pattern best suited to the content and the purpose for writing	Writing Prompt	32, Writing Prompt
11W1.5 determine whether the ideas and information gathered are accurate and complete, interesting, and effectively meet the requirements of the writing task	Writing Prompt	Writing Prompt
11W2.0 IS MISSING		
11W2.1 write for different purposes and audiences using a variety of literary, informational, and graphic forms	Writing Prompt	Writing Prompt
11W2.2 establish a distinctive voice in their writing, modifying language and tone skilfully and effectively to suit the form, audience, and purpose for writing	Writing Prompt	Writing Prompt
11W2.3 use appropriate descriptive and evocative words, phrases, and expressions imaginatively to make their writing clear, vivid, and interesting for their intended audience	Writing Prompt	Writing Prompt
11W2.4 write complete sentences that communicate their meaning clearly and effectively, skilfully varying sentence type, structure, and length to suit different purposes and making smooth and logical transitions between ideas	Writing Prompt	Writing Prompt
11W2.5 explain, with increasing insight, how their own beliefs, values, and experiences are revealed in their writing	Writing Prompt	Writing Prompt
11W2.6 revise drafts to improve the content, organization, clarity, and style of their written work, using a variety of teacher-modelled strategies	Writing Prompt	Writing Prompt
11W2.7 produce revised drafts of texts, including increasingly complex texts, written to meet criteria identified by the teacher, based on the curriculum expectations	Writing Prompt	Writing Prompt
11W3.0 IS MISSING		
11W3.1 use knowledge of spelling rules and patterns, a variety of resources, and appropriate strategies to recognize and correct their own and others' spelling errors	Writing Prompt	Writing Prompt
11W3.2 build vocabulary for writing by confirming word meaning(s) and reviewing and refining word choice, using a variety of resources and strategies, as appropriate for the purpose	29, 30, 35, 44, 45, 56, 57, Writing Prompt	Writing Prompt
11W3.3 use punctuation correctly and effectively to communicate their intended meaning		56
11W3.4 use grammar conventions correctly and appropriately to communicate their intended meaning clearly and effectively	42, Writing Prompt	Writing Prompt
11W3.5 regularly proofread and correct their writing	Writing Prompt	Writing Prompt
11W3.6 use a variety of presentation features, including print and script, fonts, graphics, and layout, to improve the clarity and coherence of their written work and to heighten its appeal and effectiveness for their audience	Writing Prompt	Writing Prompt
11W3.7 produce pieces of published work to meet criteria identified by the teacher, based on the curriculum expectations	Writing Prompt	Writing Prompt

Practice Test 1 = 58/64 = 91%

Practice Test 2 = 56/61 = 92%

PRACTICE TEST 1

Read the following passage to answer questions 1 to 10.

BIG WORDS

With the Lord of Loquacity on trial in Chicago and schools playing down language to level the playing field, is the mind-expanding power of a well-stocked vocabulary becoming a thing of the past? Ian Brown digs into his dictionary.

The last days of long words! The sunset of syntactical surplusage!

In Chicago, in a downtown courtroom, lawyer Edward Greenspan won't let Conrad Black take the stand.

The problem is Mr. Black's fondness for whacking big words: *tricoteuses* (knitters of yarn, used to describe reporters and gossips, augmented by the adjective "braying"), *planturous* (fleshy), *poltroon* (a coward, a.k.a. former Quebec premier Robert Bourassa), *spavined* (lame), *dubiety* (doubt: Mr. Black rarely uses a simple word where a splashy lemma will do), *gasconading* (blustering) and *velleities* (distant hopes), to list just a few of his verbal smatterings. Mr. Greenspan fears the Lord's lingualism will turn off the jury.

Meanwhile in Toronto, at the Ryerson School of Journalism, Ivor Shapiro is teaching his class to write clearly. The I is Early Modern Factory—flat window, false ceiling of black metal grille to make the room seem less cavernous, giant TV suspended in a corner like a moody spider.

"One has to tell students in journalism school to express themselves simply, because they have been taught in high school to use big words in an effort to impress their professors," Mr. Shapiro says.

To do this, he has handed out a story called "Dead Reckoning," by journalist Veronica Cusack, an account of an autopsy performed on a 17-year-old boy who committed suicide. The students—and this happens every time, without exception—object to the last paragraph, in which the writer employs the word "quiddity."

"'Why would she use a big word when she could use "essence?"' they ask," Mr. Shapiro says. "So there is something about a $10 word that calls out to them. I feel, myself, really caught. If she makes you go and use a dictionary because you didn't know the word, is that really so terrible a thing?"

These days, apparently, it is. A number of people are getting alarmed. And this isn't just a minor trend, or a sentimental longing for long-word-ed days of yore. It turns out that having a good vocabulary is shatteringly important.

It's fairly easy to teach our little geniuses to read. But how well they understand, and how much they learn for the rest of their lives, depends directly on how many words they acquire before they turn 18.

Which is a gargantuan (*adj*. enormous, gigantic) problem. "While North American teachers have become more effective at teaching students to read words, we have virtually ignored the impact of teaching students to understand words, especially in the primary grades," is the conclusion reached in a new and frighteningly comprehensive study by Andrew Biemiller, a professor at the University of Toronto.

This is the revenge of the Flashcard parents. If Little Princess is an average child, she'll know 6,000 root-word meanings by the end of Grade 2. That's okay, but nothing special: At that point, the top 25 per cent of children already know twice as many words as the lowest 25 per cent, and the gap grows exponentially. Roughly 35,000 more words get stuffed into Little Princess's average head by the time she leaves high school.

But by then the foundation of her so-called mind has hardened. Limited by early lexical laxity, the average North American adult knows only 30,000 to 60,000 words, out of a potential "working vocabulary" of 700,000. If only Little Princess had learned more words earlier! If only you were a better parent!

Children who live in "advantaged" homes—where new words are considered important and bandied about—hear three times as many words as kids who don't. And those who don't are at "considerable risk of continued low achievement," Prof. Biemiller says.

You don't need a vocabulary to see the point: A home, a city or a society where people appreciate and share their vocabularies, where they take public pleasure in using language, is a place with a future where the lights are on.

NO LONGER PUT TO THE TEST

Unfortunately, the trend across society is in the exact opposite direction. Debate and confusion over the value of having a vocabulary have even infected international politics. Last spring, Gilles de Robien, France's Education Minister, declared that schools in suburban Paris would teach more grammar and vocabulary to integrate immigrants and prevent future riots. The British Minister of State for Schools, Jim Knight, immediately called this Frenchie rot. He insisted that grammar and vocabulary are elitist, and therefore are what *cause* youth riots.

In the U.S., the Educational Testing Service has spent the past decade snipping vocabulary-specific bits and pieces off the Scholastic Aptitude Test (the SAT), its famous college-entrance exam. Jonathan Arak, a tutor and trainer for the Princeton Review, a company that preps students for such exams, maintains that 40 per cent of American colleges pay little or no attention to sections of the test that emphasize vocabulary. (Then again, 730 colleges use no entrance test at all.) The ETS in turn takes its orders from the College Board, the organization of U.S. colleges and secondary schools that has overseen university admission since 1900.

In 1994, the ETS dropped its antonym test, in which prospective students had to pick the opposite of a given word from a list of choices. The even subtler analogy test (collar is to dog as yoke is to___) was next to go, in 2005. The latest SAT is longer, emphasizes more math and relies on essays and sentence completion tasks instead.

"The last two changes have de-emphasized vocabulary," Mr. Arak admits. "I would guess it's to even the playing field for students who have English as a second language."

Completing a sentence with a word from a list is easier because the sentence provides context. Mr. Arak, who is 42, openly admits that the verbal comprehension of students he has today is no match for that of kids he taught 19 years ago. He blames a generation of baby-boom educators and a school system that began to fail when he was a student.

"I didn't have weekly vocabulary quizzes," he admits. "I never took grammar."

No wonder a small industry has popped up to serve holdouts who still believe it's important to learn new words. Last March, during "Win With Words Week," the GSN Corporation and Princeton Review sponsored the first televised National Vocabulary ConteSt. High-school students across the country competed for $40,000 in prizes.

Harriet Brand, director of public relations for Princeton Review, thinks the National Vocabulary Contest might eventually wipe the National Spelling Bee off the blackboard.

"The reality is," Ms. Brand insists, "God gave us spell-check. And what is spelling? It's about precocious kids, most of whom are homeschooled. A vocabulary competition, on the other hand, is just very different and special. It's literally going to improve their lives. So it's a much more practical skill than a spelling bee."…

THE WORD WARIORS

Where the argument over the importance of big words is now set to rage anew, however, is in universities across North America, in the Next Great Battle between the linguists and the logophiles.

The linguists, who have the upper hand at the moment, are very much of a type. They tend to be acolytes of American scholar William Labov, who developed the concept of code-switching. Standard vocabulary doesn't need to be taught, the Labovites claim, because there's no such thing as a standard vocabulary.

"I think that the status of one's vocabulary varies with the context," says Duke University's Cathy Davidson, a professor of English and a Labovite herself. "What linguists call 'code switching' is more prevalent than ever. And that's typically where you're moving from one economic level to another: You practise one vernacular in the 'hood and then, if you're a lawyer, say, you switch."

One Labovates oneself up or down the social ladder by mastering a new vocabulary at each rung. In the old days, this was a straightforward trick of learning the language of the establishment….

But that was before television, technology and immigration fractured the very idea of a standard vocabulary and a standard establishment. These days, students in public schools in cities such as Toronto and Los Angeles hail from at least 50 different language groups. Prime-time TV has its own specialized (and simplified) vocabulary, as do pop culture and cellphones and the Internet. Teaching a standard vocabulary today isn't just ineffective: According to the linguists, it's undemocratic and limiting.

Some of the most militant linguists are Canadian. Clive Beck, a professor of education at the Ontario Institute for Studies in Education, relishes the collapse of the standard Western vocabulary. "I think it's partly democratization, of getting teachers to have a closer relationship with their students, and being able to talk on the same level. I love correctness in speech and in writing. But I think to some extent I have to go with the change."

Betwixt, for instance, "is just an old-fashioned word. So you shouldn't use it. *Nefarious*, people don't understand it, so don't use it. I think it does put a distance between you and especially young people if you use an old-fashioned word. True, some people like to be old-fashioned. But I think the world is changing so rapidly that we should change with it. So if you don't explain what it means, you waste people's time."

And the pleasure, the actual fun of knowing and using and privately sharing a word like, say, *sciagraphy*?

"My advice to people is to get pleasure out of explaining things clearly. You have to give up things you love. But then you can have a really great connection with people." …

'I REALY DO DESPAIR'

The logophiles, meanwhile, are merely waiting. They know this battle—between those who believe words should be useful and those who believe they should be beautiful too—is age-old, and stretches back to what even Cathy Davidson calls "grumpy ancient Roman orators."

Thomas Delworth, a senior ambassador in Canada's foreign service in Germany, Sweden, Hungary and Indonesia, and a former provost of Trinity College at the University of Toronto, is a classic of the type.

Verbal precision matters to diplomats, even when they have to be intentionally imprecise. Mr. Delworth is the kind of guy who, when you ask how many dictionaries he owns, says, "You mean just the ones in English?" and means it unpretentiously….

He blames the cheesy easiness of e-mail for the barren state of our word cupboards. He also blames the linguists, "who believe all is flux and change. I think that's just absurd. How can a dictionary be anything other than normative? What's it for? A word is as it has been used by educated people to convey an idea. Although I realize I must sound like something out of Noah's Ark."…

Why bother to go fancy when plain would suffice? Because you can. Veronica Cusack, who wrote the article that Ryerson students love to hate, fished out *quiddity* "because it was so unbearably sad—a 17- or 18-year-old man, and who he was had been obliterated by stepping off a 20-storey balcony. And who was he? And what was he? And there was something about that word that said it." Something ancient, as timeless as the end of life. *Quiddity* is an old word from medieval Latin, from the root *quid*, "what." She was describing the *what* of the boy.

And the junior journalists who are upset that she used a word they didn't know? "I don't think there is really anything wrong with expecting a reader to go to a dictionary," Ms. Cusack says, "though not in the Conrad Black sense, where you have to use it four times in a sentence. There are people who tell me they don't understand some of the words I use. But probably, being a total snob, I just think, 'Well, that's your problem.'"

Will Sheff, the lead singer and songwriter for the Austin, Tex., band Okkervil River, claims to be offended when his band is described as literary and bookish—"as if pop music is ennobled when it has some kind of literary aspirations," he recently told the magazine *The Believer*. But Mr. Sheff also wrote "So Come Back, I Am Waiting", a song, by his own description, "with all these big words in it": *Killing softly and serial/ He lifts his head, horned, handsome, magisterial He's the smell of the moonlight wysteria/ He's the thrill of the abecedarian.*

Mr. Sheff said he was being ironic. “I would hope that people don’t think that the big words are what makes the song good. The big words are my attempt to be pretentious in a way that’s hopefully, maybe, wry? ‘Oh, my God, can I really get away with this?’”

But Mr. Sheff is a logophile, make no mistake. To be serious about language, and all it can do—which is anything—means playing its game, taking pleasure in it.

Vivian Rakoff, chairman emeritus of the department of psychiatry at the University of Toronto, and one of the more articulate human beings on the planet, believes our resistance to big words is part of a bigger crankiness—“the suspicion of smart people, the well-rehearsed criticism of the Churchillian stance, that you shouldn’t appear to be smart.... There is a general suspicion of the man of many words. It’s ancient, but it’s still there.”

Shakespeare knew that. His most courageous characters, the advisers and soldiers who dare to tell their lords the truth, are all plain speakers...

But Shakespeare loved all words, so he used the big ones too, to make constant fun of vain, loquacious men...

‘SCINTILATE, SCINTILATE’

The truth is that we mistrust and love long words at the same time, drawn to simplicity, longing for complication. The dilemma is built into the English language itself—its Germanic roots short and feisty, its Latinate legs longer and knotted, veined with “skeins of verbosity." (Dr. Rakoff illustrates the difference by reciting the Latinate version of “Twinkle, Twinkle, Little Star”: “Scintillate, scintillate, globule vivific/Would I could fathom thy matter specific/Lustily proud in the ether capacious/Strongly resembling a gem carbonaceous.”)

At times a culture or a profession or a mind gets stuck in one river or the other; sometimes we take them on as national traits. “It was striking when I came to Canada,” Dr. Rakoff says. “I didn’t learn it enough, but there is general value placed here on shutting up.”

The Irish (novels), the Italians (opera), the Germans (philosophy), the English (more lyric poetry than any culture on earth) are more famously blabbermouthed: They can’t stop words spilling from their lips because they can’t shut off their brains. “The more words you have,” Dr. Rackoff says, “the more ideas you have.”

Conrad Black may be so verbose as to have given big words a bad name, and he may or may not be guilty of some legal malfeasance, but what we notice, and are wary of, and can’t help listening to night after night on the news, is the way his mind keeps shouting out through his vocabulary.

“There may be two Blacks,” Dr. Rakoff speculates. “There’s obviously the businessman. And then there’s the other guy, who is genuinely excited by history and by words and by facts. Oddly, I think the businessman would like most to be admired as the writer and thinker he is." That would explain the endless e-mails.

Because this is the solid thing about words, long or short: They wait for anyone who wants them, and cost nothing. You can use rare words for an ultra-efficient purpose, and you can juggle them for pleasure. But take the pleasure out of their use, and people stop using them.

"I don't think there is any goal in having a vocabulary," Thomas Delworth says from his perch toward the end of his rich spoken and written life. "I think it is its own reward. I can't give you a cost-effectiveness breakdown. You simply have a somewhat larger grasp of this vast empire you might command."

The alternative is that we use fewer and fewer of them, until the world is small enough that one word alone will suffice: *Duh.* (*Interjection.* Used to express actual or feigned ignorance or stupidity.)

—*by* Ian Brown

1. Mr. Greenspan does not want Mr. Black to take the stand because

A. Mr. Black's vocabulary may irritate the jury.

B. Mr. Black is disrespectful of flowery language.

C. Mr. Black may seem intolerant in the jury's view.

D. Mr. Greenspan does not wish to appear uneducated.

2. The main function of paragraph three is to

A. raise an objection and propose a reasonable way to correct it

B. clarify the nature of an annoying habit and its inevitable effect

C. present a dilemma and argue for the less harmful of two choices

D. identify a personal quirk and offer suggestions to minimize its effect

3. The quotation "giant TV suspended in a corner like a moody spider" contains an example of which of the following literary devices?

A. Simile

B. Metaphor

C. Hyperbole

D. Personification

4. The description "Early Modern Factory" is best understood to imply that the decor is

A. outdated, cold, and work-oriented

B. cluttered, business-like, and practical

C. comfortable, functional, and spacious

D. stuffy, formal, and extremely confining

5. Mr. Shapiro's **main** stylistic concern is to have his students write
   - **A.** simply, so as to make their thoughts clear
   - **B.** with effectively placed, challenging words
   - **C.** with a rich vocabulary to show their knowledge `
   - **D.** factually, by downplaying the use of descriptive details

6. The fact that teachers have become more effective in teaching their students to read is ironic because
   - **A.** students are no longer taught how to comprehend what they have read
   - **B.** the potential working vocabulary in the English language is 700 000 words
   - **C.** an individual's capacity to learn begins to shrink around the time of graduation
   - **D.** students learn a little more than 16% of their word power by the end of Grade 2

7. Which of the following statements **best** summarizes Dr. Biemiller's implied thesis?
   - **A.** Children living in disadvantaged homes are inclined to work harder.
   - **B.** North American teachers are failing to prepare their students adequately.
   - **C.** Aging reduces an individual's capacity to learn and to use richer vocabulary.
   - **D.** Children should be encouraged to experiment with new vocabulary at a young age.

8. The British Minister of State for Education is against the teaching of more grammar and vocabulary because
   - **A.** he is against French methods of education
   - **B.** it is extremely expensive and of dubious academic value
   - **C.** it promotes a feeling of superiority and may very well contribute to civil unrest
   - **D.** most British colleges are dropping entrance exams, so these higher standards are not necessary

9. The **best** definition of the word "analogy" as it used in this passage is a
   - **A.** solution to a mathematical problem
   - **B.** scientific procedure for recording sounds
   - **C.** type of dilemma that favours one element
   - **D.** favourable comparison between two things

10. According to the speaker, the move away from higher expectations in the area of vocabulary instruction is the result of the following conditions **except**
   - **A.** an inability to maintain adequate funding for educational institutes
   - **B.** an invasive pop culture that generates its own common vocabulary
   - **C.** the failure of school systems to maintain higher language standards
   - **D.** a desire to meet the needs of an increasing and varied ESL population

Read the following passage to answer questions 11 to 19.

OF CHILDREN

And a woman who held a babe against her bosom
said, Speak to us of Children.
And he said:
Your children are not your children.
They are the sons and daughters of Life's longing for itself.

They come through you but not from you,
And though they are with you yet they belong not to you.

You may give them your love but not your thoughts,
For they have their own thoughts.
You may house their bodies but not their souls,
For their souls dwell in the house of tomorrow, which you cannot visit, not even in your dreams.
You may strive to be like them, but seek not to make them like you.
For life goes not backward nor tarries with yesterday.

You are the bows from which your children as living arrows are sent forth.
The archer sees the mark upon the path of the infinite, and He bends you with His might that His arrows may go swift and far.
Let your bending in the archer's hand be for gladness;
For even as He loves the arrow that flies, so He loves also the bow that is stable.

—*by* Kahlil Gibran

11. The male figure to whom the woman speaks at the beginning of the poem is **most likely**

A. her doctor

B. a wise man

C. her husband

D. a mature teen

12. The phrase "Life's longing / for itself" **most likely** means that

A. Life must patiently await what the future brings

B. Life ends and changes in substance and form

C. living things naturally desire to reproduce

D. living things are attracted to each other

life keeps continuing for it's own purpose

13. The last three lines of the first stanza are **best** summarized by the phrase

A. children are often disobedient

B. parents must hang on to their children

C. parents cannot buy their children's love

D. children are free and independent beings

children are not your children but's life children.

14. The phrase "Speak to us of Children" is **most likely** a request for advice on how to

A. raise children

B. shape children's thoughts

C. protect children from harm

D. motivate children to be successful

15. In Stanza 2, the speaker cautions parents to avoid doing all of the following actions **except**

A. encouraging your children to live as you do

B. supporting your children in developing their interests

C. choosing the type of people your children should befriend

D. teaching your children to believe that wealth leads to happiness

16. According to the speaker, one problem with encouraging children to be like their parents is that

A. children can pick up bad habits from even the most caring parents

B. parents can be overprotective, and they sometimes bend the truth

C. a child's evolving world differs from that of his or her parents'

D. children typically find it difficult to learn from their parents

17. Which of the following statements **best** paraphrases the implied meaning of the quotation "For life goes not backward nor tarries with/yesterday"?

A. What was good enough for my grandfather is good enough for me.

B. What was valid and true on Monday may not be so on Friday.

C. You will be a success if you learn how to "go with the flow."

D. There is little to be gained in crying over spilt milk.

18. The quotation, "You are the bows from which your children as / living arrows are sent forth," contains an example of which of the following literary devices?

A. Personification

B. Metaphor

C. Allusion

D. Simile

19. The archer is **most likely** representative of

A. Mother Nature

B. an omnipotent god

C. a soldier of fortune

D. a respected ancestor

Read the following passage to answer questions 20 to 30.

A FABLE FOR TOMORROW

Rachel Carson (1907–64) was an American scientist and writer. She is best known for her popular books about oceanography, Under the Sea Wind *(1941) and* The Sea Around Us *(1951), and for* Silent Spring *(1962), which fired one of the first shots in what has come to be called the environmental movement. The book discusses the pollution resulting from the massive and indiscriminate use of fertilizers and pesticides, a problem which most Americans were ignorant of until Carson's warning. The following paragraphs are the opening of* Silent Spring.

There was once a town in the heart of America where all life seemed to live in harmony with its surroundings. The town lay in the midst of a checkerboard of prosperous farms, with fields of grain and hillsides of orchards where, in spring, white clouds of bloom drifted above the green fields. In autumn, oak and maple and birch set up a blaze of colour that flamed and flickered across a backdrop of pines. Then foxes barked in the hills and deer silently crossed the fields, half hidden in the mists of the autumn mornings.

Along the roads, laurel, viburnum and alder, great ferns and wildflowers delighted the traveller's eye through much of the year. Even in winter the roadsides were places of beauty, where countless birds came to feed on the berries and on the seed heads of the dried weeds rising above the snow. The countryside was, in fact, famous for the abundance and variety of its bird life, and when the flood of migrants was pouring through in spring and autumn people travelled from great distances to observe them. Others came to fish the streams, which flowed clear and cold out of the hills and contained shady pools where trout lay. So it had been from the days many years ago when the first settlers raised their houses, sank their wells, and built their barns.

Then a strange blight crept over the area and everything began to change. Some evil spell had settled on the community: mysterious maladies swept the flocks of chickens; the cattle and sheep sickened and died. Everywhere was a shadow of death. The farmers spoke of much illness among their families. In the town the doctors had become more and more puzzled by new kinds of sickness appearing among their patients. There had been several sudden and unexplained deaths, not only among adults but even among children, who would be stricken suddenly while at play and die within a few hours.

There was a strange stillness. The birds, for example—where had they gone? Many people spoke of them, puzzled and disturbed. The feeding stations in the backyards were deserted. The few birds seen anywhere were moribund; they trembled violently and could not fly. It was a spring without voices. On the mornings that had once throbbed with the dawn chorus of robins, catbirds, doves, jays, wrens, and scores of other bird voices there was now no sound; only silence lay over the fields and woods and marsh.

On the farms the hens brooded, but no chicks hatched. The farmers complained that they were unable to raise any pigs—the litters were small and the young survived only a few days. The apple trees were coming into bloom but no bees droned among the blossoms, so there was no pollination and there would be no fruit.

The roadsides, once so attractive, were now lined with browned and withered vegetation as though swept by fire. These, too, were silent, deserted by all living things. Even the streams were now lifeless. Anglers no longer visited them, for all the fish had died.

In the gutters under the eaves and between the shingles of the roofs, a white granular powder still showed a few patches; some weeks before it had fallen like snow upon the roofs and the lawns, the fields and streams.

No witchcraft, no enemy action had silenced the rebirth of new life in this stricken world. The people had done it themselves.

This town does not actually exist, but it might easily have a thousand counterparts in America or elsewhere in the world. I know of no community that has experienced all the misfortunes I describe. Yet every one of these disasters has actually happened somewhere, and many real communities have already suffered a substantial number of them. A grim spectre has crept upon us almost unnoticed, and this imagined tragedy may easily become a stark reality we all shall know.

What has already silenced the voices of spring in countless towns in America? This book is an attempt to explain.

—*by* Rachel Carson

20. A fable can **best** be described as

A. an imaginative story usually set in nature
B. a brief narrative illustrating a moral truth
C. an historical account of a famous person
D. a humorous tale often featuring animals

21. The phrase "a checkerboard of prosperous farms" refers to the

A. geometric arrangement of farm houses and barns
B. crisscross pattern of the town's streets and alleys
C. alternating colours of fields growing different crops
D. clear differences between successful and rich farmers

22. The phrase "white clouds of bloom" contains an example of which of the following literary devices?

A. Simile
B. Paradox
C. Hyperbole = exaggeration
D. Metonymy = expression used as a substitute

washington for US federal gov

23. The phrase "white clouds of bloom" refers to

A. swirling blossoms caught in the wind

B. billowing dust created by a harvester

C. flocks of birds returning to the farm

D. the chemical haze of fertilizer spray

24. The phrase "a blaze of colour that flamed and flickered across a backdrop of pines" contains an example of which of the following literary devices?

A. Simile

B. Alliteration

C. Onomatopoeia

D. Personification

25. The phrase "delighted the traveller's eye" refers to the

A. bountiful and neatly arranged fields of many crops

B. variety and beauty of nature's untamed plant life

C. groomed and landscaped estates of the wealthy

D. white farm fences framing the various crops

26. The phrase "flood of migrants" refers to

A. birds arriving to feed off the crops

B. the types of fish caught in the spring

C. people arriving in the spring and fall

D. the many labourers who harvested crops

27. In the phrase "So it had been from the days many years ago when the first settlers raised their houses," the word "so" means

A. how

B. thus

C. since

D. therefore

28. The first two paragraphs of the opening of *Silent Spring* accomplish all of the following literary purposes **except**

A. creating a positive atmosphere

B. establishing a clear conflict

C. implying a regrettable loss

D. describing a rural setting

29. A synonym for the word "blight," as it is used in "Then a strange blight crept over the area," is

A. curse

B. disease

C. creature

D. darkness

30. The word "moribund" means

A. dead

B. quiet

C. dying

D. energized

Read the following passage to answer questions 31 to 43.

DO SEEK THEIR MEAT FROM GOD

One side of the ravine was in darkness. The darkness was soft and rich, suggesting thick foliage. Along the crest of the slope tree-tops came into view—great pines and hemlocks of the ancient unviolated forest—revealed against the orange disk of a full moon just rising. The low rays… lit strangely the upper portion of the opposite steep—the western wall of the ravine, barren … with great rocky projections and harsh with stunted junipers….

Out of a shadowy hollow behind a long white rock, on the lower edge of that part of the steep which lay in the moonlight, came softly a great panther… . He lifted his smooth round head to gaze on the increasing flame, which presently he greeted with a shrill cry… a summons to his mate, telling her that the hour had come when they should seek their prey. From the lair behind the rock, where the cubs were being suckled by their dam, came no immediate answer… .

The panther walked restlessly up and down, half a score of paces each way, along the edge of the shadow, keeping his wide-open green eyes upon the rising light. His short, muscular tail twitched impatiently, but he made no sound. Soon the breadth of confused brightness had spread itself farther down the steep, disclosing the foot of the white rock, and the bones and antlers of deer which had been… devoured.

By this time the cubs had made their meal, and their dam was ready… . She glided supplely forth into the glimmer, raised her head, and screamed at the moon in a voice as terrible as her mate's… and the two beasts, noiselessly mounting the steep, stole into the shadows of the forest that clothed the high plateau.

The panthers were fierce with hunger. These two days past their hunting had been… fruitless. What scant prey they had slain had for the most part been devoured by the female: for had she not those small blind cubs at home to nourish, who soon must suffer at any lack of hers? The settlements of late had been making great inroads on the world of ancient forest, driving before them the deer and smaller game. [Consequently] the sharp hunger of the panther parents and hence it came that on this night they hunted together. They purposed to steal upon the settlements in their sleep, and take tribute of the enemies' flocks. Through the dark of the thick woods, here and there pierced by the moonlight, they moved swiftly and silently… . For an hour the noiseless journeying continued… . Suddenly there fell upon their ears, far off and faint, but clearly defined against the vast stillness of the Northern forest, a sound which made those stealthy hunters pause and lift their heads. It was the voice of a child crying–crying long and loud, hopelessly, as if there were no one by to comfort it. The panthers turned aside from their former course and glided toward the sound. They were not yet come to the outskirts of the settlement, but they knew of a solitary cabin lying in the thick of the woods a mile and more from the nearest neighbour… they bent their way, fired with fierce hope. Soon would they break their bitter fast.

Up to noon of the previous day the lonely cabin had been occupied. Then its owner, a shiftless fellow, who spent his days for the most part at the corner tavern three miles distant, had suddenly grown disgusted with a land wherein one must work to live, and had betaken himself with his seven-year-old boy to seek some more indolent clime. During the long lonely days when his father was away at the tavern the little boy had been wont to visit the house of the next neighbour, to play with a child of some five summers, who had no other playmate. The next neighbour was a prosperous pioneer, being master of a substantial frame-house in the midst of large and well-tilled clearing. At times, though rarely, because it was forbidden, the younger child would make his way by a rough wood road to visit his poor little disreputable playmate. At length it had appeared that the five-year-old was learning unsavoury language from the elder boy, who rarely had an opportunity of hearing speech more desirable. To the bitter grief of both children the companionship had at length been stopped by unalterable decree of the master of the frame-house.

Hence it had come to pass that the little boy was unaware of his comrade's departure. Yielding at last to an eager longing for that comrade, he had stolen away late in the afternoon, traversed… the lonely stretch of wood road, and reached the cabin, only to find it empty. The door, on its leathern hinges, swung idly open. The one room had been stripped of its few poor furnishings. After looking in the rickety shed… the child had seated him self on the hacked threshold, and sobbed passionately with a grief that he did not fully comprehend. Then seeing the shadows lengthen across the tiny clearing, he had grown afraid to start for home. As the dusk gathered, he has crept trembling into the cabin, whose door would not stay shut. When it grew quite dark, he crouched in the inmost corner of the room, desperate with fear and loneliness, and lifted up his voice piteously… startling the unexpectant night and piercing the forest depths, even to the ears of those great beasts which had set forth to seek their meat from God.

The lonely cabin stood some distance, perhaps a quarter of a mile, back from the highway connecting the settlements. Along this main road a man was plodding wearily. All day he had been walking, and now as he neared home his steps began to quicken with anticipation of reSt. Over his shoulder projected a double-barrelled fowling-piece, from which was slung a bundle of such necessities as he had purchased in town that morning. It was the prosperous settler, the master of the frame-house. His mare being with foal, he had chosen to make the tedious journey on foot.

The settler passed the mouth of the wood road leading to the cabin… when his ears were started by the sound of a child crying in the woods. He stopped, lowered his burden to the road, and stood straining ears and eyes in the direction of the sound. It was just at this time, that the two panthers also stopped and lifted their heads to listen. Their ears were keener than those of the man, and the sound had reached them at a greater distance.

Presently the settler realized whence the cries were coming. He called to mind the cabin, but he did not know the cabin's owner had departed. He cherished a hearty contempt for the drunken squatter; and on the drunken squatter's child he looked with small favour, especially as a playmate for his own boy. Nevertheless, he hesitated before resuming his journey.

'Poor little devil!' he muttered, half in wrath. 'I reckon his precious father's drunk down at "the Corners", and him crying for loneliness!' Then he reshouldered his burden and strode on doggedly.

But louder, shriller, more hopeless and more appealing, arose the childish voice, and the settler paused again, irresolute and with deepening indignation. In his fancy he saw the steaming supper his wife would have awaiting him. He loathed the thought of retracing his steps, and then stumbling a quarter of a mile through the stumps and bog of the wood road. He was foot-sore as well as hungry, and he cursed the vagabond squatter with serious emphasis; but in that wailing was a terror which would not let him go on. He thought of his own little one left in such a position, and straightway his heart melted. He turned, dropped his bundle behind some bushes, grasped his gun, and made speed back for the cabin.

'Who knows,' he said to himself, 'but that drunken idiot has left his youngster without a bite to eat in the whole miserable shanty? Or may be he's locked out, and the poor little beggar's half scared to death. Sounds as if he was scared'; and at that thought the settler quickened his pace.

As the hungry panthers drew near the cabin and the cries of the lonely child grew clearer, they hastened their steps, and their eyes opened to a wider circle, flaming with a greener fire. It would be thoughtless superstition to say the beasts were cruel. They were simply keen with hunger and alive with the eager passion of the chase. They were not ferocious with any anticipation of battle, for they knew the voice was the voice of a child, and something in the voice told them the child was solitary. Theirs was no hideous or unnatural rage, as it is the custom to describe it. They were but seeking with the strength, the cunning, the deadly swiftness given them to that end, the food convenient for them. On their success in accomplishing that for which nature had so exquisitely designed them depended not only their own but the lives of their blind and helpless young, now whimpering in the cave on the slope of the moonlit ravine. They crept through a wet alder thicket, bounded lightly over the ragged brush fence, and paused to reconnoitre on the edge of the clearing in the full glare of the moon. At the same moment the settler emerged from the darkness of the wood-road on the opposite side of the clearing. He saw the two great beasts, heads down and snouts thrust forward, gliding toward the open cabin door.

For a few moments the child had been silent. Now his voice rose again in pitiful appeal, a very ecstasy of loneliness and terror. There was a note in the cry that shook the settler's soul. He had a vision of his own boy, at home with his mother, safeguarded from even the thought of peril. And here was this little one left to the wild beasts! 'Thank God! Thank God I came!' murmured the settler, as he dropped on one knee to take a sure aim. There was a loud report (not like the sharp crack of a rifle), and the female panther, shot through the loins, fell in a heap, snarling furiously and striking with her forepaws.

The male walked around her in fierce and anxious amazement. As the smoke lifted he discerned the settler keeling for a second shot. With a high screech of fury, the lithe brute sprang upon his enemy, taking a bullet full in his chest without seeming to know he was hit. Ere the man could slip in another cartridge the beast was upon him, bearing him to the ground and fixing keen fangs in his shoulder. Without a word, the man set his strong, fingers desperately into the brute's throat, wrenched himself partly free, and was struggling to rise when the panther's body collapsed upon him all at once, a dead weight which he easily flung aside. The bullet had done its work just in time.

Quivering from the swift and dreadful contest, bleeding profusely from his mangled shoulder, the settler stepped up to the cabin door and peered in. He heard sobs in the darkness.

'Don't be scared, sonny,' he said in a reassuring voice. 'I'm going to take you home along with me. Poor little lad, I'll look after you if folks that ought to don't."

Out of the dark corner came a shout of delight, in a voice which made the settler's heart stand still. 'Daddy, daddy,' it said, 'I knew you'd come. I was so frightened when it got dark!' And a little figure launched itself into the settler's arms and clung to him trembling. The man sat down on the threshold and strained the child to his breaSt. He remembered how near he had been to disregarding the far-off cries, and great beads of sweat broke out upon his forehead.

Not many weeks afterwards the settler was following the fresh trail of a bear which had killed his sheep. The trail led him at last along the slope of deep ravine, from whose bottom came the brawl of a swollen and obstructed stream. In the ravine he found a shallow cave, behind a great white rock. The cave was plainly a wild beast's lair, and he entered circumspectly. There were bones scattered about, and on some dry herbage in the deepest corner of the den he found the dead bodies, now rapidly decaying, of two small panther cubs.

—*by* Charles G.D. Roberts

31. The setting featured in the first two paragraphs is **best** described as

A. noisy and eventful

B. rugged and majestic

C. quiet but threatening

D. pitch black and mysterious

32. In the quotation "He lifted his smooth round head to gaze on the increasing flame, which presently he greeted with a shrill cry," the word "flame" **most likely** refers to

A. a threatening fire

B. the panther's mate

C. the early rising sun

D. light from the moon

flame emits light

33. The panther walks "restlessly" **most likely** because he

A. is frustrated by having to stand and wait for his mate

B. fears the dangers that likely lurk close by

C. has been kept up all night by his fidgety cubs

D. wants the joyful release associated with exercise

34. Viewed symbolically, the antlers and bones of the dead deer mentioned in the passage serve all of the following purposes **except** to

A. suggest that a kind of sickness exists in the forest

B. foreshadow the possibility of injury or death

C. establish the panther as a powerful predator

D. imply a dark, gloomy, or threatening setting

35. As it is used in the phrase "She glided supplely forth into the glimmer," the word "supplely" means

A. smoothly or nimbly

B. timidly or hesitantly

C. weakly and awkwardly

D. secretively but aggressively

supply smoothly.

36. Which of the following figures of speech is contained in the quotation "the shadows of the forest that clothed the high plateau"?

A. Simile

B. Metaphor

C. Hyperbole

D. Onomatopoeia

37. The female panther was likely **less** hungry than her mate because

A. she was a far better hunter than her mate

B. she was kept fed so that she could feed her cubs

C. as a hunter, the larger male required more food for energy

D. relaxing with her cubs most of the day meant she needed less food

38. The panthers were having difficulty finding food because

A. they had killed off most of the game in the region

B. the influx of settlers had forced the wild game away

C. they were unfamiliar with their new hunting territory

D. winter caused the hibernation or migration of their prey

inroads / house

39. The character of the crying child is **most likely** introduced to

A. develop sympathy for the blind and abandoned cubs

B. contribute to a setting seen as hostile and threatening

C. add to the plot by creating a dilemma for the panthers

D. create suspense by foreshadowing a threatening conflict

40. The phrase "The panthers turned aside from their former course" is **best** understood to mean that the panthers

A. were frightened by the sound of a human voice

B. planned to double back in order to hunt for deer

C. changed their plan when presented with easy prey

D. committed themselves to hunting nearby livestock

41. The style of language used in this passage is **best** described as

A. technical and lacking suspense

B. satirical and bitter, but insightful

C. dated, but rich in descriptive detail

D. casual or colloquial, but entertaining

42. Which of the following grammatical elements is not found in the quotation "He turned, dropped his bundle behind some bushes, grasped his gun, and made speed back for the cabin"?

A. Shift in tense

B. Parallel structure

C. Compound verbs

D. Prepositional phrases

43. The settler's initial reaction to the stranded child's wailing reveals him to be

A. calm and patient

B. decisive but cowardly

C. insensitive and self-centred

D. frustrated but compassionate

Read the following passage to answer questions 44 to 53.

ENCOURAGEMENT IS A TWO-EDGED SWORD

Please don't take exception to the fact that I'm a young aboriginal woman who's finishing her undergraduate degree.

Since I've started writing on this page, I've received e-mails from a few readers congratulating me on being in university.

"It's good to see that you're in university," is the general sentiment that's expressed, although one reader advised me that I must finish my studies in order to enhance my professional credibility as a journalist.

Now you're probably wondering why I'm bringing this up. It's good to have one's achievements and hard work recognized, right? Encouragement is desirable, isn't it? Well, of course, but what's undesirable are the implicit assumptions underlying the "encouragement" I've received.

If I weren't a young aboriginal woman who's finishing her undergraduate degree, but rather a young Euro-Canadian woman who was finishing her undergraduate degree, would any reader pick up on it and make a point of telling me what a fine example I'm setting? Would somebody tell me that I'd hurt my professional credibility as a journalist if I failed to complete my degree requirements? I doubt it, yet nobody seems to question the professional credibility of Avril Benoit and Naomi Klein, two young celebrated Canadian journalists who openly admit they're university dropouts. In fact, judging from biographical profiles of both women that I've read in the popular press, both regard their failure as a sign of their journalistic gifts; they were simply too much in demand as journalists to finish their studies. So what gives?

My aboriginal background and some people's perception of what it means to be an aboriginal in Canada today is what gives. To some, I'm an exception to the rule, which then begs the question: The rule of what? If I'm exceptional because I'm an aboriginal person who's dedicated the past few years of my life to my studies, then those who write me to congratulate me don't expect such behaviour from an aboriginal person. The implicit assumption is that I'm doing really well for an aboriginal person because we're perceived widely as being incapable of attaining certain levels of success as defined by non-aboriginal society.

This reasoning usually follows through to one of two predictable conclusions: Those aboriginal people who are "successful" must either be exceptional to escape their pathetic circumstances or they were raised with middle-class values in assimilated middle-class families, therefore, they're privileged, inauthentic representatives of aboriginal society.

Both conclusions are false and damning.

According to Plains Cree Métis writer and academic Emma LaRocque, being "exceptional is but another rung on the ghettoization ladder."

Those who are deemed exceptional are perceived as belonging to neither aboriginal society nor non-aboriginal society. They don't belong to aboriginal society because many Canadians assume that there's nothing inherent in contemporary aboriginal society that fosters excellence and success, only despair. (You've no idea how many non-aboriginal people who, upon meeting me for the first time, decry the pain I must have experienced, what with the high suicide rate and all those homeless aboriginal people living on the street!)

And they don't belong to non-aboriginal society because they're, quite frankly, aboriginal. In either case, they're suspect and must be segregated into another category known as the Aboriginal Intellectual Elite, which by its very moniker smacks of self-service.

The other extreme assumption, which is the question of privilege, is countered brilliantly by Cree/Métis writer Kim Anderson in her book *A Recognition of Being: Reconstructing Native Womanhood.* Anderson is the daughter of an upper-middle-class woman of predominantly English Protestant ancestry and a man of mixed Scottish, Cree, French and Saulteaux ancestry who is often taken to task by aboriginal and non-aboriginal people for her relatively privileged upbringing, which includes a university education, and her lighter skin.

She admits she's never experienced overt or violent prejudice, poverty, abuse and family breakdown that is accepted as the lot of the aboriginal majority. But she then turns this around by asking why these basic human rights are taken for granted as commonplace for most non-aboriginal Canadians, yet deemed as privileges for aboriginal people?

Why, indeed. For my part, I don't see much about my life or my choices that's exceptional, nor do I feel I'm breaking free from a predetermined life script that's dictated and imposed by cultural stereotypes about aboriginal people. I write, I study and I work for the same reasons everybody else does—their own—and fortunately I have the opportunity to do so. My only hope is that everybody has such freedom, because freedom isn't an exception to the rule, it is the rule we should all uphold, for your sake and mine.

—*by* Alison Blackduck

44. In the phrase "in order to enhance my professional credibility as a journalist," the word "credibility" means

A. salary

B. education

C. connections

D. believability

45. In the phrase "the implicit assumptions underlying the 'encouragement' I've received," the writer uses quotation marks around the word "'encouragement'" in order to indicate

A. recorded dialogue

B. a slang expression

C. technical language

D. a unique interpretation

46. Which of the following literary techniques does the writer primarily use in the fourth and fifth paragraphs of the passage?

A. Descriptive language

B. Supporting examples

C. Rhetorical questions

D. Humorous asides

47. The writer's reason for mentioning Avril Benoit and Naomi Klein in paragraph 5 is to

A. draw attention to two successful aboriginal women

B. show the negative consequences of dropping out

C. question the need for a course in journalism rehtorical questions

D. indicate the value of a university education

48. The "implicit assumption" underlying the encouragement the writer receives is that

A. non-aboriginals demand good English

B. aboriginals are typically unsuccessful

C. she writes exceptionally well

D. she is aboriginal

49. The sentence "So what gives?" is an example of

A. colloquialism or slang

B. professional jargon

C. a regional dialect

D. an ironic pun

50. The phrase, "being 'exceptional is but another rung on the ghettoization ladder'" contains an example of which of the following literary devices?

A. Simile

B. Metaphor

C. Hyperbole

D. Personification

51. The phrase "being 'exceptional is but another rung on the ghettoization ladder'" is best understood to mean that

A. education is a step-by-step process that eventually leads to achieving one's goals

B. following the rules forces a creative person to restrict his or her imagination

C. aboriginals must accomplish many things to overcome limiting stereotypes

D. all exceptionally gifted people eventually climb the ladder of success

52. The word that best expresses the meaning of the word "inherent" as it is used in the sentence "there's nothing inherent in contemporary aboriginal society that fosters excellence and success" is

A. inbred

B. magical

C. negative

D. uncommon

53. The fact that "successful" aboriginals are seen as not belonging in either aboriginal society or non-aboriginal society is a clear example of

A. foreshadowing

B. paradox

C. satire

D. irony

Read the following passage to answer questions 54 to 64.

FIELD OF VISION

I remember this woman who sat for years
In a wheelchair, looking straight ahead
Out the window at sycamore trees unleafing
And leafing at the far end of the lane

Straight out past the TV in the corner,
The stunted, agitated hawthorn bush,
The same small calves with their backs to wind and rain,
The same acre of ragwort, the same mountain.

She was steadfast as the big window itself.
Her brow was clear as the chrome bits of the chair.
She never lamented once and she never
Carried a spare ounce of emotional weight.

Face to face with her was an education
Of the sort you got across a well-braced gate—
One of those lean, clean, iron, roadside ones
Between two whitewashed pillars, where you could see

Deeper into the country than you expected
And discovered that the field behind the hedge
Grew more distinctly strange as you kept standing
Focused and drawn in by what barred the way.

—*by* Seamus Heaney

54. The phrase "sycamore trees unleafing/And leafing" suggests that

A. time is passing

B. the trees are diseased

C. it is a windy countryside

D. farmers harvest the leaves

55. The repetition of the phrase "the same" in the second stanza of the poem **most likely** suggests that the woman's view is

A. monotonous

B. challenging

C. comforting

D. unpleasant

56. A synonym for the word "steadfast" is

A. bored

B. trapped

C. unfeeling

D. unwavering

57. The setting described in the second stanza can **best** be characterized as

A. hostile

B. boring

C. natural

D. confusing

58. The sentence "Her brow was clear as the chrome bits of the chair" contains an example of which of the following figures of speech?

A. Simile

B. Metaphor

C. Oxymoron

D. Personification

59. The phrase "she never / Carried a spare ounce of emotional weight" suggests that the woman is

A. nervous

B. stubborn

C. accepting

D. unemotional

60. The phrase "those lean, clean, iron, roadside ones" contains an example of which of the following literary devices?

A. Onomatopoeia

B. Alliteration

C. Assonance

D. Metaphor

61. The speaker suggests that the woman received an education by

A. bringing the world closer through television

B. focusing attentively on the world around her

C. accepting her inability to see beyond her room

D. limiting the importance of what she could not touch

62. Which of the following literary devices is used in the title of the poem, "Field of Vision"?

A. Pun

B. Imagery

C. Paradox

D. Oxymoron

63. The speaker's attitude toward the woman in the wheelchair is **most likely** one of

A. pity

B. admiration

C. resentment

D. bewilderment

64. This type of poem is **best** referred to as

A. modern sonnet

B. free verse lyric

C. modified Haiku

D. traditional limerick

Writing Prompt

Write a narrative or essay that shows how an experience you have had has shaped or altered your life.

The following material may give you ideas for your writing.

A new member in the family

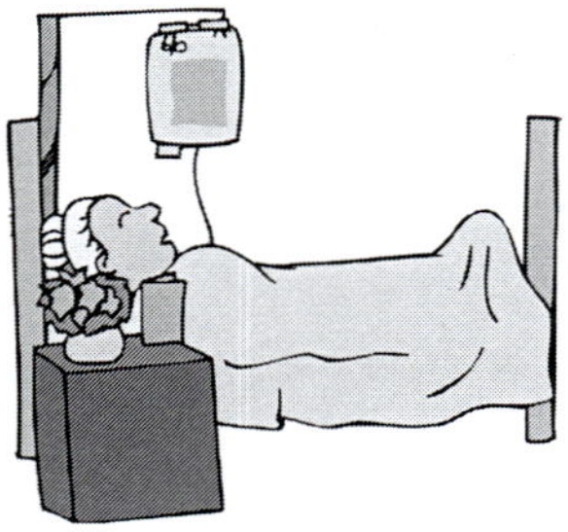

Being sick and in hospital

Changing Schools

Immigrating to a new country

A wedding in the family

Elderly grandparents moving in with you and your family

First they came for the Socialists, and I did not speak out—
because I was not a Socialist.

Then they came for the Trade Unionists, and I did not speak out—
because I was not a Trade Unionist.

Then they came for the Jews, and I did not speak out—
because I was not a Jew.

Then they came for me—and there was no one left to speak for me.

Martin Niemoller

Nothing is a waste of time if you use the experience wisely.

Auguste Rodin

Do you know the difference between education and experience? Education is when you read the fine print; experience is what you get when you don't.

Pete Seeger

If we could sell our experiences for what they cost us, we'd all be millionaires.

Abigail Van Buren

ANSWERS AND SOLUTIONS—PRACTICE TEST 1

1. A	14. A	27. B	40. C	53. D
2. B	15. B	28. B	41. C	54. A
3. A	16. C	29. B	42. A	55. A
4. A	17. B	30. C	43. D	56. D
5. A	18. B	31. B	44. D	57. A
6. D	19. B	32. D	45. D	58. A
7. C	20. B	33. A	46. C	59. C
8. C	21. C	34. A	47. C	60. C
9. D	22. D	35. A	48. B	61. B
10. A	23. A	36. B	49. A	62. A
11. B	24. B	37. B	50. B	63. B
12. C	25. B	38. B	51. C	64. B
13. D	26. A	39. D	52. A	

1. A

The lawyer, Mr. Greenspan, "fears the Lord's lingualism will turn off the jury." Since the colloquial expression "turn off" means to displease or irritate to the point of indifference, alternative **A** is the correct answer.

2. B

Paragraph three identifies Mr. Black's tendency to use "big words." His lawyer supports this by listing a series of uncommon vocabulary choices and their accompanying definitions. He then states that the effect of this habit of using inflated or uncommon word choices will "turn off the jury." With this in mind, alternative **B** is the most appropriate choice.

3. A

The comparison of the TV to a spider using the signal word *like* is an obvious example of a simile. **A** simile is an expressed comparison between two unlike objects using the linking words like or as.

4. A

The description is best understood to mean the decor is outdated, cold, and work-oriented. This is well-supported if one considers that the modern era began at the turn of the 20th century. Early Modern is consequently referring to the early 1900s. The decor from that period would certainly be considered outdated today. Furthermore, the reference to a turn-of-the-century factory connotes a variety of images: cold, spacious, production-oriented, noisy, dirty, and possibly dangerous. Each of the incorrect alternatives contains at least one descriptor that is unsuitable to such an image.

5. A

Shapiro is quoted as saying, "One has to tell students in journalism school to express themselves simply." Alternative **A** is the only alternative listed that is clearly supported by the text.

6. A

Since irony is the revealing of a discrepancy between what is logically expected and what actually takes place, alternative A is the answer to this question. One would expect that when teachers are more effective in teaching their students to read, this would be a sign of progress in literacy. However, the revelation that being able to read (presumably, to sound out words correctly) does not guarantee that students will actually understand what they read is ironic. The irony lies in the fact that because teachers are doing a better job in one area, students are doing poorly in another area.

7. D

Much of what Dr. Biemiller says develops the central idea that a larger vocabulary will likely lead to a brighter and consequently more successful individual, not to mention an enlightened society "where people appreciate and share their vocabularies, where they take public pleasure in using language." This belief is supported by the fact that there is a gap in word power that begins in elementary school and grows throughout life. That gap means that those at the lower end of vocabulary retention are at "considerable risk of continued low achievement." However, if conscientious parents encourage their children to experiment with vocabulary at a young age (**D**), both the child and society will ultimately be served.

8. C

The Minister's point is clearly summarized in the following statement: "He insisted that grammar and vocabulary are elitist, and therefore are what *cause* youth riots." Since "elitist" means superior or discriminatory, alternative **C** is the correct answer.

9. D

An analogy is defined as a likeness in some way between two things that are otherwise unlike. Alternative **D** is correct.

10. A

The speaker never mentions funding as a reason for the move away from higher vocabulary expectations. All of the other conditions listed in the alternatives are mentioned. The speaker states that the ability to capitalize on knowing the "language of the establishment" was easier when there was a standard language: "But that was before television, technology and immigration fractured the very idea of a standard vocabulary." The speaker also cites Mr. Arak, a tutor and trainer for the Princeton Review, who "blames a generation of baby-boom educators and a school system that began to fail when he was a student." Arak himself declared, "I didn't have weekly vocabulary quizzes… I never took grammar."

11. B

The woman is most likely addressing someone of age and experience in an attempt to gain advice. She is a young mother, and her husband would likely be close to the same age as her and equally inexperienced. Her doctor would be knowledgeable about children's physiology and the common health problems they encounter. However, it would be a wise man who imparts the advice featured in this poem, for he clearly appreciates the unique roles allotted to parent and child. Such wisdom would not likely come from a teen, no matter how mature, because a teenager has yet to experience the role of mature parent. Alternative **B** is best supported by the text.

12. C

In the context of a discussion about children, the speaker indicates that children are a product of something greater than the union of one man and one woman. He suggests that there is a natural stream of life that has gone on since the beginning of time. This stream or life force is a part of all living things and is manifest in the desire to regenerate or create a duplicate of oneself. In that respect, human sons and daughters are a product of "Life's longing for itself."

13. D

The speaker states that parents bear children ("They come through you") but acknowledges that they are part of a far greater life force than that of their parents ("but not from you"). They are part of "Life's longing / for itself," and consequently they are Life's children, not their parents'. The speaker is cautioning parents to avoid considering their children as their property—something they own and control. Rather, children should be viewed as free and independent beings.

14. A

Having read the first stanza, the student should be able to appreciate that the parents are seeking guidance on how best to raise their children. The woman who asks for advice is holding a baby to her breast, which suggests that she is a young mother. She is understandably seeking some indication as to what she should do for her child. Although each of the alternatives presents a possible choice, alternative A is the most general request. Each of the other choices implies an agenda or plan related to "shaping," "protecting," or "motivating" the children.

15. B

Only alternative **B** comes close to the expression of unconditional love that is implied in the stanza's opening line: "You may give them your love but not your / thoughts." Each of the other alternatives suggests that the parent should exert some sort of control over the child. In the opinion of the speaker, such control or manipulation of one's child should be avoided.

16. C

The only one of the alternatives that is clearly mentioned by the speaker is alternative **C**, which paraphrases the speaker's statement "for life goes not backward nor tarries with/yesterday."

17. B

Each of the alternatives addresses some aspect of change over time. However, the only one which clearly addresses the speaker's message that "times change" is alternative **B**: "What was valid and true on Monday may not be so on Friday." Alternative **A** argues that one should use in the present that which was successful in the past; alternative **C** encourages people to follow the crowd or do what everyone else is doing; and alternative **D** suggests one cannot change the past. Each of the three incorrect choices fails to address the differing natures of past and present.

18. B

The likening of parents to bows and children to arrows is a metaphor, an implied comparison between two different things; a figure of speech in which a word or phrase that ordinarily means one thing is used to identify another thing in order to suggest a likeness between the two.

19. B

The reference to the archer as "He" suggests, through the capitalization, that this individual is singularly significant. That connotation would eliminate a "soldier of fortune" and a "respected ancestor." Since the pronoun reference is masculine, it is logical to assume that Mother Nature is also incorrect. "An omnipotent god" allows for a variety of interpretations and is the most encompassing and best answer.

20. B

The definition of a fable is a brief narrative in either verse or prose that illustrates some moral truth. The characters are often animals, as in Aesop's fables, but not invariably so. Carson's passage fits the definition in as much as her imaginative view of the future states the moral truth that man is capable of destroying his environment, and unless he curbs his abusive ways, he will be forced to live on a dying planet.

21. C

The phrase in question is followed by a series of examples: "fields of grain and hillsides of orchards…above the green fields." These suggest not only different colours, but also different textures, since a grain field and an orchard would create unique impressions if viewed from above. The town itself would not relate to the description, for it is separate from the checkerboard. The most dominant impression one takes from a checkerboard is the geometric nature of its squares and the alternating colour pattern. These two features are far more likely to be associated with large farm fields containing different crops than with the comparatively small rooftops which crown both houses and barns.

22. D

The phrase identifies the blossoms and/or the pollen associated with the blooming orchards as "clouds of bloom." The figure of speech in which the name of some object or idea is substituted for another to which it has some relation is called metonymy.

23. A

The phrase in question appears directly after the mention of "hillsides of orchards." The word "bloom" is more likely associated with fruit than with grain, which strongly suggests that this cloud is caused by swirling blossoms caught in the wind. Each of the other alternatives, although relatable to this agrarian scene, is not as clearly supported by the text.

24. B

In this phrase, the *b* sound is repeated in the words "blaze" and "backdrop," and the *f* sound is repeated in the words "flamed" and "flickered." The repetition of initial consonant sounds in two or more words is called alliteration.

25. B

The phrase is preceded by a description of that which caught the traveller's eye. In that description, the speaker lists a variety of plants and trees, including wildflowers that would not be cultivated as crops, but rather grew "along the roads." These plants and trees would certainly be "wild" and, unlike the planned crops, would likely provide seasonal colour changes "through much of the year." Each of the incorrect alternatives contains at least one illogical descriptor: "many crops," "groomed estates," and "white fences."

26. A

The phrase is preceded by the statements that "countless birds came to feed on the berries," and that the countryside was famous for "the abundance and variety of its bird life."

27. B

In this phrase, the word "so" means *thus* or *along these lines*.

28. B

The first two paragraphs of the passage accomplish all of the listed literary purposes except establishing a clear conflict. That is done in subsequent paragraphs, where the negative effects of human interference are described first, followed by the speaker's statement that "the people had done it themselves." The only alternative that may cause students some difficulty is "implying a regrettable loss." However, the use of the past tense in the first and last sentences of this two-paragraph introduction implies that the beautiful rural setting Carson describes no longer exists. She writes, "There was once a town in the heart of America," and later, at the end of the second paragraph, "So it had been from the days many years ago."

29. B

Alternative **B** is well-supported by the text. The examples that follow the introductory phrase "Then a strange blight crept over the area" suggest sickness from an unknown disease as the cause for concern. "Mysterious maladies," "sickened," "illness," "unexplained deaths," and "stricken" all support that disease, rather than the less likely alternatives of a curse, a creature, or darkness, caused changes to the area.

30. C

The meaning of the word "moribund," although a challenge for most students, is easily understood if context is considered. This word describes "the few birds seen anywhere." Their actions are limited to trembling violently, and they "could not fly." Their living state but obvious ill health eliminates alternatives **A** and **B** as possible answers. Given the choice between the last two alternatives, alternative **C** best defines a bird that shakes violently and has lost the ability to fly.

31. B

The setting described in the first two paragraphs features a darkened forest partly lit by moonlight. The writer develops a blend of images, some positive and others negative. He begins by describing the darkened forest on one side of a ravine as "soft and rich, suggesting thick foliage." The trees that can be seen are identified as "great pines and hemlocks of the ancient unviolated forest." Contrasting this rather majestic setting is the writer's description of the other side of the ravine. It is described as "barren…and harsh with stunted junipers." Its exposed and rugged nature effectively contrasts with the other side of the ravine. Each of the other alternatives contains one or more unsuitable descriptors. For example, the quiet arrival of a single panther initiates the plot. Although he utters a terrible cry, it is the only noise mentioned in these opening paragraphs, and the action is limited, not eventful. The story does begin at night, and although such a setting may be mysterious to a human, it would not be so to a forest creature. Furthermore, the writer describes the full moon rising, providing the panther with light, and although the panther is likely hunting, the setting itself is not particularly threatening, especially to him.

32. D

The phrase in question appears shortly after the speaker's description of "the orange disk of a full moon just rising." Shortly after describing the panther's gaze, the speaker again mentions the fact that the panther kept "his wide-open green eyes upon the rising light." Since there was no mention of a fire, the panther's mate was not present, and the initial setting is clearly a night setting, alternative **D** is the best answer.

33. A

The most likely reason the panther walks "restlessly" is that he is frustrated by having to stand and wait. When the male calls to his mate, there is "no immediate answer." The waiting male is also described as being impatient.

34. A

Skeletal remains are traditionally associated with death, so by mentioning the deer's antlers and bones, a more serious mood is created. The fact that the ominous imagery occurs very close to the beginning of the story raises the possibility of danger or even death occurring later on in the story. What is not particularly likely is that the imagery is being used to suggest that a kind of sickness exists in the forest. There is nothing else in the story to support this interpretation.

35. A

In the sentence, the word "supplely" appears alongside "glided"—a word that suggests a smooth, continuous, and coordinated motion. The descriptors "awkwardly" and "hesitantly" do not describe a smooth movement, and the word "secretively" does not agree with the fact that she moved into the light ("glided…into the glimmer) and "screamed at the moon." The word "supplely" means smoothly or nimbly.

36. B

The likening of shadows to clothing is an example of metaphor, in that the word choice is an implied comparison between two different things. In this example, the "shadows of the forest" cover the high plateau similar to how clothing covers a person's body.

37. B

The writer never suggests that the female was a better hunter, that the male was larger than his mate, or that her life was particularly passive or "relaxing." The writer does disclose, however, that "what scant prey they had slain had for the most part been devoured by the female: for had she not those small blind cubs at home to nourish…?"

38. B

The speaker directly states that "The settlements of late had been making great inroads on the world of ancient forest, driving before them the deer and smaller game." This clearly supports alternative **B**. On the other hand, there is no mention of the coming on of winter, the panthers' lack of familiarity with the territory in which they hunt (on the contrary, they seemed to be very familiar with their environment—the settlement and the one isolated cabin), or their killing off of most of the region's game.

39. D

The introduction of the crying child initiates conflict by drawing the panthers into the fringes of man's world. In that respect, the writer no doubt intends to create suspense through the foreshadowing of a threatening conflict. It is less likely that the writer wishes to develop sympathy for the abandoned cubs, since their appearance at the end of the story does that far more dramatically. Similarly, the idea that the crying child creates a "dilemma" for the panthers is unlikely, since they turn immediately to hunt the easy prey. Lastly, since the story is written primarily from the panthers' point of view, a crying child would not be viewed as adding hostility or threat to the setting.

40. C

The phrase in question appears shortly after the panthers hear the child crying. The panthers had originally planned to "steal upon the settlements… and take tribute on their enemies' flocks." However, when they realized a child was crying "as if there were no one by to comfort it" and that the cabin housing this unhappy child lay "in the thick of the woods a mile and more from the nearest neighbour," they changed their plan, deciding instead to stalk the defenceless and isolated prey. With that in mind, alternative C presents the most logical explanation. As far as the other options are concerned, there is no support for the notion that the panthers were frightened or planned to double back and hunt deer. And they had clearly changed their minds regarding their original plan to hunt for settlers' livestock.

41. C

The language is clearly not technical, but it does effectively develop suspense in the latter half of the story. Although entertaining, the language is not casual or colloquial, but rather rich in beautiful and detailed descriptions. At times, the language is dated. This is apparent when the writer employs such expressions as "the steep," "they purposed," "hence," and "thither." Lastly, the story, although bittersweet and insightful, is not satirical, since there is no obvious intent to expose a human vice or folly.

42. A

This sentence contains two prepositional phrases ("behind some bushes" and "for the cabin"), as well as compound verbs arranged in a parallel structure ("turned," "dropped," "grasped," and "made"). However, there is no shift in tense, since all of the verbs appearing in this sentence are in the past tense.

43. D

The paragraph in question finds the settler pulled in a number of directions. He is exhausted from his long walk and clearly wants to reach the rest and comfort of his home ("the steaming supper his wife would have awaiting him"). He also feels anger and resentment towards the squatter, whom he accuses of abandoning his own son ("he cursed the vagabond squatter with serious emphasis"). The emotional tug-of-war that raged within him ends as he thinks of his own son. With that in mind, alternative D best captures the frustration brought on by his mixed emotions and the compassion that triggered his decision to aid his "helpless neighbour."

44. D

The word "credibility" means the quality or power of inspiring belief; thus, of the alternatives listed, alternative **D**, believability, is the best response.

45. D

The quotation marks around the word "encouragement" signal a unique interpretation of the word, since the writer prefaces her use of the word with the statement "but what's undesirable are the implicit assumptions underlying the 'encouragement' I've received." This punctuation signals to readers that the encouragement is suspect and should not be taken seriously because the person who is offering the encouragement is harbouring prejudices at the same time.

46. C

The writer uses rhetorical questions in the fourth and fifth paragraphs of the passage. Although supporting examples appear in paragraph 5, none appear in paragraph 4. There are five rhetorical questions dotted throughout the two paragraphs. The writer begins with "It's good to have one's achievements and hard work recognized, right?" and ends with, "So what gives?"

47. C

The writer mentions Benoit and Klein to provide examples of two successful women whose "journalistic gifts," not their university training, led to their popularity. "They were simply too much in demand as journalists to finish their studies." This information eliminates alternatives **A** and **D**, and alternative **B** is not clearly established, since Benoit and Klein may or may not be aboriginal.

48. B

The "implicit assumption" is correctly defined at the end of the paragraph: "The implicit assumption is that I'm doing really well for an aboriginal person because we're perceived widely as being incapable of attaining certain levels of success as defined by non-aboriginal society." The other alternatives are not supported in the passage.

49. A

The sentence "So what gives?" is an example of colloquialism or slang, which is defined as a form of informal English of a novel type that is not accepted as part of the standard language: an idiom whose meaning cannot be understood literally by the words in the expression. Alternatively, jargon is usually understood to mean the language of a particular group or profession whose "modified language" is specific to its activities. Regional dialect relates to a geographical area or class of people and is usually understood to mean a distinct form of language. Lastly, the pun is a play on words whereby two quite different meanings are derived from one expression. Each of the incorrect alternatives are clearly unsupported by the text.

50. B

Comparing the state of being "exceptional" to a "rung on the ghettoization ladder" is a good example of a metaphor: the comparing of two fundamentally different things whereby a word or phrase that ordinarily means one thing is used for another thing in order to suggest a likeness between the two. None of the other alternatives are supported by the text.

51. C

Understanding this comparison requires the reader not only to recognize the restrictions that are imposed upon aboriginals as a result of stereotyping, but also to be aware of the meaning of the word "ghetto." A ghetto is understood to mean a part of a community where a racial minority is forced to live in order to sustain its culture. Essentially this phrase suggests that any aboriginal, even the very brightest, is forced to "climb a number of rungs" or successfully complete a number of steps to prove that he or she is as worthy of recognition as are the members of the dominant culture. This is because aboriginals are often considered to be less capable than non-aboriginal members of mainstream culture.

52. A

In this phrase, the word "inherent" means *inbred.* The phrase appears just before the writer states that non-aboriginal people believe pain, suffering, and homelessness are a constant part of the aboriginal experience. Clearly, the impression of aboriginal society is a negative one, eliminating alternatives B and D, which each suggest that there is nothing stopping aboriginals from succeeding. The statement implies a failing, a lack of something that prevents the encouraging of excellence. In this light, the only logical answer is alternative is A.

53. D

When an outcome occurs that is contrary to that which would naturally be expected, it is defined as situational irony. In the situation cited by the writer, "successful" aboriginals should be celebrated by their own people, but it would seem instead that they are viewed with a degree of suspicion because they do not fit the stereotype of the typical aboriginal. Alternatively, one would expect that members of the dominant culture would be equally quick to welcome successful members of society; however, the dominant society refuses to move beyond the belief that these successful individuals are aboriginals and must be classed as such: a group apart. Each of the remaining alternatives is incorrect, since the current situation need not be a prediction of the future (foreshadowing), does not contain an apparently truthful assertion that implies two contradictory meanings (paradox), and is not intended to poke fun at an unacceptable practice (satire).

54. A

Apart from the hint that the woman sat and observed "for years," the process of losing and gaining leaves is most commonly associated with the change in seasons and the passing of time.

55. A

By repeating the phrase "the same," which literally means "alike" or "showing no difference," the poet suggests monotony.

56. D

The word *unwavering* is the best choice of synonym for "steadfast." Both words convey the idea of being firm in belief or determination.

57. A

The "stunted" and "agitated" bush and the "calves with their backs to wind and/rain" both suggest an unwelcoming or hostile environment. Even the mention of the ragwort plant connotes torn clothing or poverty.

58. A

A simile is a comparison between two things using either of the linking words *like* or *as*.

59. C

Despite the negative nature of the first two stanzas and the use of the word "never" twice in the third stanza, the speaker states that the woman "never lamented once," which indicates that she has accepted her handicap.

60. C

Assonance is the repetition of vowel sounds in the middle of the word, as is heard in this phrase in the repetition of the long *e* in the words "lean" and "clean."

61. B

The woman's inability to move beyond her window is likened to the individual whose way is blocked by a locked gate. In both cases, however, the individuals are forced to stop and stare. As a result, they see far more because they are forced to focus, which allows them to be drawn in and truly learn from what might well have passed unnoticed.

62. A

A pun, or double entendre, is word play involving the use of a word having two different meanings. The expression "field of vision" can refer to the rural field the handicapped woman sees or to the quality and range of what one understands when one looks at anything. In the woman's case, she sees much more in her natural surroundings, which she finds both strange and attractive.

63. B

Because the woman is able to rise above her handicap and learn to appreciate what she can do, it is clear that the speaker admires her for her strength of character. This admiration is evident in descriptors such as "steadfast," "clear of brow," and "face to face with her was an education."

64. B

The free verse poem lacks regular meter, rhyme, and line length. The lyric poem is a shorter poem reflecting the thoughts and feelings of a single speaker. Heaney's poem has all of these characteristics and none of those that define the sonnet, the limerick, or the Haiku.

Writing Prompt

Throughout the year, you will most likely be given writing prompts and will be expected to fulfill the task provided demonstrating the following:

- Knowledge of content
- Understanding of content
- Use of planning skills
- Use of processing skills
- Use of critical/creative thinking processes
- Expression and organization of ideas and information
- Communication for different audiences and purposes
- Use of conventions
- Application of knowledge and skills
- Transfer of knowledge and skills
- Making connections within and between various contexts

The following section of the practice test will provide you with writing prompts with which to practise your writing, as well as sample responses.

The Achievement Chart for English

You may already be familiar with the Achievement Chart shown below. Each example of writing in this section is given a level of 1, 2, 3, or 4 based on the Achievement Chart. There is a short explanation about why the example is given a level. Try to use these writing samples to improve your writing and to understand what is needed to achieve a high level.

Categories	**50–59% (Level 1)**	**60–69% (Level 2)**	**70–79% (Level 3)**	**80–100% (Level 4)**
Knowledge and Understanding – Subject-specific content acquired in each course (knowledge), and the comprehension of its meaning and significance (understanding)				
	The student:			
Knowledge of content (e.g., forms of text; strategies used when listening and speaking, reading, writing, and viewing and representing; elements of style; literary terminology, concepts, and theories; language conventions)	demonstrates limited knowledge of content	demonstrates some knowledge of content	demonstrates considerable knowledge of content	demonstrates thorough knowledge of content

Understanding of content (e.g., concepts; ideas; opinions; relationships among facts, ideas, concepts, themes)	demonstrates limited understanding of content	demonstrates some understanding of content	demonstrates considerable understanding of content	demonstrates thorough understanding of content
Thinking – The use of critical and creative thinking skills and/or processes				
	The student:			
Use of planning skills (e.g., generating ideas, gathering information, focusing research, organizing information)	use planning skills with limited effectiveness	uses planning skills with some effectiveness	uses planning skills with considerable effectiveness	uses planning skills with a high degree of effectiveness
Use of processing skills (e.g., drawing inferences, interpreting, analysing, synthesizing, evaluating)	uses processing skills with limited effectiveness	uses processing skills with some effectiveness	uses processing skills with considerable effectiveness	uses processing skills with a high degree of effectiveness
Use of critical/creative thinking processes (e.g., oral discourse, research, critical analysis, critical literacy, metacognition, creative process)	uses critical/ creative thinking processes with limited effectiveness	uses critical/ creative thinking processes with some effectiveness	uses critical/ creative thinking processes with considerable effectiveness	uses critical/ creative thinking processes with a high degree of effectiveness
Communication – The conveying of meaning through various forms				
	The student:			
Expression and organization of ideas and information (e.g., clear expression, logical organization) **in oral, graphic, and written forms, including media forms**	expresses and organizes ideas and information with limited effectiveness	expresses and organizes ideas and information with some effectiveness	expresses and organizes ideas and information with considerable effectiveness	expresses and organizes ideas and information with a high degree of effectiveness
Communication for different audiences and purposes (e.g., use of appropriate style, voice, point of view) **in oral, graphic, and written forms, including media forms**	communicates for different audiences and purposes with limited effectiveness	communicates for different audiences and purposes with some effectiveness	communicates for different audiences and purposes with considerable effectiveness	communicates for different audiences and purposes with a high degree of effectiveness
Use of conventions (e.g., grammar, spelling, punctuation, usage), **vocabulary, and terminology of the discipline in oral, graphic, and written forms, including media forms**	uses conventions, vocabulary, and terminology of the discipline with limited effectiveness	uses conventions, vocabulary, and terminology of the discipline with some effectiveness	uses conventions, vocabulary, and terminology of the discipline with considerable effectiveness	uses conventions, vocabulary, and terminology of the discipline with a high degree of effectiveness
Application – The use of knowledge and skills to make connections within and between various contexts				

	The student:			
Application of knowledge and skills (e.g., literacy strategies and processes; literary terminology, concepts, and theories) **in familiar contexts**	applies knowledge and skills in familiar contexts with limited effectiveness	applies knowledge and skills in familiar contexts with some effectiveness	applies knowledge and skills in familiar contexts with considerable effectiveness	applies knowledge and skills in familiar contexts with a high degree of effectiveness
Transfer of knowledge and skills (e.g., literacy strategies and processes; literary terminology, concepts, and theories) **to new contexts**	transfers knowledge and skills to new contexts with limited effectiveness	transfers knowledge and skills to new contexts with some effectiveness	transfers knowledge and skills to new contexts with considerable effectiveness	transfers knowledge and skills to new contexts with a high degree of effectiveness
Making connections within and between various contexts (e.g., between the text and personal knowledge and experience, other texts, and the world outside the school)	makes connections within and between various contexts with limited effectiveness	makes connections within and between various contexts with some effectiveness	makes connections within and between various contexts with considerable effectiveness	makes connections within and between various contexts with a high degree of effectiveness

Achievement Chart Level 3 Student Response

TRAVELLING

Travelling to other countries and meeting new people changes your life. Once you have travelled you realize how much there is to see and how many different places there are to see your life changes because you notice that your world at home is pretty small and the world is pretty big.

Every country is different, and there are different things to see like how people dress and what food they eat. In Canada there are lots of mcdonalds resterants to eat at but when you travel to Japan you notice there is not so many mcdonalds but there are lots of resterants that sell suchi and noodles and rice and things. Japanese food is good to eat and you have to try the new food. Some people in Japan wear the same cloths as us but sometimes they wear Japanese cloths. They are very pretty when they dress up in their Japanese cloths.

When you travel to a different country like Japan you get to visit interesting places that are different. The buildings in Japan are sometimes different especially the temples and the palaces, and the Japanese gardens are very beautiful with different plants and flowers and bridges which go over little streams and rivers and ponds. If you could sell your experience of travelling to places like Japan you would be millionaires. This means that travelling makes us rich with experiences.

Travelling changes your life when you open your eyes to everything there is to see. You do not have to learn the language because lots of people in Japan speak English but you do have to except their customs and do things the way they do things so that you do not embarass yourself and them. By travelling you learn other peoples customs and about their food and you see their buildings and gardens which changes you because you now know about somewhere else that is not in Canada. I think everyone should travel if they can.

- **The student's exploration of the topic** about how travelling to Japan can change one's perspective when you examine the different foods, clothing, and buildings is **clear and logical**.
- **The student's purpose** (to look at how travel can change a person) **is evident**, though somewhat simplistic.
- **The ideas presented by the student**, as in "there are lots of resterants that sell suchi and noodles and rice and things…." and "They are very pretty when they dress up in their Japanese cloths**," are appropriate and predictable**.
- **Supporting details**, such as "In Canada there are lots of mcdonalds resterants" and "The buildings in Japan are sometimes different especially the temples and the palaces, and the Japanese gardens are very beautiful with different plants and flowers and bridges which go over little streams and rivers and ponds," **are relevant but general**.
- **The writing is straightforward**, as in "Every country is different, and there are different things to see like how people dress and what food they eat," and generalized, as in "Some people in Japan wear the same cloths as us but sometimes they wear Japanese cloths. They are very pretty when they dress up in their Japanese cloths," **and occasionally arouses the reader's interest**, as in "Travelling changes your life when you open your eyes to everything there is to see."
- **The introduction is functional and establishes a focus** "Travelling to other countries and meeting new people changes your life..." **that is generally sustained** through the discussion of experiences had while travelling to Japan.

- **Details** such as the discussion about Japanese food, clothing, and the different architectural styles of the buildings **are developed in a discernible order**, though coherence may falter occasionally, as in "If you could sell your experience of travelling to places like Japan you would be millionaires."
- **Transitions** such as "This probably means" and "But that was what it was like," **which are generally used to connect details within sentences and between paragraphs, tend to be mechanical**.
- **Closure is related to the focus**, "By travelling you learn other peoples customs and about their food and you see their buildings and gardens which changes you because you now know about somewhere else that is not in Canada," **and is mechanical**.
- **Sentence structure is generally controlled**, as in "When you travel to a different country like Japan you get to visit interesting places that are different," **but lapses** (such as the run on sentence "Once you have travelled you realize how much there is to see and how many different places there are to see your life changes because you notice that your world at home is pretty small and the world is pretty big") **may occasionally impede meaning**.
- **Sentence type and length are sometimes effective** (such as in "They are very pretty when they dress up in their Japanese cloths" and "When you travel to a different country like Japan you get to visit interesting places that are different") **and/or varied.**
- **Some variety of sentence beginnings is evident**, as in "In Canada there are," "The buildings in Japan are," and "You do not have to learn."
- **Words**—such as "suchi and noodles", and "over little streams and rivers"—**and expressions**—such as "Travelling changes your life when you open your eyes to everything there is to see"—**are generally used appropriately.**
- **General words and expressions are used adequately to clarify meaning**—such as "there are lots of resterants that sell suchi and noodles and rice and things" and "The buildings in Japan are sometimes different especially the temples and the palaces."
- **The voice/tone created by the student is discernible** (as in "I think everyone should travel if they can") **but uneven**.
- **The quality of the writing is sustained through generally correct use of conventions**, as in "Every country is different, and there are different things to see like how people dress and what food they eat."
- **Errors occasionally reduce clarity** (such as in mechanics—the incorrect spelling of "resterants," "suchi," and "embarass," and in usage, such as "there is not so many" and "peoples") **and sometimes interrupt the flow of the response**, as in "Some people in Japan wear the same cloths as us but sometimes they wear Japanese cloths" in the second paragraph and "you do not have to except their customs" in the final paragraph.

Achievement Chart Level 4 Student Response

DRAMA CLASS

Experiences are everywhere for us to live through. They help us to learn new things and when we face these experiences then our lives become changed or altered. Imagine a drama class where students can experience different roles. We can pretend to be different characters, or we can use our imagination to see things that are not really there. We also have the chance to act in ways that might get us into trouble if we were not in drama class. In school, drama class is an experience that will shape and alter the life of anyone who comes in the door.

Imagine being able to play the fool and jump around or just act plain silly. One minute we are allowed to pretend to be kings and queens and the next minute we can try to be a poor raggedly dressed beggar, and then we can be the fierce robbers or even the aggressive policeman trying to catch the robbers. Imagine how by playing these roles our lives are altered. As we get into the character we are trying to be, we sometimes get a better understanding of how that person might feel and why he might act the way he does. Why does a beggar keep his eyes down and walk slowly? Why does a king hold his head up high? You have to think about these things if you really want to take on the character. Once our teacher told us to observe how all the people on the bus behaved and to try to think about why they might act the way they did.

Pretend a newspaper is not a newspaper. Do you see it as a walking stick or a stylish hat or a bed sheet, or even as a football? This is what we learn in drama class. We learn to see things that are not really there and to use our imagination to create all sorts of things out of newspaper's, or shoe's, or a pencil or whatever object we like or that the teacher gives to us. These experiences help us to be more creative and to think the way other people do not think. It has changed my life by making me a more imaginative and interesting person.

In school and at home we would get into trouble if we climbed on furniture like the desks or chair or tables, in drama class we are allowed to as long as it is part of the acting. We can yell or whisper, we can act crazy or we can act very calm, we can show our anger or love or hate for something. We can do all these things as long as it is part of the act or the character we are playing. When we are allowed to do things that we are not usually allowed to do we get to experience other peoples emotions and we also learn how to show our emotions in a controlled way. Even when we are angry we must not show our anger in the wrong way. However we feel there are still wrong ways to express feelings.

Being in drama class has altered my life because it has taught me so much. It has taught me that people act a certain way because of whom they are, and that we can imagine anything to be whatever we want, and that we must act appropriatly even when we are angry or sad or hateful or excited. My life is changed because I have a better understanding of people and actions.

- **The student's explanation of the topic is adept**—in that the student has examined the various ways that experiences in a drama class can alter or shape a person's life—**and plausible**, in that a greater understanding of people and a creative imagination are certain to make people see life differently.
- **The student's purpose**—to show how the experience of drama class can influence and alter one's life because "It has taught me that people act a certain way because of whom they are, and that we can imagine anything to be whatever we want, and that we must act appropriatly even when we are angry or sad or hateful or excited"—**is intentional**.

- **The ideas presented by the student are thoughtful**—such as "Why does a beggar keep his eyes down and walk slowly? Why does a king hold his head up high? You have to think about these things if you really want to take on the character" **and sound**—such as "Do you see it as a walking stick or a stylish hat or a bed sheet, or even as a football?"

- **Supporting details**—such as "One minute we are allowed to pretend to be kings and queens and the next minute we can try to be a poor raggedly dressed beggar, and then we can be the fierce robbers or even the aggressive policeman trying to catch the robbers," "create all sorts of things out of newspaper's, or shoe's, or a pencil or whatever object we like," and "We can yell or whisper, we can act crazy or we can act very calm, we can show our anger or our love or our hate for something"—**are relevant and specific.**

- **The writing is considered** ("We can pretend to be different characters, or we can use our imagination to see things that are not really there. We also have the chance to act in ways that might get us into trouble if we were not in drama class") **and draws the reader's interest** ("Imagine being able to play the fool and jump around or just act plain silly" and "Pretend a newspaper is not a newspaper").

- **The introduction is purposeful**—"In school, drama class is an experience that will shape and alter the life of anyone who comes in the door"—**and clearly establishes a focus that is capably sustained** throughout the essay by discussing the ways that drama class allows a student to experience what another's life might be like and to use the imagination creatively.

- **Details are developed in paragraphs in a sensible order**, in that each paragraph thoughtfully expands on the ideas of characterization, imagination development, and role playing that are presented in the introduction, **and coherence is generally maintained**.

- **Transitions** such as "and when we face these experiences" and "When we are allowed to do things" **clearly connect details within sentences and between paragraphs**, such as "However we feel there are still wrong ways to express feelings" and "Being in drama class has altered my life."

- **Closure is appropriate**—"Being in drama class has altered my life because it has taught me so much. It has taught me that people act a certain way because of whom they are, and that we can imagine anything to be whatever we want, and that we must act appropriatly even when we are angry or sad or hateful or excited. My life is changed because I have a better understanding of people and actions"—**and related to the focus**.

- **Sentence structure is consistently controlled**, as in "As we get into the character we are trying to be, we sometimes get a better understanding of how that person might feel and why he might act the way he does."

- **Sentence type**, such as "Why does a beggar keep his eyes down and walk slowly? Why does a king hold his head up high?" **and sentence length**, "This is what we learn in drama class. We learn to see things that are not really there and to use our imagination to create all sorts of things out of newspaper's, or shoe's, or a pencil or whatever object we like or that the teacher gives to us," **are usually effective and varied**.

- **Sentence beginnings**, as in "We can pretend to be," "One minute we are," and "Do you see it," **are often varied**.

- **Words and expressions**, such as "anyone who comes in the door," "to play the fool and jump around," and "We can yell or whisper, we can act crazy or we can act very calm, we can show our anger or love or hate," **are often used accurately**.

- **Specific words**, such as "poor raggedly dressed beggar, and then we can be the fierce robbers or even the aggressive policeman" and "stylish hat," **show some evidence of careful selection and some awareness of connotative effect.**
- **The tone created by the student**—"Being in drama class has altered my life because it has taught me so much"—**is distinct.**
- **The quality of the writing is sustained because it contains only minor convention errors**, such as "if we climbed on furniture like the desks or chair or tables."
- **Any errors that are present** (in mechanics: "peoples emotions" and "appropriatly" and in usage: "whom they are," and the comma splice in "or tables, in drama class we are allowed") **rarely reduce clarity and seldom interrupt the flow of the response.**

Achievement Chart Level 4 Student Response

MOUNTAIN CLIMBING

Taking up mountain climbing as a hobby is an experience that will alter and change forever the life of those who do it. It did for me. The experiences encountered while climbing mountains, the trust that is developed in your climbing partner, and the determination to overcome the impossible overhangs and steep slopes will give you new confidence and strength. Since every climb is different and offers different challenges, it is easy to understand that each experience on the mountain will shape and alter your life as a mountain climber and as a person.

Dealing with all the expected difficulties you face when you are climbing is hard enough without have to deal with what you don't expect. Even before the climb you have to be sure you have the right ropes, the necessary clamps, and other essential equipment. Now that you are up the mountain you need to be prepared for a rain squall or strong winds or even a sudden blizzard: "be prepared" is a great motto for all mountain climbers because you never know what lies ahead. Is there a firm foothold ahead? Am I at my physical best or will I get tired before I reach the top? And then you must have enough energy to come back down the mountain after your climb.

Never climb alone, it is too dangerous and risky. Trusting your climbing partner is a very important rule. Your partner hold your life in his hands at the end of the rope. As you hang in mid-air because you have lost your hold, your partner will lower you down to a safe ledge or flat area where you can once again start your climb. It is important that you not only trust your partner but you must also be a trustworthy climber. Others rely on you for their safety, just like you rely on them for your safety. Climbing has made me a more responsible and trustworthy person. I know that others can rely on me for all sorts of things—not just for climbing. If I say I will do something or pick up my younger brother, I do it. I never forget. I know how important it is to be reliable.

Lots of times people give up when things get difficult. When Billy didn't make the hockey A team he gave up straight away and stopped playing hockey. When Tom failed the math test he never asked for extra help, he just said it was the stupidest test he had ever done. If you gave up on mountain climbing because there are difficult crevasses to be crossed, or steep chimneys to be climbed, or dangerous overhangs to be conquered you will never be able to reach the top and say I did it. You will miss out on the thrill of conquering a mountain and standing at the top and feeling like you are the king of the world. My father has taught me to never give up and to attack events in everyday life like I treat the obstacles I meet on the mountain. There is the thrill of making a team because you have worked out hard and done your very best, or there is the satisfaction of getting good marks at school because you study hard and always do your best. But there is nothing like the thrill of standing at the bottom of a mountain and looking up at it and saying "I climbed that."

You can clearly see why that mountain climbing as a sport will change your life in more ways than you can imagine. You will become healthier and stronger, and you will enjoy being outdoors but you will also learn to be prepared for emergencies, to not give up in difficult times, to trust and be a trustworthy person. My life is so different to what it was like before I took up mountain climbing.

- **The student's exploration of the topic**, "The experiences encountered while climbing mountains, the trust that is developed in your climbing partner, and the determination to overcome the impossible overhangs and steep slopes," **is insightful**.
- **The student's purpose**—to examine how the mountain climbing experience can alter and change a person's life in the everyday world and, as a result, give that person characteristics that will enable them to face the many difficulties they will encounter in life—**is deliberate**.
- **The ideas presented by the student are perceptive**, as in "Now that you are up the mountain you need to be prepared for a rain squall or strong winds or even a sudden blizzard: 'be prepared' is a great motto for all mountain climbers because you never know what lies ahead," **and carefully chosen**, as in "When Billy didn't make the hockey A team he gave up straight away and stopped playing hockey. When Tom failed the math test he never asked for extra help, he just said it was the stupidest test he had ever done."
- **Supporting details**, such as "Even before the climb you have to be sure you have the right ropes, the necessary clamps, and other essential equipment" and "As you hang in mid-air because you have lost your hold, your partner will lower you down to a safe ledge or flat area where you can once again start your climb," **are precise and original**—in so much as the student acknowledges some of the necessary equipment and some hazards of mountain climbing.
- **The writing is confident**, as in "If you gave up on mountain climbing because there are difficult crevasses to be crossed, or steep chimneys to be climbed, or dangerous overhangs to be conquered you will never be able to reach the top and say I did it," and holds the reader's interest, as in "Since every climb is different and offers different challenges, it is easy to understand that each experience on the mountain will shape and alter your life as a mountain climber and as a person."
- **The introduction is engaging and skilfully establishes a focus**—"Taking up mountain climbing as a hobby is an experience that will alter and change forever the life of those who do it. It did for me"—**that is consistently sustained** in the discussions of how the experience of mountain climbing has changed and altered the writer's life.
- **Details are developed in paragraphs in a judicious order** (by discussing in detail the "expected difficulties," the importance of trust, and "to never give up"), and **coherence is maintained** throughout the essay, as all details relate to what can be learned from mountain climbing experiences and situations.
- **Transitions fluently connect details within sentences**, such as in "Since every climb," "Now that you are up," and "because you have worked," **and between paragraphs**, as in "Dealing with all the expected difficulties" and "You can clearly see why."
- **Closure is effective**—"You will become healthier and stronger, and you will enjoy being outdoors but you will also learn to be prepared for emergencies, to not give up in difficult times, to trust and be a trustworthy person"—and **related to the focus** that the hobby of mountain climbing will shape and alter a person's life.

- **Sentence structure is effectively and consistently controlled**, as in "Even before the climb you have to be sure you have the right ropes, the necessary clamps, and other essential equipment" and "Others rely on you for their safety, just like you rely on them for your safety."
- **Sentence type**, as in "Is there a firm foothold ahead? Am I at my physical best or will I get tired before I reach the top?" **and sentence length**, as in "I never forget" and "There is the thrill of making a team because you have worked out hard and done your very best, or there is the satisfaction of getting good marks at school because you study hard and always do your best," **are consistently effective and varied**.
- **Sentence beginnings**, such as "Now that you are up," "Trusting your climbing partner," "If I say," and "When Billy didn't make," **are consistently varied**.
- **Words and expressions**, as in "difficulties you face when you are climbing" and "Your partner hold your life in his hands at the end of the rope," **are accurately and deliberately used**.
- **Precise words and expressions**—in phrases such as "even a sudden blizzard," "hang in mid-air," "he just said it was the stupidest test he had ever done," and "dangerous overhangs to be conquered," **are used to create vivid images and enrich details**.
- **The tone created by the student is convincing**, as in "You will miss out on the thrill of conquering a mountain and standing at the top and feeling like you are the king of the world."
- **The quality of the writing is enhanced because it is essentially error free**, as demonstrated in "But there is nothing like the thrill of standing at the bottom of a mountain and looking up at it and saying 'I climbed that.' "
- **Any errors that are present** (in usage: "Your partner hold your life" and "My life is so different to what…") **do not reduce clarity and do not interrupt the flow of the response**.

PRACTICE TEST 2

Read the following passage to answer questions 1 to 10.

ANITA'S DANCE

It was a morning fit to convert any pessimist, and a Sunday to boot. Anita spent part of it in the garden virtuously weeding; then she poured enough coffee to float an army into her special mug and brought it out into the garden. Instead of reading, she sat stretching her neck to the sun and thinking how lucky she was; nothing to do but please herself all day. From time to time friends lectured her about being selfish and set in her ways, an old maid. And it was true she was sometimes lonely. She had, however, no reason to feel sorry for herself when she compared her life to theirs. She had a house, a garden, a car, a piano. A good job. A greedy, bad-tempered cat. Two eyes, a nose, and ten fingers, all in good working order. What did she have to feel sorry about? And was happiness selfish?

She mused over her library book. She had never really wanted to get married, except for a brief and embarrassing episode when she was at university. A boy she was very fond of had wanted her to drop her scholarship, marry him and put him through law school. Her fondness had ceased abruptly when he argued that, being male, he had more right to an education than she had. Winning the argument had hurt a lot.

Those days were over, she thought, and if she was wrong, she had no daughter to tell her so in exemplary form. I have company in the form of a bad-tempered cat. What is more, I have a date with Clive this afternoon. I feel good with Clive. The something that is between us is nothing; there is no self-consciousness. All's right with the world.

She had wanted to study literature but on practical grounds had chosen economics instead. She still, however, attempted to keep up with good books and now she was reading a novel by a man in England called Berger.

It was good. It took place in a small employment agency; both characters, the owner and his clerk, were weighing large changes in their private lives while appearing to deal with clients.

She looked up and smiled at the sun. She read on.

A woman came into the agency to look for a housekeeping job. A largish, comfortable, middle-aged woman. The proprietor had an instant vision of the comfort she could provide for him: a sort of comfy English house, fish and chips for tea, a kettle on the hob.

"I could live with that," Anita said to herself. "What I couldn't live with, not ever, is a set-up like this plus a job, plus three children and entertaining for a junior executive now portly and senior. No wonder I'm the way I am."

She frowned at the book, closed it, and put it down. It was cosy, and it was basically English working class, and basically (except for a mob of children) what she had come from.

She had never wanted her mother's life, one of flying elbows and fits of bad temper and aspirations that were a muddle of impulses. Her mother had never seemed to be able to think anything through, she was always anaemic from childbearing and exhausted from scrubbing; crying out "You girls…" Get this, fetch that, turn off the soup, scrub the sink, do the dishes, iron that. When she was an old woman they had bought her an automatic washing machine with a window in the door and found her sitting on the basement steps watching it like television. Anita shuddered: that dream of cosy domesticity was a male dream: she'd been living in a man's world too long. The real thing she'd lived through and it was what had made her so happy to get a scholarship to university. Never mind that she'd had to char and work in a grocery store to put herself through.

She stretched lazily. The cat was scowling at her through the kitchen window; he didn't like her to be happy. Too bad for him. She was going to enjoy this day. Clive and she weren't meeting until two and she didn't even have to change.

She heard scuffling footsteps on the gravel, the footsteps of her brother Jack. "Oh damn," she thought. "He's found me."

"Hi Nita, how's tricks?"

"Where did you come from, Jack?"

He was big and he was stupid, something of a bad dream: the one who hadn't succeeded. "Oh well, you know," he said, plunking himself down on the chaise lounge so it clicked and shivered. "I was wondering if you had any jobs for me, like."

"Broke again, eh? Want some coffee?"

"Sure."

She slammed the kitchen door as she went in. The cat gave her a satisfied look, pleased that her moment of glory was over. She poured Jack a coffee, creamed and sugared it, and stumbled as she went out, staining her white summer pants. "Here," she thrust it at him.

He sat up like a patient in bed and began not so much to drink as to inhale it. "What have you been doing lately?" she asked.

"I been doing … well, littla this, littla that. Delivering leaflets. You know."

She knew. He was no good, Jack, and that was that.

"I keep up with the work around here myself," she said. "I don't really have anything for you to do."

"There must be something, the way you lie around reading all the time."

She refused to rise to the bait.

"Lanie's poorly," he said. "I was there yesterday."

He must be making the rounds again, she thought, borrowing from all of us.

"She's got cancer," he said, almost with satisfaction: the voice of the child at school announcing family bad news for current events class. "She looks awful, and she can hardly move."

"She's doing all right," Anita said.

"Gotta get worse before you get better, eh? I don't think she'll get better. Ross is scared out of his wits. You should take the kids."

"I can't. I go out to work, remember?"

"I remember," he said and continued to stare at her, trying to put her in the wrong before he asked her for money.

"I wrote to Rosie but she's just had an operation. Kit's on the sick list too. Bill won't open the door to me."

"Look, I have to go out and see a man about a dog. If ten dollars would do you, I could see you on your way."

"Drop me off somewhere?"

It wasn't the clothes he was wearing, it was the condition he was in: tousled and dirty.

"Ten bucks and a subway ticket. That's it, Jack."

"You always were a tight old broad."

She went inside again, slamming the door. She dashed upstairs and changed into another pair of trousers. As she went down again she made sure the front door was locked, then the back. "Here," she said, handing him ten dollars and a ticket. "You can stay and finish your coffee. I have to be off."

She was meeting Clive at the end of the subway line and they were going out in the country to browse through antique shops.

She had known him for only a few months and hadn't taken him seriously at firSt. Indeed there was nothing special about him except the fact that they got on together, very well indeed. He was divorced, and he had made it plain he wanted to set up housekeeping with someone again. She didn't know whether she wanted to live with anyone else: it had been so long since she hadn't had the morning paper and the morning clock and the morning coffee to herself that she was afraid she would resent an intruder.

She saw him swing into the parking lot and smiled to herself. An intruder! "Hi," she said, and ran towards him. "Marvellous day."

"Wonderful." He put her into the car like the gentleman he was, said, "Belt up, now," and headed north.

Ordinarily, this act of merely strapping herself in beside him made her happy, but today it was different. Jack niggled and danced in her mind. Being mean to Jack made her feel like the mean, ignorant child she no doubt had been, that Jack still was.

"What's the matter?" Clive said. "You're twitchy."

"I'm mean-tempered today," she said. "As bad as Martha the cat. My brother Jack turned up. The no-good one."

"I was having such a good time," she said. "reading in the garden. Then in stomped Jack, and I still feel shattered."

"Look, about your brother, you'd better tell me about him and get it off your mind. No use having a day in the country if we're not in good spirits. Was he mother's blue-eyed boy?"

Suddenly she heard her mother yell, "You girls, Nita, Rosie, look after that Jackie and make sure he don't fall in the well." She hunched herself and said, "First, you have to understand we were small-town people and not what you'd call well off." She had used the genteel phrase for so long it didn't surprise her any more.

"Born with a plastic spoon?"

"Tin. My father was a sergeant in the army."

"Powerful influence?"

"When he was there. There were four girls, then Jackie and Bill. Jackie tore the wings off flies and drowned our kitten in the rain barrel; we hated him. I'm sure he was disturbed or something, but I don't bleed for him; he was an awful kid and he's an awful man."

"Where is he now?"

"In my backyard on the chaise, I suppose. I gave him ten bucks and a subway ticket. But there's no real hope he's gone yet."

Clive looked at her and slowed the car down. "I think," he said, 'that we'd better go back…"

"Clive, I don't want to spoil your day in the country."

"You're more important than a day in the country and you're miserable."

He turned the car and drove very fast down the half-empty Sunday highway into town. They were home in twenty minutes.

They went in the front door and found Jack reclining with his work boots on the white corduroy sofa.

"Jack!" she roared.

"Snob," he said with an impish smile. "So you caught me, you and your fine feller here. Nice coat he's got on. You're coming up and up and up in the world, aren't you, girl? Ma would be proud of you." But he swung his boots off the chesterfield.

"I think you'd better go," Clive said. "You're bothering Anita."

"Do you think so, Mr. Prettyboy? What are you doing hanging around our Nita? Don't you know she's our Educated Woman, too good for a man? Why, all she cares about is white velvet and books and doilies. She don't even go to visit the sick and the dying."

"Jack," she said. "Get out."

"And why would I want to get out, with a fine house to come to and a fine sister to look after me?"

"You should go," said Clive, being reasonable, trying, being also, Anita thought, very sweet and middle class, "because your sister has asked you to go."

"Oh, I never did nothing Nita told me. It was Rosie had the good left hook. Nita was nothing, all skin and bone and no bust."

On the one hand, Anita wanted to laugh because he was being a self-defeating grotesque, asking for punishment, exile, anything; he had always been like that. But she was also very, very angry. The rest of us reclaimed ourselves, she thought, as Mother wanted us to. We got out of misery and brutality. We stopped swearing, read books, got at least a smattering of education: cleaned up the family act.

Clive balled his fists. Nita looked at the two of them and sized them: Clive was taller, but Clive was nervous. Clive had never had to punch anyone out.

Nita took his measure and lashed out, one two, one two, and bang bang bang on his falling head with her fists. Jack went down like a lamb.

Nita sat down on the sofa and started to cry. Clive sat down beside her and put his arm around her. Jack came to.

"Nita, you shouldn't ought to have done that. Nita, you damn well broke me false teeth."

"Get out, Jack," she said. "Get flaming well out of this house and don't come back. If you don't, or if you ever come back. I'll flaming well … I'll call your probation officer."

Jack stood up, holding his head, trying again. "Nita, you're a hard woman."

"Shut up, Jack, and go and tell your government psychiatrist you're persecuted by your sister," Nita said. "Get out. Get on with you."

He went.

Anita sat trying to pull herself together. She sat up and sighed. She looked at Clive.

"Well," she said. "Now you know."

"Look," he said, "there's something I should tell you, but I want to know first how you did that?"

"What?"

"That's wonderful kayo; I've never seen anything like it."

"I wasn't born a lady and a scholar," she said. "I was born on the outskirts of Camp Borden. I was one of six children. Circumstances were not good. But in addition to being a sergeant, my father was a fighter, and when he got a beer or two into him he'd spar with anyone he could find. We saved my mother a lot."

Clive disappeared for a moment. She looked at herself in the mirror, smoothed down her hair. Thought desperately: now he knows. It's over.

Clive reappeared.

She managed to look up at him and smile.

"I don't care what happens between us; I know it won't bore me. But if we ever do take up living together and things get all sedate and cosy, would you…"

"I'd do anything for you," she heard herself say, not believing she had said it, but hearing it anyway.

—*by* Marian Engel

1. The sentence "It was a morning fit to convert any pessimist" suggests that the morning is

A. full of hard work

B. bright and promising

C. gloomy and depressing

D. a time for religious reflection

2. Anita is **best** described as

A. lazy and insensitive

B. grateful and practical

C. timid but good natured

D. sociable but easily influenced

3. The university student Anita was attracted to is **best** described as

A. ambitious

B. sensitive

C. romantic

D. selfish

4. The sentence "Winning the argument had hurt a lot" **most strongly** suggests that

A. the young man was an extremely abusive individual

B. Anita sacrificed her feelings in order to maintain her beliefs

C. Anita gave up her scholarship and left university broken hearted

D. the young man won the argument, but he no longer cared for Anita

5. Anita's choice to study economics at university **most strongly** suggests that her character is
   A. artistic
   B. realistic
   C. creative
   D. mathematical

6. The **most likely** reason Anita closes the book she is reading in a less than pleasant mood is that
   A. Jack's noisy arrival disturbs her peace and quiet
   B. the characters in the book are predictable and flat
   C. the book triggers unpleasant thoughts and memories
   D. her cat is scowling at her through the kitchen window

7. Anita's mother's life can **best** be described as
   A. hard but clearly gratifying
   B. controlled but prosperous
   C. frantic and unrewarding
   D. boring and middle class

8. Anita was **most likely** motivated to go to university by her desire to
   A. avoid the marriage trap that had caught her mother
   B. earn enough money to support her anaemic mother
   C. find a husband who was educated and refined
   D. allow herself to satisfy her love of literature

9. The sentence "that dream of cosy domesticity was a male dream" **most strongly** suggests that
   A. only men view working to make a comfortable home as a good thing
   B. housewives do not earn the money needed to purchase their own dream home
   C. most men dislike having to work out of the house and would rather work at home
   D. women like Anita's mother lack the time to dream about all the comforts of home

10. Jack can **best** be described as
   A. sensitive and thoughtful
   B. thoughtless but naive
   C. caring but awkward
   D. lazy and parasitical

→ annoying

Read the following passage to answer 11 to 17.

A JANUARY MORNING

The glittering roofs are still with frost; each worn
Black chimney builds into the quiet sky
Its curling pile to crumble silently.
Far out to westward on the edge of morn,
The slender misty city towers up-borne
Glimmer faint rose against the pallid blue;
And yonder on those northern hills, the hue
Of amethyst, hang fleeces dull as horn.
And here behind me come the woodmen's sleighs
With shouts and clamorous squeakings; might and main
Up the steep slope the horses stamp and strain,
Urged on by hoarse-tongued drivers—cheeks ablaze,
Iced beards and frozen eyelids—team by team,
With frost-fringed flanks, and nostrils jetting steam.

—*by* Archibald Lampman

11. The phrase "Its curling pile to crumble silently" **most likely** describes

A. smoke from houses climbing irregularly into the air
B. a poorly made stone chimney slowly collapsing
C. low, drifting clouds disappearing into the forest
D. steam rising from the ice-covered roof

12. The phrase "the edge of morn" refers to the

A. boundary between city and country
B. dome shape of the partially risen sun
C. barely lit horizon farthest from the sun
D. darkness yet untouched by the sun's rays

13. In the phrase "hang fleeces dull as horn," the word "fleeces" refers to

A. a newly awakened flock of sheep
B. a ridge of violet-coloured trees
C. the drifting smog from the city
D. clouds lying over the hills

14. The phrase "on those northern hills, the hue / of amethyst, hang fleeces dull" contains an example of which of the following literary devices?

A. Simile

B. Hyperbole exageration

C. Alliteration

D. Personification

?

15. Which of the following elements are **most notably** contrasted by the poet?

A. A dark and gloomy nighttime with a bright and spirited daytime

B. The cold and inhospitable outdoors with the warm and cozy indoors

C. A peaceful and passive background with a noisy and bustling foreground

D. The luxury and ease of city life with the harshness and toil of country life

16. The rhyme scheme used in the first four lines of this poem is

A. *aabb*

B. *abab*

abba

C. *abba*

D. *abca*

17. The phrase "frost-fringed flanks" refers to the

A. ice-caked ridges of the road

B. edges of the frozen sleighs

C. cold faces of the labourers

D. chilled sides of the horses

Read the following passage to answer questions 18 to 27.

HIDDEN LESSONS

David Suzuki is a scientist who, as host of the CBC's popular and long-lived television series The Nature of Things, *has become one of Canada's best-known public figures. Born in Vancouver in 1936, he earned a Ph.D. at the University of Chicago in 1961, specializing in genetics, then quickly gained an international reputation for his genetic research on fruit flies. In 1969 he won a prize as "outstanding research scientist in Canada," and since then has received many other awards, grants and honourary degrees. He lectures internationally, writes a syndicated newspaper column, and in addition to scholarly publications has written many books for a larger audience, among them* Metamorphosis *(auto-biography, 1987),* Inventing the Future: Reflections on Science, Technology and Nature *(1989), and many books explaining nature to children. Suzuki rejects the narrowness that sometimes underlies the specialized vision of the research scientist, and instead has for years used his broadcasts and newspaper columns as platforms from which to educate the larger public about both the promise and dangers of science: the application of little-understood technologies; unchecked economic and industrial expansion; and the consequent devastation of other plant and animals species through our consumption of their habitat. The essay that follows, from the February 7, 1987 Toronto* Globe and Mail, *makes the point in an especially concrete way.*

In spite of the vast expanse of wilderness in this country, most Canadian children grow up in urban settings. In other words, they live in a world conceived, shaped and dominated by people. Even the farms located around cities and towns are carefully groomed and landscaped for human convenience. There's nothing wrong with that, of course, but in such an environment, it's very easy to lose any sense of connection with nature.

In city apartments and dwellings, the presence of cockroaches, fleas, ants, mosquitoes or houseflies is guaranteed to elicit the spraying of insecticides. Mice and rats are poisoned or trapped, while the gardener wages a never-ending struggle with ragweed, dandelions, slugs and root-rot. We have a modern arsenal of chemical weapons to fight off these invaders and we use them lavishly.

We worry when kids roll in the mud or wade through a puddle because they'll get "dirty." Children learn attitudes and values very quickly and the lesson in cities is very clear—nature is an enemy, it's dirty, dangerous or a nuisance. So youngsters learn to distance themselves from nature and to try to control it. I am astonished at the number of adults who loathe or are terrified by snakes, spiders, butterflies, worms, birds—the list seems endless.

If you reflect on the history of humankind, you realize that for 99 per cent of our species' existence on the planet, we were deeply embedded in and dependent on nature. When plants and animals were plentiful, we flourished. When famine and drought struck, our numbers fell accordingly. We remain every bit as dependent upon nature today—we need plants to fix photons of energy into sugar molecules and to cleanse the air and replenish the oxygen. It is folly to forget our dependence on an intact ecosystem. But we do whenever we teach our offspring to fear or detest the natural world. The urban message kids get runs completely counter to what they are born with, a natural interest in other life forMs. Just watch a child in a first encounter with a flower or an ant—there is instant interest and fascination. We condition them out of it.

The result is that when my 7-year-old daughter brings home new friends, they invariably recoil in fear or disgust when she tries to show them her favorite pets—three beautiful salamanders that her grandfather got for her in Vancouver. And when my 3-year-old comes wandering in with her treasures—millipedes, spiders, slugs and sowbugs that she catches under rocks lining the front lawn—children and adults alike usually respond by saying "yuk."

I can't overemphasize the tragedy of that attitude. For, inherent in this view is the assumption that human beings are special and different and that we lie outside nature. Yet it is this belief that is creating many of our environmental problems today.

Does it matter whether we sense our place in nature so long as we have cities and technology? Yes, for many reasons, not the least of which is that virtually all scientists were fascinated with nature as children and retained that curiosity throughout their lives. But a far more important reason is that if we retain a spiritual sense of connection with all other life forms, it can't help but profoundly affect the way we act. Whenever my daughter sees a picture of an animal dead or dying, she asks me fearfully, "Daddy, are there any more?" At 7 years, she already knows about extinction and it frightens her.

The yodel of a loon at sunset, the vast flocks of migrating waterfowl in the fall, the indomitable salmon returning thousands of kilometres—these images of nature have inspired us to create music, poetry and art. And when we struggle to retain a handful of California condors or whooping cranes, it's clearly not from a fear of ecological collapse, it's because there is something obscene and frightening about the disappearance of another species at our hands.

If children grow up understanding that we are animals, they will look at other species with a sense of fellowship and community. If they understand their ecological place—the biosphere—then when children see the great virgin forests of the Queen Charlotte Islands being clearcut, they will feel physical pain, because they will understand that those trees are an extension of themselves.

When children who know their place in the ecosystem see factories spewing poison into the air, water and soil, they will feel ill because someone has violated their home. This is not mystical mumbo-jumbo. We have poisoned the life support systems that sustain all organisms because we have lost a sense of ecological place. Those of us who are parents have to realize the unspoken, negative lessons we are conveying to our children. Otherwise, they will continue to desecrate this planet as we have.

It's not easy to avoid giving these hidden lessons. I have struggled to cover my dismay and queasiness when Severn and Sarika come running in with a large wolf spider or when we've emerged from a ditch covered with leeches or when they have been stung accidentally by yellowjackets feeding on our leftovers. But that's nature. I believe efforts to teach children to love and respect other life forms are priceless.

—*by* David Suzuki

18. According to the writer, a problem with most Canadians growing up in urban settings is that
   A. city dwellers live in a world that is designed for and dominated by people
   B. farmland is scarce and farms are more beneficial to people than animals
   C. urban landscapes tend to be more polluted than vast natural spaces
   D. city dwellers easily lose any meaningful connection with nature

19. In the quotation "We have a modern arsenal of chemical weapons to fight off these invaders," the word "arsenal" means
   A. type
   B. supplier
   C. stockpile
   D. producer

20. Which of the following points does the writer make about human history?
   A. Humankind is dependent on plants and animals.
   B. Crop failures have been a result of human failure.
   C. Plants and animals live in independent ecosystems.
   D. Humans are traditionally trained to fear and hate nature.

21. According to the writer, the irony in the "urban message" children receive about nature is that
   A. species born in the wild naturally fear humans
   B. children never spend much time in nature anyway
   C. nature found in urban areas is groomed by humans
   D. children are naturally attracted to other living species

22. In the sentence "children and adults alike usually respond by saying 'yuk'," the word "yuk" is an example of
   A. exaggeration
   B. onomatopoeia
   C. a colloquialism
   D. a biological term

23. The sentence "Does it matter whether we sense our place in nature so long as we have cities and technology?" is an example of a
   A. red herring
   B. false analogy
   C. rhetorical question
   D. hasty generalization

24. According to the writer, which of the following attitudes is responsible for creating many of today's environmental problems?

A. Humans are special creatures different and apart from nature.

B. Millipedes, spiders, slugs, and bugs are dirty and threatening creatures.

C. The pollution from cities and technology has a minimal impact on nature.

D. Children are inclined to believe that other species are amusing but unimportant.

25. The writer considers a spiritual connection with nature to be extremely important because it will

A. reduce the pain associated with environmental harm and ecological collapse

B. make children far more sensitive to the complex needs of their own species

C. allow us to look at other species with a sense of fellowship and community

D. give society the motivation to move out of our cities and into the country

26. The sentence "The yodel of a loon at sunset, the vast flocks of migrating waterfowl in the fall, the indomitable salmon returning thousands of kilometres—these images of nature have inspired us to create music, poetry and art" contains examples of which of the following literary devices?

A. Exaggeration and interjection

B. Irony and subordinate clauses

C. Alliteration and onomatopoeia

D. Imagery and parallel structure

27. In the context of this passage, the term "ecological place" is **best** defined as

A. the interconnectedness of the species

B. a natural setting unharmed by pollution

C. an animal habitat, such as a game reserve

D. a scientific facility for the study of a species

Read the following passage to answer questions 28 to 35.

AN ODE TO THE USER-FRIENDLY PENCIL

"Anyone can write," says Bonnie Laing, "it's the rewrites that kill you." She gave her own essay three drafts on the very computer whose behaviour she describes below. When it "stops dead" she plans to acquire a faster model like the ones she uses at work. Laing is a freelance advertising copywriter, who has also written speeches and press releases for government. She regularly publishes essays and fiction as well; her humorous articles have appeared in Toronto Life, The Toronto Star *and* Canadian Living, *and her short fiction in* Fiddlehead, Quarry *and* Montreal. *In 1992 was published* The Marble Season, *a collection of her short stories about French-English relations in the East End of Montreal where she grew up. She also writes plays; since 1990 summer theatres across Canada have produced her comedy* Peggy and Grace. *Laing says that after completing an Honours B.A. in English at Queen's, she spent two years as a hippie in England. But once arrived in Toronto, she quickly entered advertising. As a "social marketer" of food and other "lifestyle products," Laing needs a keener sense of audience than even the essayist; in producing "target-specific" text, she says, you have to keep asking yourself "Who is this person I'm writing for?" Although she did have publication in mind, the audience for "An Ode to the User-Friendly Pencil" was herself: she vented her frustrations, felt better, then found that others liked the piece too. On April 29, 1989, The Toronto* Globe and Mail *published it.*

Recently I acquired a computer. Or perhaps I should say it acquired me. My therapist claims that acknowledging the superior partner in a destructive relationship is the first step toward recovery. I should point out that prior to this acquisition, my idea of modern technology at its best was frozen waffles. My mastery of business machines had advanced only as far as the stapler.

I was persuaded to make this investment by well-meaning friends who said the word-processing capacity of a computer would (a) make me a better writer (b) make me a more productive writer and (c) make me a richer writer. I pointed out that Chaucer was a pretty good writer even though he used a quill, and Dickens managed to produce 15 novels and numerous collections of short stories without so much as a typewriter. But I have to admit that option C got to me, even if I couldn't figure out how spending $3,000 on a piece of molded plastic was going to make me wealthier.

To date, my association with the computer has not been too successful. It has proved to be very sensitive to everything but my needs. At the last breakdown (its, not mine) the service man commented that it should have been called an Edsel, not an Epson, and suggested an exorcist be consulted. Needless to say, I am not yet in a position to open a numbered Swiss bank account.

But they say hardship teaches you who your friends are. And so, my computer experience has forced me to spend a lot more time with an old friend, the pencil. Its directness and simplicity have proven to be refreshing. In fact, the more I wrestled with my microchips (whatever they are), the more convinced I became that the pencil is superior to the computer. Allow me to cite a few examples.

To start with the purchase decision, you don't have to ask for a bank loan to buy a pencil. Since most pencils are not manufactured in Japan, you don't feel you're upsetting the nation's balance of trade by buying one.

In fact, pencils are constructed in part from that most Canadian of natural resources—wood. By buying pencils you create employment and prosperity for dozens of people in British Columbia. Well, a few anyway.

Of course, like most people I rarely *buy* a pencil, preferring to pick them up free from various places of employment, in the mistaken belief that they are a legitimate fringe benefit. It's best not to make that assumption about office computers.

Operationally, the pencil wins over the computer hands down. You can learn to use a pencil in less than 10 seconds. Personally, at the age of 2, I mastered the technology in 3.2 seconds. To be fair, erasing did take a further 2.4 seconds. I've never had to boot a pencil, interface with it or program it. I just write with it.

Compared to a computer, a pencil takes up far less space on a desk and it can be utilized in a car, bathroom or a telephone booth without the aid of batteries. You can even use one during an electrical storm. Pencils don't cause eye strain and no one has ever screamed, after four hours of creative endeavor, "The ——— pencil ate my story!"

Pencils are wonderfully singleminded. They aren't used to open car doors, make the morning coffee or remind you that your Visa payment is overdue. They're user-friendly. (For the uninitiated, see comments on vocabulary.)

Of course, the technologically addicted among you will argue that the options of a pencil are rather limited. But the software of a pencil is both cheap and simple, consisting of a small rubber tip located at one end of the unit. A pencil is capable of producing more fonts or typefaces than any word processor, depending on the operator's skill.

—*by* Bonnie Laing

28. Which of the following words **best** describes the speaker's relationship with technology?

- **A.** Deceitful
- **B.** Competitive
- **C.** Incompetent
- **D.** Sophisticated

29. The speaker refers to Chaucer and Dickens in order to

- **A.** prove how far writing has come
- **B.** show off her knowledge of literature
- **C.** suggest how much money could be made
- **D.** point out what was done without computers

30. The speaker was **most motivated** to buy her first computer by the belief that it would enable her to

A. earn more money

B. be more productive

C. work more efficiently

D. become famous quickly

31. Which of the following quotations does not contain a clear example of personification?

A. "Or perhaps I should say it acquired me"

B. "It has proved to be very sensitive to everything but my needs"

C. "the more convinced I became that the pencil is superior to the computer"

D. "Pencils are wonderfully singleminded"

32. The method the writer uses **most** to develop the argument that the pencil is superior to the computer is

A. cause and effect

B. descriptive detail

C. statistical evidence

D. comparison and contrast

33. Which of the following statements **best** reflects the speaker's opinion of Japanese-made computers?

A. They are cheaper than Canadian machines.

B. Their repair is simple and can be done at home.

C. Buying them may influence our country's balance of trade.

D. Japanese computers are of higher quality than Canadian machines.

34. The speaker compares a pencil eraser with which of the following computer components?

A. Software

B. Delete key

C. Memory chip = different section

D. Font selection button

35. The speaker's reference to Edsel is an example of the rhetorical device of

A. paradox

B. allusion

C. simile

D. irony

Read the following passage to answer questions 36 to 46.

MIRROR

I am silver and exact. I have no preconceptions.
Whatever I see I swallow immediately
Just as it is, unmisted by love or dislike.
I am not cruel, only truthful—
The eye of a little god, four-cornered.
Most of the time I meditate on the opposite wall.
It is pink, with speckles. I have looked at it so long
I think it is a part of my heart. But it flickers.
Faces and darkness separate us over and over.

Now I am a lake. A woman bends over me,
Searching my reaches for what she really is.
Then she turns to those liars, the candles or the moon.
I see her back, and reflect it faithfully.
She rewards me with tears and an agitation of hands.
I am important to her. She comes and goes.
Each morning it is her face that replaces the darkness.
In me she has drowned a young girl, and in me an old woman
Rises toward her day after day, like a terrible fish.

—*by* Sylvia Plath

36. A synonym for the word "exact," as it is used in the sentence "I am silver and exact," is

A. precise

B. straight

C. beautiful

D. unforgiving

37. Which of the following statements **best** explains the phrase "unmisted by love or dislike"?

A. Love can never dislike what it is attracted to.

B. Emotions can lead people to swallow their pride.

C. Passions like love and hate can obscure the truth.

D. Love and dislike can often cause tearful outbursts. – not in that stanza

38. The phrase "The eye of a little god" **most likely** refers to the

A. denial that conceals honest feelings

B. mirror's divine ability to show truth

C. kind and giving nature of eternal love

D. human ability to see love in common things

39. Which of the following statements **best** explains the quotation "But it flickers./Faces and darkness separate us over and over"?

A. The mirror is frequently picked up, used, and placed face down.

B. Light is never constant and as a result, impressions can change.

C. A person in love experiences heartfelt but conflicting emotions.

D. The wall is frequently redecorated on the whim of its owner.

40. The figure of speech **most** used in the first half of the poem is

A. paradox

B. hyperbole

C. onomatopoeia

D. personification

41. Which of the following statements **best** describes the meaning of the line "Now I am a lake"?

A. Like a tidal pull, the mirror pulls the woman closer.

B. At times, the mirror's reflective surface is blue-green in colour.

C. The mirror's surface is moistened by the bitter tears of its owner.

D. Laid flat, the horizontal surface of the mirror is reflective, like the surface of a lake.

42. Which of the following statements **best** explains why the candles and the moon are described as "liars"?

A. Candles eventually burn out, and the moon regularly changes its form.

B. People still believe in the moon's power to alter moods, just as candles do.

C. Insincere lovers frequently tell flattering lies in order to steal a kiss as darkness falls.

D. With subdued lighting, the woman would not get a true impression of her appearance.

43. The quotation "In me she has drowned a young girl" **most likely** refers to the fact that the

A. mirror has taken revenge on the woman in response to her negligence

B. woman wasted too much of her youth absorbed with her own appearance

C. woman has turned her back on a close friend and now regrets her decision

D. mirror was the only witness to the drowning death of the woman's daughter

44. The quotation "and in me an old woman / Rises toward her day after day, like a terrible fish" contains an example of which of the following literary devices?

A. Simile

B. Allusion

C. Oxymoron = less is more

D. Onomatiopoeia = Boom

45. The implied attitude of the speaker is **best** described by which of the following descriptors?

A. Quiet but logical

B. Proud but frustrated

C. Unreliable but friendly

D. Inquisitive but guarded

46. "Mirror" is an example of which of the following types of poetry?

A. Playful haiku

B. Modern sonnet

C. Free verse lyric

D. Traditional ballad

Read the following passage to answer questions 47 to 61.

GENIUS WITHOUT THE GENETICS?

In the spring of 2004 I received a letter from a doctor asking if I would talk to the mother of one of his patients. Her nine-year-old son, Matthew, had been assessed as being in the 0.1 percentile in mathematical ability and he was having a very rough time at school.

Matthew's doctor wasn't sure he would ever develop a sense of numbers: even at age 9, after a great deal of specialized help and therapy, he seemed to have little sense of the relative size or order of numbers, and he could only add pairs of small numbers consistently. I found out later that Matthew, who is autistic, was so anxious about math that he would regularly throw up at school.

For Matthew's first lesson I had decided to use an approach that works well with children who have lost their confidence in math. I told Matthew that I assumed he was very intelligent, so I would skip him ahead a few grade levels. I said that even though he was in Grade 4, I would teach him how to add fractions, which is something children don't usually learn to do until grade 6 or 7.

After he had successfully added several pairs of fractions, such as 1/4 + 1/4 Matthew was clearly growing more confident—so I decided I would take a risk. I asked him if he could add a triple sum: 1/7 + 1/7 + 1/7.

But when Matthew saw the triple sum he panicked. It occurred to me that the only way I could raise the bar for Matthew would be to increase the size of the denominators. I said, "Matthew, you're very smart. Could you add these fractions?" and I wrote 1/17 + 1/17. When he had written the answer I said, "You're amazing! Could you add these?" 1/39 + 1/39.

As I continued to increase the size of the denominators, Matthew became more and more excited. After he had successfully added a pair of fractions with denominators in the hundreds, he was beside himself. Clearly overjoyed to be able to do a calculation involving such enormous numbers, he said, "I think I can do that other question." So I wrote 1/7 + 1/7 + 1/7—and he quickly gave me the answer: 3/7.

This may seem like a very small victory, but for Matthew it was something of a new experience. He had solved the problem subconsciously. For the first time, perhaps in years, his intellect wasn't paralyzed by his fear of mathematics and he was able to draw on the processing power of his unconscious mind.

Matthew now attends math classes at school. He has advanced four or five grade levels in many areas of the curriculum. He has begun to develop a sense of numbers that has transferred into his daily life.

Over the past five years, I have taught in regular public schools as well as in inner-city schools, private schools and first nation schools. My observations have led me to believe that we must change our expectations of weaker students. The extreme differences between the weakest and strongest students in our schools are, in my opinion, a product of the way the children are taught.

The idea that all kids can do well in math, or in any subject, is foreign to our culture. People are inclined to talk about innate gifts in any field, but their opinions about intelligence are most evident when they talk about mathematics.

Math is widely thought to be a subject for which either you are born with ability or you aren't. People who can't read usually try to hide this fact, but people who can't do math are happy to reveal publicly how innumerate they are, particularly in stores and restaurants. No real stigma is attached to being bad at math: to be embarrassed about your inability to do math would be like being embarrassed about the colour of your eyes—it's something you're born with.

Our views of what kids can and can't do are generally based on very old science. In his book *The Mind and the Brain*, neurologist Jeffrey Schwartz gives a picture of how far our understanding of the brain has come:

"A mere 20 years ago neuroscientists thought that the brain was structurally immutable by early childhood and that its functions and abilities were programmed by genes. We now know that this is not so.

"To the contrary: the brain's ensembles of neurons change over time, forming new connections that become stronger with use, and letting unused synapses weaken until they are able to carry signals no better than a frayed string between two tin cans in the old game of telephone. The neurons that pack our brains at the moment of birth continue to weave themselves into circuits throughout our lives...

"The life we lead, in other words, leaves its mark in the form of enduring changes in the complex circuitry of the brain—footprints of the experiences we have had, and the reactions we have taken. This is neuroplasticity."

One of the most striking discoveries in neuroplasticity, which I believe is connected to the changes I have seen in the children I've taught, was made by Edward Taub in experiments with stroke patients in the 1980s.

Before his experiments, physicians thought that "whatever function a patient has regained one year after stroke is all he ever will: His range of motion will not improve for the rest of his life." Taub was convinced that people who suffered from strokes were unable to recover function in the affected limbs because they only ever used the unaffected limbs after the stroke, and the brain modified itself to compensate.

He developed a routine called constraint-induced movement therapy, in which stroke patients would wear a sling on their good arm for 90 per cent of their waking hours. For six hours a day they would work at using their affected limb, eating lunch, pushing brooms, throwing balls and practicing their skills on dexterity boards and pegboards. After only two weeks of CI therapy many patients regained significant use of a limb that they thought would "forever hang uselessly at their side."

In teaching children who appear to be incapable of learning mathematics, I believe we make the same mistake that doctors made for years with stroke patients.

We can't imagine being able to break through the blank stares of these children any more than we would hope for a stroke patient's lifeless limb to gain mobility. We assume that nothing is to be gained by putting their minds and hands through the motions of calculating and manipulating symbols, because they seem to lack the spark of intelligence that would invest these activities with life and meaning.

Traditional models of learning assume that intelligence and mathematical ability are fixed and that reducing explanations to small steps can add only tiny increments to a student's knowledge. But this way of looking at intelligence does not take account of the way complex systems such as the brain actually behave; in such systems a series of small changes can have dramatic effects.

Like the chemical solution that changes colour with the addition of a single drop of re-agent or the ant colony that begins to forage for food with the arrival of a few ants, the brain can acquire new abilities that emerge suddenly and dramatically from a series of small conceptual advances.

I have witnessed the same progression in hundreds of students: a surprising leap forward, followed by a period where the student appears to have reached the limits of his or her ability, then a tiny advance that precipitates another leap.

This phenomenon, which I call emergent intelligence, has not been taken account of in education. Our schools are still based on rigid hierarchies of talent and intelligence, the product of outmoded views of the brain and of complex systems in general.

Many people still believe that children are born with vastly different mental abilities and that there is little a teacher or parent can do for a child who is born without ability.

—*by* John Mighton

47. The fact that Matthew "had been assessed as being in the 0.1 percentile in mathematical ability" is **best** understood to mean that he is

A. extremely bright but frustrated

B. unique and in a class of his own

C. at the very top of his math class

D. at the very bottom of his math class

48. The speaker's plan to boost Matthew's confidence makes use of all of the following techniques **except**

A. meaningful repetition

B. purposeful flattery

C. material rewards = no physical gifts

D. attainable goals

49. The statement "He had solved the problem subconsciously" is **best** understood to mean that Matthew

A. reasoned without being aware of doing so Conscious

B. relied on his instincts to solve the problem

C. worked through the problem without guilt

D. relied on chance and guessed the answers

50. According to the writer, the **primary** reason for the great differences between the strong and weak students is

A. differences in the way they are taught

B. the type of school the student attends

C. differences in genetic makeup

D. socioeconomic status

51. The expression "raise the bar" is an example of the figure of speech known as

A. personification

B. synecdoche

C. metaphor

D. simile

52. As it is used in the sentence "the only way I could raise the bar for Matthew would be to increase the size of the denominators," the expression "raise the bar" is **best** understood to mean that the teacher plans to

A. request that Matthew use a slide rule

B. threaten Matthew with corporal punishment

C. give Matthew an additional tool to solve the problem

D. provide Matthew with a greater mathematical challenge

53. As it is used in the phrase "people are inclined to talk about innate gifts in any field," the word "innate" means the **opposite** of

A. to come by naturally as part of one's makeup

B. not alive or useful until employed by a user

C. to acquire as a by-product of education

D. enriching skills that guarantee success

54. In the sentence "No real stigma is attached to being bad at math: to be embarrassed about your inability to do math would be like being embarrassed about the colour of your eyes—it's something you're born with," the colon is used to

A. introduce a supporting or explanatory idea

B. signal that a short list is to be itemized

C. separate two distinctly different ideas

D. indicate that a definition is to follow

55. Which of the following statements about the sentence "the brain's ensembles of neurons change over time, forming new connections that become stronger with use" is **true**?

A. It contradicts a previously stated opinion.

B. It indirectly answers a rhetorical question.

C. It supports a preceding opinion with an example.

D. It introduces a satirical comment as a distraction.

56. Which of the following experts' publications does the writer cite to explain the most recent discoveries related to the brain's structure and function?

A. Jeffrey Schwartz

B. Charles Darwin

C. John Mighton

D. Edward Taub

57. Which of the following statements related to emergent intelligence **best** reflects the thoughts of the writer?

A. Students weak in math gain only limited knowledge from taking small educational steps.

B. Small mental steps can stimulate brain changes which result in huge intellectual leaps.

C. Children are born with vastly different mental abilities that they emerge or grow into.

D. Intelligence is an elastic ability that grows as it is programmed to by one's genes.

58. The statement “unused synapses weaken until they are able to carry signals no better than a frayed string between two tin cans in the old game of telephone” uses a literary technique known as

A. irony

B. analogy

C. metaphor

D. hyperbole

59. The writer’s reference to “footprints” on the brain can best be understood to refer to

A. biological scars left behind by emotionally traumatic experiences

B. oddly shaped neuron configurations formed at the point of birth

C. neuron configurations formed in response to new brain activity

D. withered synapses that leave behind a faded mental impression

60. The practice of “constraint-induced movement therapy” is an effective treatment because it requires patients to

A. concentrate on keeping their injured limbs perfectly still to promote healing

B. force the unaffected limbs to take over the range of motion of damaged limbs

C. restrict the use of unaffected limbs in order to force the damaged limbs to work

D. practice their dexterity skills in their imaginations in order to visualize movement

61. The writer’s **main** purpose in writing this article was to

A. criticize current teaching practices

B. generate sympathy for individuals struggling with math phobias

C. reveal new scientific information concerning brain development

D. provide teachers and students with techniques for overcoming difficulties

Writing Prompt

Write a narrative or essay to show how a negative situation can be turned into something positive. The following material may give you ideas for your writing.

- You break a leg and end up in hospital—this experience so moves you that you decide to become a doctor
- You are fired from your job—you find a much better one two days later that has more opportunity for you to learn and grow
- You fail the end-of-year exams and your parents make you go to summer school—you meet new and great friends who are a positive influence on you
- Your parents ground you for the weekend— home alone, you catch a robber entering your house, and you are hailed a hero by the neighbourhood
- Your team loses a very important sports' game—your team is picked for the tournament's "Best Sportsmanship" trophy and you go to the next tournament anyway
- You are out hiking with some friends and you take a wrong turn in the forest—you find two orphaned bear cubs that would surely have died if you had not been there to rescue them
- Your parents move to another town/city/country and, against your wishes, you are made to go with them—at your new home you discover there are opportunities for you to do things/play sports/join clubs/that were never present in your previous town/city/country
- While driving the family car, you are in a minor car accident that damages the car quite extensively—your parents insist that you help pay for the repairs so you get a job at a garage where you learn all about car maintenance, as well as being paid
- The option course that you want to take is full so you have to take another course instead—by moving out of your comfort zone, you discover that you have hidden talents that you were unaware of
- You are in an accident that leaves you in a wheelchair—you join a sports league for paraplegics and make the Canadian Olympic team for one of the sports. Not only do you get to go to the Olympic games but you also do a lot of travelling with your sport
- You have to forfeit a winning prize for four to Los Angeles (all expenses paid) because your parents can't get time off work—when the promoters hear the reason, they give you a 7-day Caribbean Cruise instead, at a time when your parents will be able to accompany you

ANSWERS AND SOLUTIONS—PRACTICE TEST 2

1. B	14. C	27. A	40. D	53. C
2. B	15. C	28. C	41. D	54. A
3. D	16. C	29. D	42. D	55. A
4. B	17. D	30. A	43. B	56. A
5. B	18. D	31. C	44. A	57. B
6. C	19. C	32. D	45. B	58. V
7. C	20. A	33. C	46. C	59. C
8. A	21. D	34. A	47. D	60. C
9. A	22. C	35. B	48. C	61. D
10. D	23. C	36. A	49. A	
11 A	24. A	37. C	50. A	
12. C	25. C	38. B	51. C	
13. D	26. D	39. A	52. D	

1. B

The writer paints a picture of a pleasant, sunny Sunday morning. Anita has finished her garden work and set aside a period of time to sit down, relax, and pamper herself by enjoying a large cup of coffee in her special mug, contemplating "how lucky she was; nothing to do but please herself all day." The only alternative that reflects this scene is alternative **B**: bright and promising.

2. B

Anita thinks about how "lucky" she is, and although she admits to being lonely at times, she accepts her situation and focuses on her accomplishments: "She had a house, a garden, a car, a piano. A good job." She feels she is better off than other people she knows. Clearly, she is grateful for what she has and practical enough to realize that she may not have everything, but she is happy with what she does have. She is not lazy, for she apparently is not afraid of hard work, and she does not seem particularly timid or easily influenced, since she is not cowed by her friends' criticism. With that in mind, alternative **B** is the only accurate set of descriptors.

3. D

Anita indicates that the reason she ended the relationship with the young man in university was his belief that he had more of a right to an education than she did. He expected her to give up her scholarship in order to work and put him through law school. He may well be viewed as ambitious, but the most appropriate description of his character is alternative **D**: selfish.

4. B

It is implied that Anita was the one who was hurt, and therefore it was she who won the argument. The reader is left to conclude that Anita refused to support her boyfriend, believing that she had as much right to an education as any man. Considering the chauvinistic nature of the boyfriend, it is fair to conclude that they split up over this fundamental difference of opinion. In the end, Anita had to accept that her fondness for the young man and any thoughts of marriage were less important than her belief in gender equality (alternative **B**). Each of the other alternatives is not well supported by the text.

5. B

Anita admits that she had wanted to study literature, "but on practical grounds had chosen economics instead." The implication here is that she would make a better living with a degree in economics than a degree in literature. This practical decision indicates that Anita is realistic (alternative **B**), since her choice was based on reason and common sense, despite the fact that she might well have been both creative and artistic. Similarly, there is nothing in the text that suggests that she was particularly mathematical.

6. C

At first, Anita is entertained by the thought of the "comfy English house" envisioned by one of the book's characters; however, she then goes on to imagine the more likely modern version of the typical household, one in which the wife would be expected to deal with "three children and entertaining for a junior executive now portly and senior." These unpleasant thoughts are followed by memories of the type of life her mother was forced to live, and she concludes that she is better off with the life she has than the romanticized version in the novel. Alternative **C** best captures these thoughts, while the other alternatives are not supported by the chronological unfolding of events.

7. C

Anita's recollections of her mother's life include "fits of bad temper and aspirations that were a muddle of impulses." Furthermore, her mother "never seemed to be able to think anything through." Chores and raising children with limited help from a husband who was away a good deal of the time would make her life frantic and unrewarding. Each of the other alternatives includes at least one element that is not supported by the text. For example, her mother's life was not prosperous, boring, middle class, or gratifying, which leaves alternative **C** as the only logical choice.

8. A

After considering the kind of frantic life her mother had to live, Anita realizes that the "dream of cosy domesticity was a male dream." In Anita's view, women invariably struggle alone to bring some sense of order into their chaotic lives. She realizes that she has lived through this difficult experience already, "and it was what had made her so happy to get a scholarship to university." Education, and the financial independence that comes with it, would allow Anita to avoid becoming some man's drone. This is best reflected in alternative **A**. None of the other alternatives are supported by the text.

9. A

Many of Anita's thoughts relate to the hard life of a housewife. Clearly, she sees staying at home, running a household, and raising children as an unpleasant life path. She arrives at this conclusion after reflecting on her mother's quality of life. The sentence in question suggests that men who work away from the home and return to prepared meals, clean clothes, and disciplined children view domestic life as desirable and worth pursuing. They fail to take into account the toll it takes on the "domestic engineer" or housewife. With that in mind, alternative **A** best explains the implications of Anita's thoughts. The other alternatives, although reasonably valid, are not supported by the text.

10. D

Jack's character is developed both directly through Anita's thoughts and indirectly through his actions and comments. Initially, Anita describes him as "stupid, something of a bad dream." This establishes Jack as a negative character and thereby eliminates the two positive alternatives. The fact that he arrives requesting help, and Anita's guess that he has likely been borrowing from other members of the family, again establishes a pattern of dependency. He has no regular job, which is revealed by his comment "well, littla this, littla that. Delivering leaflets." Finally, his crafting of the conversation around other members of the family in need of help in order to gain his sister's sympathy is anything but naïve. He is an astute bargainer out to get the most for himself, and others, such as Anita, resent him for it. This is implied by Jack's comment that "Bill won't open the door to me." All things considered, alternative **D** best describes Jack: lazy and parasitical.

11. A

The reference to a "chimney" should immediately suggest heat and smoke. What is "building" from the chimney is smoke. The image of a "curling pile" refers to the meandering smoke that is simultaneously manipulated by the rising heat and the cold winter air.

12. C

This phrase is preceded by the phrase "far out to westward," which is the opposite direction from the rising sun. Conceivably, the sun's rays would travel westward, where their brightness would fade as they met the edge of darkness. These details in combination would mean that "the edge of morn" refers to the barely lit western horizon.

13. D

The phrase "hang fleeces dull as horn" suggests something suspended. Given the options, a cloud is the most likely answer.

14. C

The repetition of the *h* sound in "hills," "hue," and "hang" is a clear example of alliteration, which is the close repetition of the same first sound in two or more words.

15. C

In the first eight lines of the poem, the poet focuses primarily on the passive elements of the setting: frost, chimney smoke, a quiet sky, distant city towers, and cloud-shrouded hills. This mixture of manmade and natural elements is not described negatively, but matter-of-factly. In the six lines of the poem that follow, the poet focuses on far more active and boisterous elements that are closer at hand, like the noise and movement from the horses and their drivers. The hubbub or activity characterized by energy and strain effectively contrasts the quiet backdrop of the introduction.

16. C

The end rhyme of the first four lines is:
worn (*a*)
sky (*b*)
silently (*b*)
morn (*a*)
Thus, the rhyme scheme used in the first four lines of this poem is *abba.*

17. D

The phrase in question is separated from the rest of this descriptive passage with a dash. This indicates that the horse team with "frost-fringed flanks, and nostrils jetting steam" is the subject of the descriptive phrase.

18. D

The writer admits quite candidly that there is "nothing wrong" with an urban environment. However, he also states that in such an environment "it's very easy to lose any sense of connection with nature." Alternative **D** is the only alternative that addresses the question and is supported by the text.

19. C

The sentence refers to an arsenal of chemical weapons used "lavishly." The word stockpile is the only alternative that implies a direct use or application and that suggests more than one type of weapon. Consequently, it is the only option that might allow for lavish use. After all, one would not lavishly use either a supplier or producer to kill bugs, but a stockpile, which implies more than one type, might well do the job.

20. A

The central point of the fourth paragraph is that "for 99 per cent of our species' existence on the planet, we were deeply embedded in and dependent on nature." The writer supports this generalization by showing that this dependency became evident in the past when shortages of plant and animal life led to a dying off of humans.

21. D

The definition of irony makes clear a discrepancy between what might reasonably be understood or expected and what actually "is" or what takes place. The writer states, "The urban message kids get runs completely counter to what they are born with, a natural interest in other life forms." Since the urban message encourages children to fear what they are naturally attracted to, there is a clear discrepancy between what should be expected of children and what they are actually encouraged to do.

22. C

The term "colloquial" refers to the level of language used in everyday conversation; it is typically informal. Expressions such as "yuk" or "gross" are colloquial expressions that, although informal and at times inexplicable, convey meaning simply because they are widely used, accepted, and understood.

23. C

The writer's intent in raising this question is not to solicit an answer from an audience, but rather to provide himself with a platform on which to build his own argument. That is why the writer, in this case, answers his own question in the affirmative and goes on to list reasons for his opinion. It is a stylistic element of rhetoric that can be used effectively in oral or written communication.

24. A

In paragraph 6, the writer states that the attitude of viewing other species as repulsive is tragic. He goes on to comment that "the assumption that human beings are special and different and that we lie outside nature" is creating many environmental problems.

25. C

Although the writer phrases the answer to this question in several different ways, the only one of the alternatives that makes sense and is supported by the text is found in paragraph 9: "If children grow up understanding that we are animals, they will look at other species with a sense of fellowship and community."

26. D

Alternative **D** is the only valid response. The writer supports his central thesis, that the spiritual relationship between humans and nature is inspiring, by first providing a series of images that his readers can likely relate to ("the yodel of a loon at sunset, the vast flocks of migrating waterfowl in the fall, the indomitable salmon returning thousands of kilometres—these images"). The series of images appears in parallel structure, as does the series of artistic endeavours they inspire, namely "music, poetry and art."

27. A

The term "ecological place" implies a positive attitude toward one's position in the universe. Not unlike the admonition "know your place," this term defines a respect for relationships between two or more things. The loss of our ability as human beings to know our place has led to the poisoning of the "life support systems that sustain all organisms." Logically, the knowing of "our place" in the grand scheme of things should lead to our improving those life support systems that sustain all organisms and, by extension, our acceptance and cultivation of the interconnectedness of the species.

28. C

The writer makes an effort to focus on her lack of skill, or incompetence, with technology. She begins by taking a submissive role in her relationship with her newly acquired computer ("it acquired me"). The joking statements "my idea of modern technology at its best was frozen waffles," and "My mastery of business machines had advanced only as far as the stapler" both contribute to the writer's aim of establishing her technological ineptitude.

29. D

The writer cites these two canonized literary figures as evidence that a computer is not a necessity for either good or efficient writing. The speaker cites Chaucer as an example of fine writing and Dickens as an example of prolific efficiency; both writers used only very basic technology to achieve their fame.

30. A

For the writer, increased wealth was the most compelling reason for purchasing a new computer. Although fame is implied (better writer) and productivity is clearly stated, the writer states that the idea of earning more money "got to me, even if I couldn't figure out how spending $3,000 on a piece of molded plastic was going to make me wealthier."

31. C

Something having superiority over something else does not necessitate "personhood." The fact that the writer states that the pencil is better than the computer does not give either object any human characteristics. The other alternatives all offer examples of personification, giving objects human qualities and capabilities, such as sensitivity, single-mindedness, and acquisition.

32. D

Once the writer has identified the computer as a problem source and has introduced the pencil as an alternative, her argument is built on comparing the strengths of the pencil with the weaknesses of the computer and highlighting the contrasting elements of the two devices.

33. C

The speaker argues that if one were to buy a pencil rather than a computer, "you don't feel you're upsetting the nation's balance of trade." Although it is not directly stated, the writer is implying that by buying computers made in foreign countries like Japan, consumers in North America are contributing to an economic imbalance.

34. A

The speaker compares the eraser with software, stating, "the software of a pencil is both cheap and simple, consisting of a small rubber tip located at one end of the unit."

35. B

The reference to Edsel, a failed Ford product, is an allusion to something presumably well known. What makes this question more difficult than one of medium difficulty is the range of general knowledge in the student population.

36. A

The first five lines of the poem focus on the mirror's ability to reflect with absolute precision that which it captures in its gaze.

37. C

In light of the fact that the speaker sees everything "just as it is," the word "unmisted" implies that emotions may at times obscure clear vision, acting like a mist. The mirror's precision is in this sense established as being superior to that of humans, whose feelings may colour their perceptions.

38. B

The phrase in question refers back to the "I" that is described as "silver," "four-cornered," and capable of seeing everything "just as it is." It tells the truth without bias. Moreover, the fact that the poem is entitled "Mirror" and the "I" in question remains stationary for much of the time, meditating "on the opposite wall," further supports the idea that the little god is a mirror.

39. A

A mirror can only flicker when it is reflecting a variety of images. Since the mirror meditates on the opposite wall "most of the time," it is reasonable to assume that it is typically placed in a vertical position, reflecting the opposite wall until it is picked up to examine the owner's face, and then it is placed facedown where it sees nothing but darkness.

40. D

Through narration, the mirror exhibits the power to see, reason, meditate, and feel: all human actions not normally ascribed to an inanimate object. By bestowing human qualities on an inanimate object, the poet has made use of personification.

41. D

The line in question is followed by the statement "A woman bends over me." For this to occur, the mirror would have to be lying flat, providing the woman with a reflection of herself looking down, as though looking into a lake's reflective surface.

42. D

The woman turns away from the mirror after bending over it and "searching [its] reaches for what she really is." The fact that tears and wringing of hands follow suggests that the woman is not satisfied with what she sees in her mirror. By turning to "those liars," the flattering light of candles or the moon, the woman seems to be searching for a more pleasing, albeit less accurate, reflection of herself.

43. B

The reference to the drowning of a young girl "in me" suggests that the woman's youth has been drowned or lost in the mirror. The woman's former beauty has faded away with time. She "drowned" her youth in the mirror, focusing excessively on her appearance.

44. A

The comparison of the old woman to a terrible fish meets the definition of a simile: the expressed comparison between two unlike elements using the words *like* or *as*.

45. B

The first five lines of the poem focus on the mirror's description of itself. The mirror proudly describes itself as the "eye of a little god" and uses a direct tone that is hardly modest. However, the mirror's frustration is evident as the passage progresses. The mirror's mistress frequently leaves the mirror in the dark face down and refuses to accept the mirror's honest reflection, seeking out the opinions of others.

46. C

The poem is short and expresses a central idea or feeling typical of the modern lyric poem. It has neither a rhyme scheme nor any apparent rhythm. It is best defined as a free verse lyric. Each of the other alternatives is incorrect.

47. D

The percentile ranking could be used to denote the top 0.1% or the bottom 0.1%; however, context clues clearly indicate that Matthew is struggling; therefore, the lower ranking is clearly the intended meaning.

48. C

The tasks assigned to Matthew involved purposeful flattery ("I assumed he was very intelligent"; "Matthew, you're very smart."), meaningful repetition (repeated the adding of fractions until confidence was achieved), and attainable goals (kept the addition of fractions to two numbers until the student felt comfortable with three). However, at no point in this initial lesson does the speaker offer Matthew any material reward for succeeding at the various challenges.

49. A

"Subconsciously" means to reason without being consciously aware of doing so. Matthew solved the math problem without realizing he was doing it.

50. A

This is a basic fact retrieval question. The writer states, "The extreme differences between the weakest and strongest students in our schools are, in my opinion, a product of the way the children are taught." Although the writer mentions genetics and the types of schools in which he has taught, he does not consider these things to be determining factors in student achievement. Socioeconomic status, although a popular factor in the student achievement debate, is not mentioned in this article.

51. C

The expression "raise the bar" is a comparison between Matthew's mathematical struggles and the struggles faced by a high jumper or pole vaulter. This implied comparison between two different things is intended to take a phrase that ordinarily means one thing and apply it to another thing in order to suggest a likeness between the two. Such a comparison is called a metaphor.

52. D

The expression "raise the bar" is a comparison between Matthew's mathematical struggles and the struggles faced by a high jumper. When the bar is raised for the jumper, he is given a greater height to successfully jump. The raised bar in the athletic metaphor is being applied to Matthew's mathematical challenges. In order to provide Matthew with a "higher bar," or greater challenge, the speaker believes he would have to establish a level of confidence in his student by having him successfully complete less difficult tasks that appear more difficult due to an increase in the size of the denominators.

53. C

The word "innate" means something that comes to you naturally or something you are born with. If you do not have a certain skill or an ability when you are born, you must acquire it as a by-product of education and study.

54. A

Although the colon can introduce or announce any number of things, usually it is not intended as a mark of separation. Of the three remaining options, the only one that is supported by the text is alternative **A**: introduce a supporting or explanatory idea. In this sentence, the general statement concerning a lack of stigma is supported by a more specific example suggesting that one would not feel any stigma about the colour of one's eyes.

55. A

The statement in question is only part of the full thought, which begins "To the contrary." This introductory phrase should make it obvious that the speaker is planning to contradict a previously stated opinion. That opinion is the belief that the brain does not change and is primarily programmed by the genes.

56. A

This is a basic fact retrieval question. The writer directly states, "In his book *The Mind and the Brain*, neurologist Jeffrey Schwartz gives a picture of how far our understanding of the brain has come." He goes on to explain how the brain adapts as the neurons "change over time," which debunks the original theory that the brain does not change and its structure is determined by genetic coding alone. Although two of the other three scientists are named in the article (the writer himself and Edward Taub), the speaker does not cite any publications written by them. Charles Darwin is not mentioned in the article.

57. B

Toward the end of the article, the writer compares the growth of muscle intelligence in stroke victims forced to manipulate weakened limbs to intellectual growth in math students required to process simple mathematical problems. In both cases, brain stimulation leads to "a tiny advance that precipitates another leap. This phenomenon, which I call emergent intelligence, has not been taken account of in education."

58. B

The comparison between frayed nerves and an ineffective telephone system designed by children is an example of an analogy. Like the simile, the analogy shows a similarity between two different things. Of the alternatives listed, metaphor may be considered a possible alternative; however, a metaphor typically states that something is another thing. The other two alternatives are not supported by the text.

59. C

The reference to "footprints" is made as a way of describing the physiological effects of repeated actions or thoughts on the brain's neuron configurations. As thought or action patterns change, so too does the shape of the "complex circuitry of the brain."

60. C

As stated by the writer, "constraint-induced movement therapy" involves restricting the patient's use of unaffected limbs in order to force the damaged limbs to work. For some stroke victims, binding the undamaged limb so that "they would work at using their affected limb" resulted in the patient regaining

61. D

Beginning with a case study involving one of his own students, the writer explains how some individuals fail to grasp math. He goes on to discuss some of the misconceptions about the nature of the brain and its development, which in turn have led to the failure of many educators to help students weak in math. He concludes by establishing a parallel between those who suffer from stroke damage and those who, for a variety of reasons, struggle with basic math problems. He proves that by taking incremental steps and building confidence, even weak students can make significant intellectual leaps. The fact that the writer has helped many students himself and admits that "we must change our expectations of weaker students" strongly suggests that he wishes to improve the lives of struggling students by providing both students and teachers with the insight, motivation, and tools needed to achieve success.

Writing Prompt

Throughout the year, you will most likely be given writing prompts and will be expected to fulfill the task provided demonstrating the following:

- Knowledge of content
- Understanding of content
- Use of planning skills
- Use of processing skills
- Use of critical/creative thinking processes
- Expression and organization of ideas and information
- Communication for different audiences and purposes
- Use of conventions
- Application of knowledge and skills
- Transfer of knowledge and skills
- Making connections within and between various contexts

The following section of the practice test will provide you with writing prompts to practise your writing with as well as example responses.

The Achievement Chart for English

You may already be familiar with the Achievement Chart shown below. Each example of writing in this section is given a level of 1, 2, 3, or 4 based on the Achievement Chart. There is a short explanation about why the example is given a level. Try to use these examples of writing to improve your writing and to understand what is needed to receive a high level.

Categories	**50–59% (Level 1)**	**60–69% (Level 2)**	**70–79% (Level 3)**	**80–100% (Level 4)**
Knowledge and Understanding – Subject-specific content acquired in each course (knowledge), and the comprehension of its meaning and significance (understanding)				
	The student:			
Knowledge of content (e.g., forms of text; strategies used when listening and speaking, reading, writing, and viewing and representing; elements of style; literary terminology, concepts, and theories; language conventions)	demonstrates limited knowledge of content	demonstrates some knowledge of content	demonstrates considerable knowledge of content	demonstrates thorough knowledge of content

Understanding of content (e.g., concepts; ideas; opinions; relationships among facts, ideas, concepts, themes)	demonstrates limited understanding of content	demonstrates some understanding of content	demonstrates considerable understanding of content	demonstrates thorough understanding of content
Thinking – The use of critical and creative thinking skills and/or processes				
	The student:			
Use of planning skills (e.g., generating ideas, gathering information, focusing research, organizing information)	use planning skills with limited effectiveness	uses planning skills with some effectiveness	uses planning skills with considerable effectiveness	uses planning skills with a high degree of effectiveness
Use of processing skills (e.g., drawing inferences, interpreting, analysing, synthesizing, evaluating)	uses processing skills with limited effectiveness	uses processing skills with some effectiveness	uses processing skills with considerable effectiveness	uses processing skills with a high degree of effectiveness
Use of critical/creative thinking processes (e.g., oral discourse, research, critical analysis, critical literacy, metacognition, creative process)	uses critical/creative thinking processes with limited effectiveness	uses critical/creative thinking processes with some effectiveness	uses critical/creative thinking processes with considerable effectiveness	uses critical/creative thinking processes with a high degree of effectiveness
Communication – The conveying of meaning through various forms				
	The student:			
Expression and organization of ideas and information (e.g., clear expression, logical organization) **in oral, graphic, and written forms, including media forms**	expresses and organizes ideas and information with limited effectiveness	expresses and organizes ideas and information with some effectiveness	expresses and organizes ideas and information with considerable effectiveness	expresses and organizes ideas and information with a high degree of effectiveness
Communication for different audiences and purposes (e.g., use of appropriate style, voice, point of view) **in oral, graphic, and written forms, including media forms**	communicates for different audiences and purposes with limited effectiveness	communicates for different audiences and purposes with some effectiveness	communicates for different audiences and purposes with considerable effectiveness	communicates for different audiences and purposes with a high degree of effectiveness
Use of conventions (e.g., grammar, spelling, punctuation, usage), **vocabulary, and terminology of the discipline in oral, graphic, and written forms, including media forms**	uses conventions, vocabulary, and terminology of the discipline with limited effectiveness	uses conventions, vocabulary, and terminology of the discipline with some effectiveness	uses conventions, vocabulary, and terminology of the discipline with considerable effectiveness	uses conventions, vocabulary, and terminology of the discipline with a high degree of effectiveness

Application – The use of knowledge and skills to make connections within and between various contexts				
	The student:			
Application of knowledge and skills (e.g., literacy strategies and processes; literary terminology, concepts, and theories) **in familiar contexts**	applies knowledge and skills in familiar contexts with limited effectiveness	applies knowledge and skills in familiar contexts with some effectiveness	applies knowledge and skills in familiar contexts with considerable effectiveness	applies knowledge and skills in familiar contexts with a high degree of effectiveness
Transfer of knowledge and skills (e.g., literacy strategies and processes; literary terminology, concepts, and theories) **to new contexts**	transfers knowledge and skills to new contexts with limited effectiveness	transfers knowledge and skills to new contexts with some effectiveness	transfers knowledge and skills to new contexts with considerable effectiveness	transfers knowledge and skills to new contexts with a high degree of effectiveness
Making connections within and between various contexts (e.g., between the text and personal knowledge and experience, other texts, and the world outside the school)	makes connections within and between various contexts with limited effectiveness	makes connections within and between various contexts with some effectiveness	makes connections within and between various contexts with considerable effectiveness	makes connections within and between various contexts with a high degree of effectiveness

Achievement Chart Level 3 Student Response

Negative situations are always occurring. People miss buses and airplanes and are late for work or school. Sometimes it can be a good thing that these situations happened. I am going to write about times when a negative situation became positive for a boy who fell in the river and nearly drownded, and a girl who had to go on a boring holiday with her parents, and a man who missed his plane for a very important buisness meeting.

Many children fall in rivers or swimming pools and sometimes they are nearly drownded so when this happened to Jack his mother decided that he had to have swimming lessons. He started his lessons at a swimming pool near his home and he began to like them so he went on having swimming lessons even after he could swim. He joined a swim club and became very good. He went to swim meets and began to win races and medals. When Jack was about 18 he was picked for the Canada Olympic swimming team. He was thrilled. At the Olympics he won his race and won Gold. This all happened because when he was five he fell in the river and nearly drownded.

Sometime parents have to go on business trips and the children have to go to because there is no one to look after them. Grace had to go with her parents even though she didn't want to. The trip was going to be BORING and she wanted to stay at home and hang out with her friends. At the hotel in Victoria where there was the meeting. People had organized things for the kids to do. One day they went to sea world, another day they went to the museum, another day they went to the wax museum, and on the last day they went out in a boat to see whales. Grace had a great time and learned so much and this all happened because Grace was made to go on a boring trip with her parents.

Tom was a very important buisness man and he had to make lots of trips to other places to go to meetings and to listen to lecters and to meet other important people, Tom liked travelling and he liked his job. One day Tom was in a big hurry to catch his plane to Chicago but he missed it, he was to late. He was very unhappy because he might get fired from his job for not being at the meeting in Chicago. Tom was lucky that he missed his plane because it crashed and everyone on the plane was killed but Tom wasn't because he missed his plane.

Negative situations happen in life and sometimes it ends up positive for the person but sometimes it doesn't. But look on the bright side Tom missed a plane crash, Grace did interesting things in Victoria and Jack won a Olympic Gold Medal.

- **The student's exploration of the topic** ("Negative situations are always occurring," and that sometimes there can be positive results from these experiences) **is clear and logical**.
- **The student's purpose** to show how positive results can come out of negative situations **is evident**—as in the three examples the student elaborates on in this essay.
- **The ideas presented by the student**, as in "I am going to write about times when a negative situation became positive for a boy who fell in the river and nearly drownded, and a girl who had to go on a boring holiday with her parents, and a man who missed his plane for a very important buisness meeting," **are appropriate and predictable**.
- **Supporting details**, such as "Jack won an Olympic Gold medal because he nearly drowned as a child," "Grace had a great time and learned so much and this all happened because Grace was made to go on a boring trip with her parents," and "Tom was lucky that he missed his plane because it crashed and everyone on the plane was killed" **are relevant but general**.

- **The writing is straightforward**, as in "He started his lessons at a swimming pool near his home and he began to like them," **and general**, as in "Sometime parents have to go on buisness trips and the children have to go to because there is no one to look after them," **and occasionally arouses the reader's interest**, as in "One day Tom was in a big hurry to catch his plane to Chicago but he missed it, he was to late. He was very unhappy because he might get fired from his job."
- **The introduction is functional and establishes a focus** by listing the three negative situations that had positive results that the student elaborates on in the essay, **and this focus is generally sustained**.
- **Details are developed in a discernible order** (the student discusses the positive outcomes of the negative situations of Jack, Grace, and Tom) **though coherence may falter occasionally** in that the situations are farfetched and have no relation to each other.
- **Transitions** such as "When Jack was about 18" and "At the hotel in Victoria" **are generally used to connect details within sentences and between paragraphs and tend to be mechanical**.
- **Closure is related to the focus and mechanical**: "Negative situations happen in life and sometimes it ends up positive for the person but sometimes it doesn't. But look on the bright side Tom missed a plane crash, Grace did interesting things in Victoria and Jack won a Olympic Gold Medal."
- **Sentence structure is generally controlled**, as in "Many children fall in rivers or swimming pools and sometimes they are nearly drownded so when this happened to Jack his mother decided that he had to have swimming lessons," **but lapses** (such as "At the hotel in Victoria where there was the meeting") **may occasionally impede meaning**.
- **Sentence type and length are sometimes effective** ("When Jack was about 18 he was picked for the Canada Olympic swimming team. He was thrilled") **and/or varied** ("Grace had a great time and learned so much and this all happened because Grace was made to go on a boring trip with her parents").
- **Some variety of sentence beginnings is evident**, as in "I am going to write," "This all happened because," and "But look on the bright side."
- **Words**—such as "swim meets" and "boring holiday"—**and expressions**— such as "hang out with her friends" and "look on the bright side"—**are generally used appropriately**.
- **General words and expressions are used adequately to clarify meaning**, such as "He was thrilled" and "Grace had a great time and learned so much."
- **The voice/tone created by the student is discernible**, as in "The trip was going to be BORING and she wanted to stay at home," **but uneven**.
- **The quality of the writing is sustained through generally correct use of conventions**, as in "One day they went to sea world, another day they went to the museum, another day they went to the wax museum, and on the last day they went out in a boat to see whales."
- **Errors occasionally reduce clarity** (such as the consistent misspelling of "buisness" and "drownded") **and sometimes interrupt the flow of the response** (such as "children have to go to because" and "he was to late").

Achievement Chart Level 4 Student Response

GOOD COMING OUT OF BAD

Children whose parents are in the armed forces have to spend their time moving from place to place or even country to country about every two or three years. Moving is a part of being in the armed forces. It just has to be accepted. However, this does not make it easy for the children of those whose career is in the armed forces. I know, because my father is a sergeant and not only does he go away for long lengths of time to places like Afghanistan, we also have had to move six times in my life time. This might seem really bad news to many people my age but actually it is not. I have learned so much about the world, other cultures, travelling, making friends, and excepting whatever happens—especially if it is something you have no control over. I am far more mature than the other kids in my school and I make friends easily. So, as you can see good can come out of bad situations.

It is always very hard to go to the airport to see your father and other members of his regiment go off to war to Afghanistan. The airport is crowded with people hugging each other and maybe even crying. Little children are running around chasing each other and screaming and laughing because they do not understand what is happening and do not realize they might never see their dad's again. Once dad has left I become the man of the house and I have to take responsibility for trying to make everyone happy, especially my mom. Dad has always said that he counts on me. Because I have had to be the man of the house, I am more mature than many kids my age. When my mom is working I have often had to baby sit my little brother and if she forgets the milk I go to the 7-11 to pick up some more, just like dad would have done if he had been home.

Moving is hard for all the family. Not only are there so much packing and sorting to be done, there is also the goodbyes that have to be said to grandparents, aunts and uncles, and friends. The goodbye part is never so bad if the move is only to another province because you are still quite close to everyone, but when the move is to another country then it seems more permanent. But imagine the excitement as you board the airplane for a twelve hour journey to Heidelberg in Germany. Everything is so different—the cars, the houses, the cities, and the language. There is so much to get used to but it is such a great opportunity to get to know people who live lives very different to yours. There is also the opportunity to travel and see places you had only read about in books, like the Alp mountains, the Rhine river, the old towns with their stone streets and the medeival castles that are found all over Germany.

Whenever there is a move, there is a new school and new teachers and new friends. Some people might think that this would be really hard and it is, but if you have a positive attitude then moving is easier. From grades 1 to 9, I have been to five different schools. Because I have had this opportunity I have been taught by some great and interesting teachers and I have made some excellent friends. Most of these friends and I keep in touch on facebook so we still know what each other is doing and we talk like we were in the same country. We share our experiences and we help each other when necessary. Moving has made me more outgoing so I make friends easily because there is no time to be shy or to hang back.

Because we have moved so much in my life I feel confident that I can travel anywhere, make friends easily, and being a mature responsible person who my family can rely on. Constantly moving is not easy for anyone but you can make it a positive experience if you put your mind to it and then you will enjoy all the benefits that travelling and moving will give you.

- **The student's explanation of the topic is adept**—in that the student examines the negative and the positive aspects of being a member of a military family—**and plausible** "Because we have moved so much in my life I feel confident that I can travel anywhere."
- **The student's purpose** (to look at the issues that people who are family members of military personnel have to face and how the situations that occur can have positive results) **is intentional**.
- **The ideas presented by the student are thoughtful**, such as "Once dad has left I become the man of the house and I have to take responsibility for trying to make everyone happy, especially my mom," and sound, such as "The goodbye part is never so bad if the move is only to another province because you are still quite close to everyone."
- **Supporting details**, such as "The airport is crowded with people hugging each other and maybe even crying. Little children are running around chasing each other and screaming and laughing because they do not understand what is happening and do not realize they might never see their dads again" and "There is also the opportunity to travel and see places you had only read about in books, like the Alp mountains, the Rhine river, the old towns with their stone streets and the medeival castles that are found all over Germany," **are relevant and specific**.
- **The writing is considered** ("I know, because my father is a sergeant and not only does he go away for long lengths of time to places like Afghanistan, we also have had to move six times in my lifetime") **and draws the reader's interest** ("I have learned so much about the world, other cultures, travelling, making friends, and accepting whatever happens").
- **The introduction is purposeful** ("Children whose parents are in the armed forces have to spend their time moving from place to place or even country to country about every two or three years. Moving is a part of being in the armed forces") **and clearly establishes a focus** that is capably sustained throughout the essay by discussing how the negative aspects of being a child of an armed forces member can have some positive results.
- **Details are developed in paragraphs in a sensible order** (each paragraph supports the positive aspect of a negative situation that can occur due to being a member of an armed forces family), **and coherence is generally maintained**.
- **Transitions**, such as "This might seem really bad news to many people my age," "Once dad has left," and "Whenever there is a move, there is a new school and new teachers and new friends," **clearly connect details within sentences and between paragraphs**.
- **Closure is appropriate**—"Because we have moved so much in my life I feel confident that I can travel anywhere, make friends easily, and be a mature responsible person who my family can rely on. Constantly moving is not easy for anyone but you can make it a positive experience if you put your mind to it and then you will enjoy all the benefits that travelling and moving will give you"—**and related to the focus**.
- **Sentence structure is consistently controlled**, as in "I know, because my father is a sergeant and not only does he go away for long lengths of time to places like Afghanistan, we also have had to move six times in my lifetime" and "But imagine the excitement as you board the airplane for a twelve hour journey to Heidelberg in Germany."
- **Sentence type**, such as "Not only are there so much packing and sorting to be done, there is also the goodbyes that have to be said to grandparents, aunts and uncles, and friends," **and sentence length**, "From grades 1 to 9, I have been to five different schools. Because I have had this opportunity I have been taught by some great and interesting teachers and I have made some excellent friends," **are usually effective and varied**.

- **Sentence beginnings**, as in "Not only is there so much packing and sorting," "Whenever there is a move," and "From grades 1 to 9, I have been to five different schools," **are often varied**.
- **Words and expressions**, such as "other cultures, travelling, making friends, and accepting whatever happens" and "if she forgets the milk I go to the 7–11 to pick up some more, just like dad would have done if he had been home," **are often used accurately**.
- **Specific words**, such as "I have had to be the man of the house" and "Everything is so different – the cars, the houses, the cities, and the language," **show some evidence of careful selection and some awareness of connotative effect**.
- **The tone created by the student** ("Moving has made me more outgoing so I make friends easily because there is no time to be shy or to hang back") **is distinct**.
- **The quality of the writing is sustained because it contains only minor convention errors**, such as "Not only are there so much packing and sorting to be done, there is also the goodbyes that have to be said to grandparents, aunts and uncles, and friends."
- **Any errors that are present** (in mechanics: "life time," "excepting," "dad's," and "medeival," and in usage: "and being a mature responsible person") **rarely reduce clarity and seldom interrupt the flow of the response**.

Achievement Chart Level 4 Student Response

THE CHOICE IS ALL YOURS

Robert Frost wrote something like, "Two roads diverged in a wood, and I—I took the one less travelled by and that has made all the difference." Robert Frost did not say whether one road would be difficult and have many problems along the way and the other road would be easier to travel, but that could be the case. For every choice there is an outcome and the outcome can be negative or positive. It is how we look at the negative situations in our lives and how we can do something to turn them into positive results that help us to grow and mature. Some negative things that can occur in your life such as your girl friend breaking up with you, you failing a really important test, you breaking your leg skateboarding just before football try-outs, or you missing the bus and having to walk five kilometers to school in a snow storm would be pretty bad, but they might have positive outcomes if you open your mind to all possibilities. You do not know what good may happen to you as a result of these negative situations that you found yourself in. Good can come out of bad as you will see in this essay.

Suppose you had been dating this girl since Grade 8 and she breaks up with you just before the Easter break. You would be really disappointed because you had been planning on going snow-boarding with her and you had hoped she would invite you to her family's cabin by the lake where you could have gone ski-doing and cross-country skiing and snow shoeing. You have a choice. You can mope around your house all of the break and make life miserable for yourself and the rest of your family or you can shut the door on that chapter of your life (my mother's wise saying) and get out and do some fun activities with other friends. You can still snow-board, cross country ski, snow-shoe. You just can't ski-do because you don't know anyone else who has one. But so what? It isn't the end of the world. You might even meet new and exciting friends. You might find that life is freer if you don't have a girl friend. Now you can do what you want, when you want, and with who you want.

Failing important tests in school can be serious and is definitely a wake-up call. Why did you fail? Perhaps it means you are not studying hard enough. Maybe you were spending too much time with the girlfriend (who just broke up with you) so it is a good thing that you two are not going out any more. Your parents and teachers will be disappointed because they expect better from you; so not only are you surprised but so are your parents and teachers. It doesn't matter if you fail one test in Junior High as long as you learn from it and realize that some tests (like your Grade 12 exams to get into University) are extremely important. The positive that came out of you failing a test is that you will learn how important it is to study for all tests.

You always wanted to make the high school junior football team. The senior team nearly always wins the city championships and you know that if you make the junior team you are pretty sure of a place on the senior team in Grade 11 or 12. How do you feel if the week before try-outs, you go flying down a flight of stairs while skateboarding (with a new friend that you met since you are no longer dating the girlfriend) and you end up in hospital with a badly broken leg? Imagine your frustration and anger. Now that you will have no chance to make the junior team, it is unlikely that you will make the senior team in a year's time. What good can come out of this? you wonder. Well, your new friend suggests that, since you can't do anything too active for the next two months, the two of you get together with some others and form a rock band. You like this idea as you already know how to play the guitar and can now put it to some use. Five of you (a drummer, two regular guitarists, a bass guitarist, and a saxophone player) form a band called The Frivolous Five. You have so much fun that you are almost glad you broke your leg. In Grade 12 you will be able to play in gigs around the city.

It is not likely that you will ever have to walk five kilometers to school in a snow storm. I know our parents tell us they had to (and back home, and up-hill both ways) but they exaggerate to try and make us think that our life is too easy. I think I would freeze my toes.

This essay has tried to show how positive things can result from negative situations. Maybe we learn from our mistakes (which is a positive result), or maybe new and unexpected things come our way because of the negative situation. We never know what lies ahead so when times are bad, we must never give up because as one door closes, another always opens (another of my mother's wise sayings), and new and exciting and positive life experiences could be just around the corner.

- **The student's exploration of the topic** ("As we walk along the road of life, we do not know where each path will lead us. Good can come out of bad as you will see in this essay," "The positive that came out of you failing a test is that you will learn how important it is to study for all tests," and "Maybe we learn from our mistakes [which is a positive result], or maybe new and unexpected things come our way because of the negative situation") **is insightful**.

- **The student's purpose**—to recognize how the results of unfortunate and negative situations may lead to unexpected but positive results—**is deliberate**.

- **The ideas presented by the student are perceptive**, as in "You can mope around your house all of the break and make life miserable for yourself and the rest of your family or you can shut the door on that chapter of your life (my mother's wise saying) and get out and do some fun activities with other friends," **and carefully chosen**, as in "How do you feel if the week before try-outs, you go flying down a flight of stairs while skateboarding."

- **Supporting details**, such as "your new friend suggests that, since you can't do anything too active for the next two months, the two of you get together with some others and form a rock band. You like this idea as you already know how to play the guitar and can now put it to some use," **are precise and original**, in so much as the student acknowledges some of the outcomes that might create a positive experience from a negative situation.

- The **writing is confident and holds the reader's interest**, as in "It is not likely that you will ever have to walk five kilometers to school in a snow storm. I know our parents tell us they had to (and back home, and up-hill both ways) but they exaggerate to try and make us think that our life is too easy. I think I would freeze my toes."

- **The introduction is engaging and skilfully establishes a focus**—"It is how we look at the negative situations in our lives and how we can do something to turn them into positive results that help us to grow and mature. Some negative things that can occur in your life such as your girl friend breaking up with you, you failing a really important test, you breaking your leg skateboarding just before football try-outs, or you missing the bus and having to walk five kilometers to school in a snow storm would be pretty bad, but they might have positive outcomes if you open your mind to all possibilities"—**that is consistently sustained** (by the elaboration of the examples given in the introduction).

- **Details are developed in paragraphs in a judicious order**—evident in each paragraph's detail and examples, such as "You can still snow-board, cross country ski, snow-shoe. You just can't ski-do" and "the two of you get together with some others and form a rock band," of how positive results have come out of negative situations—**and coherence is maintained** by the presentation of three different situations.

- **Transitions fluently connect details within sentences** ("Now you can do what you want, when you want, and with who you want") **and between paragraphs**, as in "Suppose you had been dating this girl since Grade 8 and she breaks up with you just before the Easter break" and "You always wanted to make the high school junior football team."

- **Closure is effective and related to the focus**—"We never know what lies ahead so when times are bad, we must never give up because as one door closes, another always opens (another of my mother's wise sayings), and new and exciting and positive life experiences could be just around the corner."

- **Sentence structure is effective and consistently controlled**, as in "Some negative things that can occur in your life such as your girl friend breaking up with you, you failing a really important test, you breaking your leg skateboarding just before football try-outs, or you missing the bus and having to walk five kilometers to school in a snow storm would be pretty bad, but they might have positive outcomes if you open your mind to all possibilities."

- **Sentence type** ("But so what? It isn't the end of the world") **and sentence length** ("It doesn't matter if you fail one test in Junior High as long as you learn from it and realize that some tests [like your Grade 12 diplomas to get into University] are extremely important") **are consistently effective and varied**.

- **Sentence beginnings**, such as "For every choice there is an outcome," "Why did you fail?" and "Well, your new friend suggests that…," **are consistently varied**.

- **Words and expressions** ("You can mope around your house all of the break and make life miserable for yourself and the rest of your family") **are accurately and deliberately used** ("Maybe you were spending too much time with the girlfriend (who just broke up with you…").

- **Precise words and expressions**, such as "you can shut the door on that chapter of your life (my mother's wise saying,)" **are used to create vivid images**, such as "Five of you (a drummer, two regular guitarists, a bass guitarist, and a saxophone player) form a band called The Frivolous Five," and enrich details.
- **The tone created by the student is convincing**, as in "Now you can do what you want, when you want, and with who you want" and "I know our parents tell us they had to (and back home, and up-hill both ways) but they exaggerate to try and make us think that our life is too easy. I think I would freeze my toes."
- **The quality of the writing is enhanced because it is essentially error free**, as demonstrated in "Robert Frost wrote something like, 'Two roads diverged in a wood, and I—I took the one less travelled by and that has made all the difference'" and "How do you feel if the week before try-outs, you go flying down a flight of stairs while skateboarding (with a new friend that you met since you are no longer dating the girlfriend) and you end up in hospital with a badly broken leg?"
- **Any errors that are present** (in usage: "you can do what you want, when you want, and with who you want" and "Maybe we learn from our mistakes (which is a positive result) **do not reduce clarity and do not interrupt the flow of the response**.

Appendices

Glossary

Abstract	Abstract terms and concepts name things that are not knowable through the senses; examples are love, justice, guilt, and honour.
Alliteration	The repetition of initial consonants.
Allusion	A reference to a pre-existing work of art or literature or to a person or event.
Ambiguity	A vagueness or lack of clarity of meaning or expression which makes possible more than one interpretation
Analogy	A comparison that is made to explain something that is unfamiliar by presenting an example that is similar or parallel to it in some significant way.
Anecdote	A brief story telling an interesting incident; often used as an introduction to a related topic for an essay.
Antagonist	The character in a drama or novel who presents the greatest opposition to the central figure. Antagonists can be sympathetic, like Macduff in *Macbeth*, or villainous, like Claudius in *Hamlet*.
Antecedent Action	Action that takes place before the story opens.
Apostrophe	A figure of speech in which animate or inanimate objects are addressed in the second person as if the object were able to understand being addressed.
Aside	A brief, often sarcastic or revealing comment made by an actor to the audience and not meant to be heard by the other characters. It allows the spectators to hear significant and sometimes foreshadowing remarks. An example of this is Iago's aside in *Othello*: "With as little a web as this will I ensnare as great a fly as Cassio."
Assonance	Repetition of similar or identical vowel sounds.
Atmosphere	The emotional tone and overall effect of a narrative or descriptive passage.
Ballad	A folk song or story in poetic form.
Blank Verse	Poetry possessing rhythm but not rhyme.
Chronological	In order of time.
Cliché	An overused expression; one that has become stale through overuse.
Colloquial	Informal writing suitable for everyday speech but not for formal writing.
Connotative Meaning	The suggested meaning of words because of personal experience and association.
Consonance	The repetition of a consonant sound within a series of words to produce a harmonious effect.
Denotative Meaning	The specific dictionary meaning of words and terms.
Diction	The choice of words in literature, usually classified using such descriptive terms as *slang* or *colloquial*, *informal*, *formal*, *elevated*, *technical*, *ordinary*, *figurative*, *archaic*, *abstract*, *concrete*, *connotative*, or *denotative*.
Discrepancy	Distinct difference between two things that should not be different or that should correspond.

Dissonance	Harsh sound or discordance; in poetry, a harsh, jarring combination of sounds.
Dramatic Monologue	A poem involving an uninterrupted speech by a character to a silent second figure. It is meant to reveal the personality of the speaker through his manner of speech, the attitudes his remarks disclose, and the implied reactions of his listener.
Dynamic Character	A character that undergoes a permanent change in some aspect of his or her character, personality, or outlook.
Epic	A long narrative poem that recounts the deeds of a legendary or historical hero or group of heroes.
Flashback	The recounting, in fleeting or extended form, of past incidents in a character's life, usually for the purpose of clarifying present events.
Flat Character	A character with only a few traits; often plays a minor role.
Foil	Any character who, by his contrast to another character, brings out the personality of the latter. Banquo is a foil of Macbeth in *Macbeth*.
Foreshadowing	Any indication or hint of a later event in a story.
Hyperbole	A figure of speech that uses exaggeration for effect.
Imagery	Language that uses imagery evokes sensory impressions.
Irony	The result of a statement's saying one thing while meaning the opposite, or of a situation developing contrary to expectation. *Verbal irony* refers to a statement in which the opposite of what is said is meant. *Dramatic irony* is based on the principle of opposition between appearance and reality. The speaker is unaware of the opposition, but the audience recognizes the ironic implications. *Irony of situation* is imbedded in circumstances themselves and does not depend on the spoken word.
Jargon	Special vocabulary of a particular group or activity; sometimes used to refer to confusing or unintelligible language.
Metaphor	A comparison made by referring to one thing as another.
Monologue	A literary form; an oral or written composition in which only one person speaks.
Mood	In a story, the atmosphere; when a writer creates the setting, action, and characters of a story so as to suggest a dominant emotion or patterns of emotions. This emotional pattern is the mood of the story. Also can refer to a person's state of mind or complex of emotions at any given time.
Ode	A poem expressing lofty emotion. Odes often celebrate an event or are addressed to nature or to an admired person, place, or thing; an example is "Ode on a Grecian Urn" by John Keats.
Onomatopoeia	The use of words that suggest the sound of the thing they describe.
Oxymoron	Phrases or ideas with an apparent contradiction.
Parable	A short, simple story that teaches or explains a lesson—often a moral or religious lesson.
Paradox	An apparently self-contradictory statement that is, in fact, true.
Parallelism	Refers to the grammatical or structural similarity between sentences or parts of a sentence.
Pathos	A term used to describe an element in literature which evokes pity or sorrow.

Personification	The attribution of human characteristics to non-human things.
Point of View: First Person	The story is told by one of the characters in the story (*I*). The narrator is in the story. First person narrators can only narrate what they can perceive.
Point of View: Objective	The story is told without describing any characters' internal thoughts and feelings. Only the characters' actions and words are told. This point of view is a lot like the camera's point of view in a movie.
Point of View: Third Person	The story is told through the eyes of one or more characters (he, she, and they). The narrator is outside the story and describes what the characters think, feel, and do. Omniscient narrators know everything that happens and what any character thinks and feels. Limited omniscient narrators only know about one character and the things that one character thinks and feels.
Prologue	An introduction to a play, often delivered by the chorus (in ancient Greece, a group, but in modern plays, usually by one actor) who plays no part in the action of the play that follows.
Protagonist	The central character of a drama or narrative.
Pun	A humorous expression that depends on a double meaning, either between different senses of the same word or between two similar sounding words.
Rhetorical Question	A question which is not posed to be answered seriously. Instead, it is used to draw attention to a point.
Rhyme	Rhyme is, loosely, the repetition of the same vowel sounds in poetry.
Ridicule	Contemptuous mocking or derision; ridicule may be an element of satire.
Round Character	A complex, many-sided, and fully developed character.
Satire	A form of writing that exposes the failings of individuals, institutions, or societies. Satire uses ridicule or scorn in order to correct or expose some evil or social injustice.
Simile	A comparison using the words *like* or *as*.
Sonnet	A lyric poem 14 lines long and usually written in iambic pentameter. The Shakespearean sonnet consists of three quatrains (four-line stanzas) and a couplet (two lines), all written to a strict end-rhyme scheme (*abab cdcd efef gg*). The Italian sonnet has the following more complex structure: *a b b a a b b a c d e c d e*. The last six lines of an Italian sonnet structure can vary in structure. The development of the poet's thoughts is also structured. There are several methods: one is to use each quatrain for different points in an argument and the couplet for the resolution of the argument. Because of the complexity of the sonnet, poets sometimes find it a suitable form for expressing the complexity of thought and emotion.
Static Character	The same sort of person at the end of the story as he or she was at the beginning of the story
Stock Character	A stereotyped figure who has occurred so often in fiction that his or her nature is immediately known.

Symbol	Anything that stands for or represents something other than itself. In literature, a symbol is a word or phrase referring to an object, scene, or action that also has some further significance associated with it. For example, a rose is a common symbol of love. Many symbols, such as flags, are universally recognized. Other symbols are not so universally defined. They do not acquire a meaning until they are defined by how they are used in a story. They may even suggest more than one meaning. For example, snow could be used to symbolize goodness because of its purity. Snow could also be used to symbolize cruelty because of its coldness. Symbols are often contained in story titles, in character and place names, and in classical, literary, and historical allusions and references. They are found in images or figures that appear at important points in a story and in images that either receive special emphasis or are repeated.
Symbolism	The use of one thing to represent something else.
Synecdoche	A figure of speech in which a part of something is used to represent the whole.
Thesis	A statement that is made as the first step in an argument or a demonstration.
Tone	The attitude toward both subject matter and audience implied in a piece of literature.

Credits

Every effort has been made to provide proper acknowledgment of the original source and to comply with copyright law. However, some attempts to establish original copyright ownership may have been unsuccessful. If copyright ownership can be identified, please notify Castle Rock Research Corporation so that appropriate corrective action can be taken.

Some images in this document are from www.clipart.com, © 2013 Clipart.com, a division of Getty Images.

Reading – Reading for Meaning

"Sanctuary" from "Speak" by Laurie Halse Anderson, New York, Farrar Straus Giroux, 1999

Reading – Understanding Form and Style

Excerpt from "Walden, or Life in the Woods", by Henry David Thoreau

"Fog" from CHICAGO POEMS by Carl Sandburg, copyright 1916 by Holt, Rinehart and Winston and renewed 1944 by Carl Sandburg, reprinted by permission of Houghton Mifflin Harcourt Publishing Company

"Mother to Son", from THE COLLECTED POEMS OF LANGSTON HUGHES by Langston Hughes, edited by Arnold Rampersad with David Roessel, Associate Editor, copyright © 1994 by The Estate of Langston Hughes. Used by permission of Alfred A. Knopf, a division of Random House, Inc.

Reading – Practice Questions

"Because I Could not Stop for Death" by Emily Dickinson

"A Nice Place to Visit" by Russell Baker, from The New York Times, © 1979

From The Thrill of the Grass by W.P. Kinsella, Copyright © W.P. Kinsella, 1984. Reprinted by permission of Penguin Group (Canada), a Division of Pearson Canada Inc.

"The Tell-Tale Heart" by Edgar Allan Poe

Reading – Unit Test

"A Work of Artifice" by Marge Piercy. Copyright © 1972 by Marge Piercy. From Circles on the Water: Selected Poems of Marge Piercy, published by Alfred A. Knopf, Inc., a division of Random House Inc

"The Express" by Stephen Spender, from "Stephen Spender Collected Poems 1928-1985", Faber and Faber Ltd. Copyright © 1986 by Stephen Spender

"Suitcase Lady" by Christie McLaren, from The Globe and Mail, January 24, 1981, pg. P5

"Old Man at the Bridge" by Ernest Hemingway, from "The Complete Short Stories of Ernest Hemingway", Scribner

"To His Coy Mistress" by Andrew Marvel

Reflecting On Skills and Strategies

"Dragon Night" by Jane Yolen. Copyright © 1980 by Jane Yolen. Currently appears in HERE THERE BE DRAGONS, published by Harcourt Brace and Company. Reprinted by permission of Curtis Brown, Ltd.

"The Fork in the Graveyard" as retold by Julie V. Watson.

Practice Test 1

"Big Words" by Ian Brown, published in The Globe and Mail, June 16, 2007, pg. F1

"Of Children" by Kahil Gibran

"A Fable for Tomorrow" from "Silent Spring" by Rachel Carson, Copyright © 1962 by Rachel L. Carson, Used by permission of Frances Collin, Trustee, Any electronic copying or distribution of this text is expressly forbidden

"Do Seek Their Meat from God" from "Earth's Enigmas", by Charles G.D. Roberts, McClelland and Stewart Limited, Toronto

"Encouragement is a Two-edged Sword" by Alison Blackduck, from the Toronto Star. Toronto, Ont.: Mar 6, 2001. pg. A.21

"Field of Vision' by Seamus Heaney, from "Opened Ground – Selected Poems 1966-1996, Farrar, Straus and Giroux, Copyright © 1998 by Seamus Heaney

Practice Test Two

"Anita's Dance" by Marian Engel, from "The Tattooed Woman" by Marian Engel, Penguin Books, 1985. Copyright © 1985 the Estate of Marian Engel

"A January Morning" by Archibald Lampman

"Hidden Lessons" by David Suzuki, from The Globe and Mail, February 7, 1987, pg D4

"Ode to the User-Friendly Pencil" by Bonnie Laing, The Globe and Mail. Toronto, Ont.: Apr 29, 1989. pg. D.6

"Mirror" by Sylvia Plath, from "Crossing the Water", Harper Perennial, 1980

"Genius Without the Genetics" excerpted and abridged from "The End of Ignorance" by John Mighton, copyright © 2007 by John Mighton. Published by Alfred A. Knopf Canada, a division of Random House of Canada Limited.

NOTES

NOTES

NOTES

NOTES

NOTES

NOTES